MORAL VALUES
IN THE ANCIENT WORLD

MORAL VALUES IN THE ANCIENT WORLD

JOHN FERGUSON

M.A. (*Cantab.*) B.D. (*London*)
Professor of Classics
University College Ibadan

BARNES & NOBLE INC.
NEW YORK

First published 1959

Printed in Great Britain
by Western Printing Services Ltd Bristol

FOR

N.M.J. C.L.H.T. C.M.

C.S.C. G.A.G. H.C.

who laid the foundations

CONTENTS

INTRODUCTION

THIS BOOK STUDIES some of the moral values which were current in the Ancient World. It is curious that, so far as I can ascertain, no such study has hitherto been made, though there have been investigations, on varying scales and of varying value, of particular topics, and innumerable books in the vaguer field of Greek ideals. Reference to particular studies will be found in the appropriate chapters.

The presentation, though not, I hope, the investigation, has been influenced by certain presuppositions which emerged in the course of the investigation. History is always continuous. But we can rightly and properly mark off certain periods as having an integrity or completeness of their own. Such is the Graeco-Roman civilization, and whether one dates its finale to the accession of Constantine at the beginning of the fourth century A.D., or the fall of Rome in 410, or some other convenient landmark, it is factually true that the change is associated with the predominance of Christianity. Christianity can thus be seen as the culmination and conclusion of the old order as well as the beginning of the new. The method by which Christianity spread suggests that it served to fulfil the aspirations of the world to which it came. One potent factor in helping it to spread was the concept of Christian love or *agape*. I have thus come to see earlier evaluations to some extent against the background of that *agape* which gave satisfaction where they had failed, and this presupposition affects the presentation. But the presupposition arises from historical fact, not religious dogma.

Secondly, the question becomes inescapable: what has *agape* got that the rest haven't got? The details of the answer lie in the remainder of this study. But the investigation forced certain con-clusions which are written back into the earlier chapters. It is a cardinal principle of science that the simplest explanation con-sistent with the facts is the most scientifically admirable. When Copernicus and his followers were able to dispense with the com-plex Ptolemaic cycles and epicycles by setting the sun at the centre of the universe, it was a scientific advance; when Newton was able to subsume Kepler's laws of motion under the single law of gravitation, it was a scientific advance. Much science consists in finding a single explanation for many phenomena. We do not know that this is reflected in reality; it is rather a necessity of the human mind. So it seems that the human mind seeks for a single ethical principle, or at least to reduce ethics to its simplest propor-tions, and principles of limited application do not satisfy. In par-ticular, at this point thinking man (it is by no means true of all societies) demands that religion and ethics come together. Think-ing man rejects unethical religion, and though he (or she) has more recently aspired towards Morals without Religion, this is scarcely important in the Ancient World, where absolute atheism was rare, and even the Epicureans had a more religious approach to ethics than was at one time believed. I have tried to show that *agape* satisfied because it was comprehensive, and have assumed it to be a defect in earlier evaluations that they were not.

I have been persuaded by the thought of the Greekless reader, combined with the exigencies of book-production, to trans-literate into English isolated Greek (or Hebrew) words in the text. Quotations I have left, but they are invariably either translated or explained. Such transliterations are not very satisfactory, like most compromises, and I hope those whom they offend will show forbearance. Greekless readers may like to be reminded that final 'e' in such words is pronounced e.g. *dike* is a two-syllable word.

My thanks are due to many people, among whom must be especially named my colleague Mr. H. F. Guite for much con-structive help, my secretary Mr. M. B. Akanji for typing the MS., and my wife for her aid with the proofs and index, and her con-tinual patience and encouragement.

I

THE HOMERIC AGE

THE TWO POEMS whose author we call Homer are difficult to use as evidence of social custom and personal belief because they reflect in part the poet's own society of the ninth or eighth century B.C., in part the traditions about the world of some centuries earlier, which he is overtly depicting. Archaeology has gone some way towards helping us to disentangle the threads, but many problems remain.[1] None the less the poems remain our earliest literary source about Greek civilization (for the recently deciphered documents of the Mycenaean age are hardly to be called literary) and it is here that our beginning must lie.

Society is aristocratic. At its head stands Agamemnon, king of kings, lord of 'many islands and of all Argos'.

'The kingship is his by hereditary right, he is the leader in war, and at his side are the council of elders and the army assembly.'[2]

The elders are, so to speak, the king's 'companions' but each of them is a king in his own right, and has his own group of 'companions'. It was the break-up of the Mycenaean dominion which gave to these kings their full independence, and brought about the city-state structure familiar in classical Greece. In turn the weakening of their own authority *vis-à-vis* that of their companions led to the transformation of monarchy into aristocracy. Meantime the seeds of a more fundamental transformation were burgeoning. The army assembly represents a concession to the voice of the people. It had no authority, but the king would be foolish lightly to flout its will. It is here that Thersites makes his

[1] See M. P. Nilsson, *Homer and Mycenae*; H. L. Lorimer, *Homer and the Monuments.* [2] M. P. Nilsson, *Homer and Mycenae*, 221.

appearance.[1] Homer's sympathies are with the aristocracy, and Thersites is caricatured by the poet and maltreated by Odysseus, but we have in him the first recorded example of democratic opposition to the aristocratic domination.[2]

Moral concepts are not yet clear-cut. Onians has shown that there is no distinction between the physical and the psychological and that terms which in their conventional translation appear abstract are in reality vividly concrete;[3] thus *thumos* is the breath, and *aion*, the stuff of life, is the liquid which flows from the eyes in the form of tears. Words are broad in their field of action, and a verb like *eidenai* has a variety of what appear to us to be different usages. *Thumos* is associated with thought, sensation and knowledge. There is no clear distinction between what is immoral and what is inexpedient. A convenient example is that of Melantheus in kicking the disguised Odysseus. His behaviour is described as 'folly', and he later suffers cruelly for it.[4] Grote indeed declared that words like *esthlos* and *agathos*, which are generally translated 'good', are related 'to power and not to worth'.[5] Certainly Autolycus is described as *esthlos* in that he is a thief and perjurer; the word obviously denotes efficiency or even success.[6] *Agathos* is sometimes found in expressions which are almost to be called ethical;[7] sometimes it refers to a particular skill.[8] We too speak of a good doctor, a good actor, or a good cricketer without reference to their morals. The general ideal of life has been described by Burckhardt as 'agonistic'—αἰὲν ἀριστεύειν καὶ ὑπείροχον ἔμμεναι ἄλλων.[9] It has to come out on top. If it points forward to anything, it is to Aristotle's *megalopsuchia*. There is in fact no word except perhaps *aidos* which expresses what is unequivocally a moral concept. There are however five Homeric concepts which bear the germ of moral development, and which it is important to understand.

Nemesis is properly the distribution of what is due, from

---

[1] Hom. *Il.* 2, 200 ff.

[2] The general picture of this paragraph is borrowed from T. B. L. Webster, *Political Interpretations in Greek Literature.*

[3] R. B. Onians, *The Origins of European Thought.*

[4] Hom. *Od.* 17, 212 ff; 22, 474 ff.   [5] G. Grote, *Hist. of Greece* II 88 n.

[6] Hom. *Od.* 19, 395.   [7] e.g. id. *Il.* 6, 162; *Od.* 3, 266.

[8] e.g. id. *Il.* 2, 732.   [9] ib. 6, 208; 11, 784.

nemein;[1] in usage however it always means retribution, the righteous anger which is aroused by injustice. Retribution, not revenge; *nemesis* is the attitude of a third party, not the injured person. Aristotle defines it as the feeling of distress occasioned by unmerited good fortune.[2] In Homer this retribution is purely human;[3] only later is it used of divine retribution;[4] later still it is rationalized and legalized.[5] In Hesiod it is personified, together with *aidos*, and fitted into his genealogical and cosmological schemes as a child of Night, being described as an affliction to mortals, but one whose absence will surely lead to further degeneration.[6] The last thought is imitated by Euripides and Cercidas.[7] Personified, Nemesis was worshipped in a celebrated shrine at Rhamnus, and acquired her own mythology. The general tone of the concept is to be seen in Pindar, whose philosophy warns against *hubris*, the scholastic sin of 'superbia', and twice speaks explicitly of the *nemesis* (or Nemesis—we cannot tell for certain) which is liable to attend those who enjoy excessive prosperity, and thereby, as we put it, 'get above themselves'.[8] It would be dangerously improper to read these back into Homer, but they serve to show how the concept developed from his handling of it. The most interesting of the Homeric passages is one in the *Iliad* where Neptune is addressing the Greeks and tells them to set in their minds *aidos* and *nemesis*,[9] that is, to keep before them a sense of shame and the thought of others' active disapprobation. Here *nemesis* is linked with the need for right action, but it is not wholly moralized. In the mouth of Helen it becomes almost the power of public opinion.[10] Its most amusing appearance is on the lips of the old men as they watch Helen on the walls 'If men fight and die for such a woman as that, οὐ νέμεσις—one can't blame them.'[11] Gladstone summed it up usefully when he wrote

[1] A. B. Cook connected it, not wholly convincingly, with the rules of the *nemos*, or pasture-land. The words have a common derivation but different history.   [2] Arist. *Rhet.* II 9; *N.E.* II 7; *E.E.* III 7, 2; *Top.* 110 a 1.
[3] e.g. Hom. *Od.* 2, 136; 22, 40, cf. Aesch. *fr.* 226.
[4] e.g. Hdt. 1, 34; Soph. *Phil.* 518; Eur. *fr.* 1040.   [5] Ael. *V.H.* 6, 10.
[6] Hes. *W.D.* 200; *Theo.* 223.   [7] Eur. *Med.* 439 ff; Cercidas *fr.* 1, 31.
[8] Pind. *Ol.* VIII 86; *Pyth.* X 44.   [9] Hom. *Il.* 13, 121.
[10] ib. 6, 351.   [11] ib. 3, 156.

'This sentiment is usually half way between *aidos* and fear because what it apprehends, though it is not force, yet neither is it simple disapproval; rather it is disapproval with heat, disapproval into which passion enters.'[1]

When it is used reflexively, as when Telemachus tells the citizens of Ithaca to show an effective indignation against themselves, it is coming near to conscience.[2]

Gladstone himself relied on *aidos* in his noble attempt to exalt the explicit morality of the Homeric poems.[3] *Aidos* is conventionally translated 'sense of shame', and is, as we have seen, linked with *nemesis* as an impulse to right action in Homer and as a personification in Hesiod. In a military context the prime meaning becomes 'sense of honour'. αἰδώς, 'Αργεῖοι 'Argives, show some sense of honour!' is a battle-cry.[4] Generally it means respect for others. This may indicate mere fear, and *aidos* is linked with fear as well as with *nemesis*.[5] More often its connotation is wider, and indeed the fact that it is linked with fear and *nemesis* shows that it is not identical with either. So Ajax expands the battle-cry.

'Be soldiers, my friends, and keep a sense of honour before you. Honour one another in the violence of conflict. When men show honour more are saved than die.'[6]

'Honour' here represents αἰδώς and cognate words. The last line recurs elsewhere in Homer[7] and shows the prudential element from which Greek morality scarcely ever got free. In the *Doloneia* Agamemnon warns Diomedes not to choose an inferior companion for his night exploit through *aidos*, that is out of fear of or deference to one of the others.[8] But it may also be used of the relations of a superior to an inferior, and in this inversion acquires a much more genuinely moral element.[9] There is an exceptionally interesting passage in the *Odyssey*, referred to above, where Telemachus tells the Ithacans to show *nemesis* towards themselves, *aidos* towards their fellows, and fear towards the gods.[10] It is at the end of the *Iliad* that its potentialities appear most clearly. Achilles

---

[1] W. E. Gladstone, *Homer and the Homeric Age*, II 436.
[2] Hom. *Od.* 2, 64; cf. *Il.* 17, 254.   [3] W. E. Gladstone, op. cit. II, 431 ff.
[4] Hom. *Il.* 15, 502; cf. 16, 422.   [5] ib. 15, 657.   [6] ib. 15, 561–3.
[7] ib. 5, 531.   [8] ib. 10, 237.   [9] ib. 1, 23; 1, 377; 21, 74.   [10] id. *Od.* 2, 64–7.

is treating Hector's body despitefully, and the gods meet in solemn conclave. Apollo speaks. 'Achilles', he says, 'has eradicated pity, and has no *aidos*.'[1] Does this mean a proper respect for Hector, a proper respect for the gods, or proper self-respect, such as was later called ἑαυτοῦ αἰδώς?[2] It is hard to be certain, but the very ambiguity is significant. Later Priam calls on him to direct *aidos* towards the gods,[3] and this may be the real meaning of the earlier passage. But the *aidos* which he finally shows he shows towards the humbled Priam, and it is here that the highest morality of the Homeric poems is to be seen. It is surprising that the concept is not central to later Greek ethical thought; the fact is that it is not, even in the classical period, and in the Hellenistic Age it has almost ceased to have any place at all. The reason may be that *aidos*, however desirable, is an emotion, which you either feel or do not. If a man did not feel it, to what was the moralist to appeal? But many Homeric ideals—the high place of women, the simplicity of the upper classes, the cameraderie of masters and servants, the worth of manual toil—seem to be evanescent in the classical period.

The third concept which contains germinal morality is that of *Moira* or *Aisa*. These words indicate a man's lot or destined portion. It may be ultimately derived from the traditional structural divisions of primitive tribal life.[4] From there it takes on an individual meaning, and is often and understandably associated with death, but not identical with it. From this follows a virtual personification, by which Fate takes hold of a man and hurries him to his death,[5] and even spins his destiny.[6] Hence all the alter mythology of the Fates with their spinning-wheel, one assigning the destiny, one spinning the thread, and one cutting it;[7] the plural is only found once in the *Iliad*, and there it may mean the different destinies attaching to different individuals.[8] Destiny is sometimes identified with the will of the gods, and we have specific reference to Zeus' *aisa* or dispensation.[9] This is in fact an early attempt to

---

[1] id. *Il.* 24, 44. The next line may be an interpolation and I have not here treated it.   [2] Hierocles, *In Carm. Aur.* 9.   [3] Hom. *Il.* 24, 503.
[4] F. M. Cornford, *From Religion to Philosophy*, esp. 40–60. G. Thomson, *Aeschylus and Athens*, 37–55.   [5] Hom. *Il.* 5, 83; 12, 116.   [6] ib. 20, 128; 24, 209.
[7] Hes. *Theog.* 901 ff.   [8] Hom. *Il.* 24, 49.   [9] ib. 9, 608; 17, 321.

solve the age-old problem of free-will and determinism. Moira fixes some things but not all. Moira provides the framework within which man is free to act. But revolt against this framework is conceived. 'Then the Argives might have accomplished their return against their destined fate, had not Hera spoken to Athene.'[1] So too it is possible by wanton folly to aggravate your destiny.[2] It is here that a moral element enters the concept. The man who accepts his destiny, who, so to speak, elects to work within the framework, who bows to the will of heaven and does not set himself up against it, is *enaisimos*, and this is a term of definite approbation.[3] Here is a concept of morality closely similar to, though not identical with, that which the Stoics were later to evolve—right action consists in acceptance of that which destiny lays upon you. But it is not a truly fruitful concept, for it is at best of limited (and very difficult) application, and it is incapable of much development, except negatively. *In la sua volontade e nostra pace* is religiously admirable, but ethically not very helpful.

Themis appears in Homer both as a common noun and as a proper name.[4] The root meaning of the word may also be something to do with dispensation, but in the sense of 'laying down' not 'distributing'. In Hesiod she is personified as mother of the Moirai.[5] She is also called daughter of Earth,[6] but elsewhere is identified with Earth.[7] She is always associated with wise counselling. Hirzel indeed pointed out the link between *themis* and *boule* (counsel).[8] In Aeschylus' *Prometheus* she appears as a prophetess and adviser;[9] in the *Eumenides* he claims that the Delphic oracle once belonged to her.[10] In Pindar she prophesies the fated future and is termed *euboulos*;[11] in Euripides she is the guardian of oaths.[12] In the ancient hymn of the Curetes the worshippers are called on to leap for full jars, fleecy flocks, fields of fruit, cities, sea-borne

---

[1] ib. 2, 155. [2] id. *Od.* 1, 34.
[3] id. *Il.* 24, 40; *Od.* 2, 123; 5, 190; 7, 299; 10, 383; 17, 363, etc.
[4] For an important but controversial treatment see J. E. Harrison, *Themis*, c. xi. See also for Themis and Dike H. Frisch, *Might and Right in Antiquity*; J. L. Myres, *The Political Ideas of the Greeks.*
[5] Hes. *Theog.* 901.   [6] ib. 135.   [7] Aesch. *P.V.* 209-10.
[8] cf. Hom. *Od.* 16, 402-3.   [9] Aesch. *P.V.* 209-10.   [10] id. *Eum.* 2.
[11] Pind. *Isth.* VIII, 34; *fr.* 30 (Bergk); cf. *Ol.* VIII 22.   [12] Eur. *Med.* 160 ff.

ships, citizens and goodly Themis—presumably the right counsel from which the rest will spring. It looks as if she was originally an oracular goddess of earth, or a title of Earth in her oracular capacity: Ge Themis was known at Athens. *Themistes* then would be her divine decrees. They are thus the rules, customs or laws by which a man lives. Nestor reminds Agamemnon that it is from Zeus that he derives his staff and rules of office.[1] It is from Zeus that the judges get the rules they keep.[2] Hence Themis is closely associated with the assembly,[3] and may even be called the spirit of the assembly, and Jane Harrison (enthusiastically followed by the Marxists) saw in the primacy of Themis an expression of the fact that man's social structure gives birth to his conception of order. The moralization of this is closely similar to that which we have just examined; indeed *athemistes* is set in contrast to *enaisimos*.[4] The concept is however more immediately useful, for it does imply obedience to a well-marked set of precedents or dooms, but it is not more fruitful, for it equally leaves no room for development. More seriously, a people like the Cyclopes may be found who acknowledge no law, but with whom each is a law unto himself[5] (the paradoxical phrase echoes the Greek). That is to say that customs and precedents can be found which do not depend on God's will. Once this is realized, all coherence dies out from the concept, and it quickly fades out.

Finally there is *dike*. Even in Homer this appears in a wide variety of meanings, which makes it difficult to discern its exact origin. It is possible that its root meaning is 'way'. So it commonly appears 'this is the way of mortals' 'this is the way of old men'.[6] Hence it comes to mean 'custom' and later again 'right'. The defect of this explanation (which may be none the less true) is that there is no evidence for a primitive usage meaning 'way'. The examples are all from the *Odyssey*, and in the *Iliad themis* is correspondingly used.[7] If this explanation is true the man who is *dikaios* (conventionally 'just') is the man who conforms with social custom. It is worth adding that in Hesiod Dike appears

[1] Hom. *Il.* 9, 99. [2] ib. 1, 238. [3] ib. 11, 807.
[4] id. *Od.* 17, 363. [5] ib. 9, 112–15.
[6] Hom. *Od.* 11, 218; 24, 255, etc. [7] id. *Il.* 2, 73, etc.

personified as one of the seasons and the child of Themis;[1] and in a magical papyrus she appears as the moon.[2] Here *dike* is surely associated with the order and constancy, the way, of nature. An alternative explanation would derive *dike* from the same root as *deiknunai* and give it an original meaning of 'judgement'. Later it would come to be 'justified claim'. According to this view the man who is *dikaios* is the man who respects the justified claims of others, gods, beggars or suppliants. Whichever be its origin its usage comes to practically the same thing. The man who is *dikaios* refuses to break the conventions (in the highest sense of that word) out of self-interest or for any other purpose. He is under obligations towards his fellows which he acknowledges and fulfils. This is a pattern of thought from which, if it be not itself accorded the name 'ethical', an ethical approach can emerge. It is not arbitrary; it acknowledges in some sense that righteous action is social action and that relationship is the basis of morality; and it bears within itself the seeds of fruitful development.

[1] Hes. *Theog.* 901.   [2] *Par. Pap. Abel* 292, 7; 49.

II

THE VALUES OF
EARLY GREEK SOCIETY

THE SEVENTH AND SIXTH centuries saw the growth of an articulate civilization in the Greek world. Much of the impulse came from the Greeks who had settled on the coast of Asia Minor, and though their claim to absolute primacy in things cultural has recently been challenged, it remains generally accepted. Literature becomes more individual and personal. The characters of Sappho, Theognis and Archilochus leap from their pages while Homer remains an enigma. In sculpture the same process takes place; we begin to learn the names of individual sculptors, and common stylization gives way to a more personal approach. The philosophers of Miletus ask searching questions about the world around them, and pave the way for those who will ask similarly searching questions about man, his character and destiny.

The predominant values of the age were aristocratic, and because aristocratic values tend to be conservative, they may properly be represented by the rather later figure of Pindar. His ideals in fact derive directly from the tradition of the Dorian aristocrats. The man who would achieve to the full that most untranslatable of Greek qualities, *arete* ('goodness'), must begin with the natural advantages of birth and wealth. Breed tells in the end, and wealth is among the greatest of external boons. But the mere possession of such external advantages is not of itself sufficient; success or failure still depends on what we do with the advantages which we possess. Inherited ability is a great thing, but it needs drawing out by education, training, discipline, work. The natural genius far outshines the technical expert, but natural genius will not of itself reach the highest point unless it is trained in the necessary techniques. Wealth and position should be used with courtesy and directed towards generosity and a liberal hospitality. Men must beware of that self-exaltation in face of heaven which the Greeks called *hubris*. These values reflect with greater poetical power and greater intellectual depth what may be found in the writings of an earlier aristocrat such as Theognis of Megara. His lines show moral contempt for those who lack both breed and riches, and he honours good-living and hospitality.

At this period *arete* means a capacity to do something. In its social context it naturally is linked with wealth, military (and athletic) prowess, and political authority. Homer can call Aegisthus *amumon* ('blameless') while at the same time condemning him for the murder of Agamemnon; this shows the connotation to be pragmatic, not moral.[1] Mimnermus shrinks from old age because it makes a man *kakos* (conventionally 'bad'), very nearly 'impotent'. Wealth and *arete* are so closely linked in Homer and Hesiod as to be at times indistinguishable. In Tyrtaeus and Callinus *aner agathos* (conventionally 'a good man') is a successful warrior. Solon speaks of strength as the mark of *arete*. This curiously recurs among the Stoics. Chrysippus links the beauty of a young man with *arete*. But the Stoics were notoriously *laudatores temporis acti*. Sometimes the prowess is intellectual. Even in the *Iliad* dominance in the political assembly is put alongside dominance on the battlefield.[2] As the notion of morality itself becomes articulate it tends to be linked with the social solidarity of the dominant class. Thus in Homer it is characteristic of a good man to love and look after his wife.[3] The moralization of the concept is increased as the aristocracy's power decays. Theognis, presented with the spectacle of impoverished aristocrats, cannot equate *arete* with wealth. Unhappily the emergence of moral concepts within this class at this period, though it did not stultify the ultimate development of moral philosophy, did have a profoundly adverse effect upon the whole future of Greek social thought, which remained consciously or unconsciously dominated by the ideas of a land-owning aristocracy. The working-man was *poneros* or *mochtheros*. Originally,

[1] cf. above p. 12. [2] Hom. *Il.* 9, 440 ff. [3] ib. 9, 341.

perhaps, this meant little more than that he was socially impotent, lacking wealth, political privilege and any opportunity for outstanding military success. It remained as a moral stigma, and Greek thought never escaped from the delusion that there is something dishonourable attaching to manual labour, even when they exalted the virtue of toil itself. So too the merchants were stigmatized with the dislike that an ancient and established landed gentry always feel for the get-rich-quick methods of trade and commerce.

As the new democratic parties arose to challenge the *status quo* they introduced their own political catchwords of Liberty and Equality.[1] It is important to notice that the second of these at least is an adaptation of an old aristocratic idea. *Homoios* ('equal') is in Homer a term of disapprobation, which is applied to war, death, old age and in general things which blot out the proper distinctions between man and man. The aristocrats however gradually took it up and applied it to themselves. At Sparta the ruling-class were known as the *Homoioi*. Herodotus speaks of the *isokratia* ('equality in power') of the Corinthian oligarchs.[2] The picture is that of a ruling-class which allowed no individual member to domineer over the rest. The democrats took the same principles and applied them over a wider field. Greek democracy is in fact only an enlarged oligarchy, and the privileges which the democrats demanded for a wider citizenry they would not dream of extending to slaves or foreigners. *Mutatis mutandis*, George Orwell's epigram, 'All animals are equal, but some are more equal than others', may justly be applied to some of the political catch-phrases of the Greeks.

The mere enunciation of these slogans is enough to make a modern student aware of a gap. The French Revolution bore on its banners LIBERTE, EGALITE and FRATERNITE. The impulses behind that revolution were in measure anti-Christian. But they were also post-Christian. Freedom and equality are assertions of rights, in the face of oppression. But brotherhood springs from a more philosophical reflection, and involves a moral judgement rather different from the other two. This the Greeks were not yet ready

[1] Eur. *Suppl.* 403, etc.   [2] Hdt. 5, 92.

to make. They were to draw near to it under the influence of more mature philosophical speculation and a wider and more understanding experience of other peoples. But that lay in the future.

What did develop during this period was a new sense of the importance of co-operative action, which may be drawn out of the writings of the lyric poets. It is interesting to trace the causes of this development. Primitive societies take social solidarity for granted. Such solidarity is the life of the people, and does not require any specific emphasis or expression. This is tribalism. An individual who dares to be unconventional is regarded in the strict sense as extra-ordinary, and cuts himself off from the life of the tribe. This excommunication is the worst possible fate in an age where everything depends on the life of the community. But when the order itself is challenged a different state of things emerges. One suspects that a potent factor in the change among the Greeks was the period of colonization. However conservative such colonies were in their original establishment, they acted on the framework of Greek ideology much as the fact of the 'moving frontier' influenced the Americans. They encouraged individualism. Once individualism is there, not just in a solitary and isolated rebel, but as part of the accepted environment, it means that the old unthinking social solidarity has no longer any force. Co-operative enterprise has ceased to be automatic response. It has to become an act of will. This is precisely what we find.

Classical Greek knew literally thousands of words compounded with *sun* (anglicized as syn, as in synthesis) and indicating complete or co-operative action. In Homer there are not more than fifty, and in the verbal forms, almost if not quite without exception, the collectivity refers to the object not to the subject, and the word connotes action rather than emotion. Thus we find *sun-halein* to call together, *sunageirein*, to bring together, *sunelaunein*, to drive together, *sunorinein*, to move together. These are typical. But in the lyric period a new group of words comes into use. They refer to the inner life of mind and spirit, not the externalities of action, and the collectivity relates to the subject not the object. They relate in fact to what we should call 'fellow-feeling'.

Such words are *sumpaschein*, *sunaschalan* and *suneidenai*, which now come to birth.

It will be noticed that though the actuality (and hence, once reflection sets in, the desirability) of such a communal sensitivity has now found expression, and though there is some transference of attention from external act to inward thought and feeling, language as yet reflects no moral judgement upon the nature of the communal experience itself. It is enough that we join together; the question has not yet been asked. 'In what are we to join together?' It is in the pages of tragedy that this question forces itself forward, when Antigone cries

οὔτοι συνέχθειν ἀλλὰ συμφιλεῖν ἔφυν

'My nature is to join in love not to join in hatred.'[1]

or when Jocasta comments

καὶ τοῦτο λυπρόν, ξυνασοφεῖν τοῖς μὴ σοφοῖς.

'It is distasteful to join with fools in their folly',[2]

and this leads us to a later stage of our enquiry.

[1] Soph. *Ant.* 523.   [2] Eur. *Phoen.* 394.

III

THE CARDINAL VIRTUES

THE ACTUAL PHRASE 'the cardinal virtues' seems to derive from St Ambrose;[1] the doctrine emerged in Greece during the fifth and fourth centuries, and is presented for the first time in Plato's *Republic*. But the process of analysis was taking place a hundred and more years previously. In a difficult passage in the third Nemean ode Pindar writes as follows.

'In the attempt is revealed the outcome of those things wherein one man may surpass his fellows, whether as a lad among young lads, as a man among men, or thirdly among those rather older, according to the several portions of life which we, the race of men, possess. Mortal life brings four virtues, and bids us face the present with prudence. From these virtues Aristoclides is not far.'[2]

It was this passage which made the great scholar Böckh remark that the longer he considered it the more obscure it became to him. Donaldson wanted to refer the words to the cardinal virtues, which he regarded as Pythagorean, each corresponding to one of the ages of man on a sort of Shakespearean principle, self-control being the virtue of youth, courage of manhood, justice of maturity, and prudence of old age. The ode was written at some interval after the event, when Aristoclides might be of an age to 'face the present with prudence'. In the second Pythian there is an association of courage with early manhood, coupled with the sense that wise counsel is an elder virtue,[3] but this is commonplace and hardly to be pressed. It should be remarked also that there are no direct grounds for associating the doctrine of four virtues with the Pythagoreans, save only the mystical quality of the number

---

[1] Ambrose, *Lib. V in Lucam*; cf. Noltenius, *Lexicon Antibarbaricum*, p. 455.
[2] Pind. *Nem.* III 70 ff.   [3] id. *Pyth.* II 63–5.

four, and the variety of doctrine in the fifth century is against any attempt to see too early a standardization. Aristarchus and the scholiasts, followed by Bury and Wilamowitz, see the passage as meaning that there are three periods of life, each with its peculiar virtue, and a fourth virtue *phronein to parkeimenon*, judgement, common to all alike. Farnell is scornful of all this, suggesting that it is ridiculous to see individual virtues as characteristic of one period of life only, but his sarcasm is uncalled for, and his own reference to the cardinal virtues as 'those of the old popular morality', and therefore easily to be comprehended without further reference, ignores the fact that they are nowhere else so coupled at this period, nor at any point in the dramatists. He sees the passage as containing three separate elements (*a*) our excellences are tested in rivalry with our contemporaries; (*b*) there are four cardinal virtues which we must show at any stage; (*c*) in addition we should face the present with prudence. I am inclined to think that the natural interpretation is to link the four virtues to the stages of life just enumerated, supplying a fourth, old age, without difficulty to follow the comparative *palaiteroisi*. But the virtues are not named, and he may not be saying more than that different ages have different fields of action and approaches to life. It would certainly be unwise to build a doctrine of the cardinal virtues upon a passage so controverted.

About contemporary with Pindar's ode is a passage in Aeschylus which singles out the

σώφρων δίκαιος ἀγαθὸς εὐσεβὴς ἀνήρ[1]

thus naming self-control, justice, goodness and piety. The affinities of Aeschylus with the Pythagoreans are well-attested and should warn us against tracing back Plato's scheme too rigidly. Here the appearance of piety is to be observed, as it recurs in Plato before the pattern of ethical thought in the *Republic* has emerged.

The difficulty in estimating the influence of Pythagoras is accentuated by a further point. Our knowledge of Pythagoras himself is limited and speculative. His very name is mentioned only five times between the years 500 and 300 B.C. What we do

---

[1] Aesch. *Sept.* 610.

know is that Plato's contact with 'the so-called Pythagoreans' (in Aristotle's phrase) in 387 radically influenced his thinking with results which are to be seen in the *Phaedo* and the *Republic*, and enabled him to develop a constructive metaphysic from the point to which Socrates had led him. The parallels between Plato's thought in the *Republic* and Hindu thought are too close to be accidental.[1] 'The mind of Plato was heavily charged with Orphic mysticism mainly derived from Asiatic sources. India, always the home of mystical devotion, probably contributed the major share.'[2] The supposition that this was mediated through the Pythagoreans is almost inescapable, and it may even be that the name Pythagoras represents Pitta-guru, 'father-teacher'. Hindu thought accepts a threefold ethical, psychological and social division. The elements of the soul are called Sattva, Rajas, and Tamas, and represent roughly intelligence combined with morality, energy and desire. They correspond in turn with the three great castes of the twice-born, the Brahmanas or priest-rulers, the Kshattryas or soldiers and executive, and the Vaishyas or producers and traders. The remarkable parallel with Plato is obvious and cannot be coincidental. There is however in the Hindu system a fourth caste, the Sudras, and these do not at first sight seem to fit into the pattern. But they are marked off from the other castes as being 'once-born' and correspond to Plato's slaves. Is there then among the Hindus a scheme of the virtues corresponding with the later cardinal virtues? Not, it seems, in any clear-cut form. But embryonically they are there. Tamas is incapable of virtue in itself; it lives in the realm of ignorance and sense-pleasure. But it is capable of obedience to the higher faculties. Rajas on its stronger side shows itself as 'go-getting', but it may appear as affectionate loyalty, and tenacious fidelity is its highest mark. Sattva is characterized by practical intelligence. The highest aim of the soul is Dharma, or 'the right performance of all duty'. This last is of great importance, for the Platonic definition of *dikaiosune* has no obvious antecedents in Greek usage, but is in many ways akin to the Hindu Dharma. The general deriva-

[1] See E. J. Urwick, *The Message of Plato*; S. Radhakrishnan, *Eastern Religions and Western Thought*. [2] Stutfield, *Mysticism and Catholicism*, p. 74.

tion of Plato's thought at this point from Indian originals appears to me to be certain, and the most probable channel of its mediation the Pythagoreans. But it is needful to emphasize again the danger of imagining a cut-and-dried scheme too early. Its precise formulation was evolved across the years and Western as well as Eastern thought went to its making.

The next relevant witness is Xenophon. Two passages in the *Memorabilia* depict Socrates as discoursing upon the virtues.[1] The first of these at a superficial glance might seem to anticipate the doctrine of the four cardinal virtues, and is certainly the closest parallel to Plato's exposition to be found in earlier Greek literature.[2] But a careful reading shows that the parallel is not to be pressed. The passage concerned is not part of a connected discourse, and the collocation of the virtues which it contains is due to Xenophon, not to Socrates. It is sharply and clearly divided into two. The earlier section deals with the question whether courage can be taught. The later comprises some scattered maxims about wisdom, under three broad headings: (*a*) there is no distinction between wisdom and self-control; (*b*) justice and all the rest of virtue is wisdom; (*c*) madness is the opposite of wisdom. It thus appears that though the four virtues are mentioned within a few lines of one another there is no sense that this is a systematic or basic analysis. This conclusion is reinforced by the second passage which lists some of those qualities whose definition Socrates was concerned to reach. The first of these is, significantly, piety (*eusebeia*). There follow justice, wisdom, goodness (*to agathon*), nobility (*to kalon*), and courage. There is no mention of *sophrosune*.

Later fourth-century evidence points in the same direction. There is no evidence either of a popular fourfold division or of an immediately accepted normative exposition. Thus in a pamphlet written about 355 Isocrates speaks of piety, self-control, justice, and virtue generally.[3] A typical passage comes in Demosthenes,[4] where he links courage, justice, and self-control. The evidence is that the fourfold scheme derives from the authority of Plato and took some time to become current.

[1] Xen. *Mem.* III 9, 1–5; IV 6, 1–12.
[2] Krohn, *Plat. Stud.*, p. 372.   [3] Isoc. *De Pace* 63.   [4] Dem. *De Cor.* 215.

Plato's own thinking is by no means standardized, as reference to a few passages will swiftly show. In the *Laches* he specifies *sophrosune, dikaiosune* and *hosiotes* (piety),[1] in the *Protagoras* the same three with justice taking precedence,[2] so too in the *Meno*.[3] In the *Gorgias* courage is added.[4] In these lists the absence of wisdom and the presence of piety is noteworthy. In the *Euthyphro* piety is defined as a part of justice,[5] but this is not apparent in any of these other analyses. As the argument of the *Protagoras* develops, however, Socrates attempts to show the identity of justice and piety, self-control and wisdom. Courage is subsequently added, and Socrates tries to reduce them all to knowledge. Piety was obviously pressing hard for inclusion in a definitive list of supreme virtues. The four which finally became dominant appear in an interesting passage in the *Phaedo*,[6] Pythagorean influence in the *Phaedo* is marked, and I take the dialogue to be Plato's first major work following his contact with Archytas and the South Italian Pythagoreans in 387. The passage runs

'The true moral ideal, whether self-control or justice or courage, is really a kind of purgation from all these emotions, and wisdom itself is a sort of purification.'

This is important for three reasons. First, it shows for the first time a clear association between the four eventually cardinal virtues. Secondly, wisdom (not justice) is set at some distance apart from the other three. Thirdly, the word for wisdom is not *sophia* but *phronesis*, which later appears as the Pythagorean name for 3, as *dikaiosune* is the Pythagorean name for 4.[7] These four recur in the Laws, where they are set in an hierarchy, with *phronesis* at the top, followed by *sophrosune, dikaiosune* and *andreia* in that order.[8] But Plato shows awareness that the actuality is a little more complex, as a translation shows.

'For wisdom is chief and leader of the divine class of goods, and next follows self-control; and from the union of these two with courage, springs justice, and fourth in the scale of virtue is courage.'

[1] Plat. *Lach.* 199 D.   [2] id. *Prot.* 329 C.   [3] id. *Meno* 78 D.
[4] id. *Gorg.* 507 C.   [5] id. *Euthyphr.* 12 D.   [6] id. *Phaed.* 69 C.
[7] *Theol. Ar.* 14; 23.   [8] Plat. *Laws* I 631 C.

In the Republic the four virtues are linked to the class structure of the community he has devised, and subsequently to the psychological analysis of the structure of the human personality which he essays. But they are apparently not derived either from his political or his psychological thinking, for he searches for the four named virtues within the structure rather than seeing what virtues he can derive from the structure.[1] In fact, as we have seen, the choice of these four virtues was neither unfamiliar nor inevitable. They were chosen because they accorded with the political and psychological scheme he had accepted from India and was here concerned to expound. Wisdom is the peculiar prerogative of the governing body, the philosopher-kings, and, as they alone possess the ultimate knowledge of good and evil, so they alone possess true virtue; the virtue of the rest is of the sort which Plato calls 'civic' or 'popular'. Courage obviously is the prerogative of the soldiers, the lower division of the Guardians of the State. Self-control schematically would pertain to the third class, the governed, but Plato attaches it to the whole community in the form of an unanimous agreement as to who should rule. Finally justice is to be seen in another principle pervading the whole community, the principle of 'a place for everyone and everyone in his place'. The individual is, in Cornford's words, 'a replica of society in miniature'. His inner personality is divided between Reason, Temper and Desire. Plato shows by an acute psychological analysis that our reason and our desire are often in conflict, and that temper sides now with one now with the other. (If we follow reason against our inclinations we are liable to say 'What a fool I am not to enjoy myself!' Equally if we follow our desires against reason we are liable to say 'What a rotter I am to behave like this!') Wisdom is the proper virtue of reason; courage belongs to temper, and is manifested when the person follows the dictates of reason no matter what the consequences; self-control as before is a pervasive harmony in accepting the rule of reason. Finally an individual is just, not merely in terms of his external behaviour, but in terms of the inner state of his soul, when each part of him is fulfilling its proper function. The most interesting

[1] Plat. *Rep.* IV 427 E; 429 A; 430 D; 432 B; 433 B.

part of this analysis, and one which has rarely excited comment, is the close similarity between the definitions of *sophrosune* and *dikaiosune* in these terms.

We must next examine more minutely each of the four qualities which thus became central to the ethical thinking of the Greek world. *Phronesis* or *sophia* is the crown of the virtues. We have seen this in the *Phaedo* and the *Laws*.[1] In the *Meno*, and in an important passage towards the end of the *Laws*, it is specifically said that the other virtues need to be under the generalship of Intelligence.[2] So in the *Republic*, where the overt attention is directed to *dikaiosune*, wisdom is the characteristic virtue of the ruling class and of the ruling element in man. In the *Protagoras* (as in Pericles' contrast of Sparta with Athens) real courage is shown to depend on the presence of *phronesis*.[3] This apparent intellectualism derives from Socrates. Socrates was nicknamed the *phrontistes*, and is represented in comedy as head of a *phrontisterion* or thinking-shop.[4] Aristotle tells us that he held that all the virtues were forms of *phronesis*.[5] That this is authentically Socratic we have seen in the pages of Xenophon.[6] But if the essence of virtue be intelligence, then the essence of vice must be ignorance. Hence the celebrated Socratic paradox that no man sins willingly. οὐδεὶς ἑκὼν κακός.[7] This reflects his theory of virtue. It accords with the introspective truth that when I do wrong I do so because I momentarily and aberrantly see it as better; if I really and fully knew what was good I could not help choosing it, for 'we needs must love the highest when we see it'. What is more, the sophistic movement of the fifth century, with which Socrates was popularly associated, but against whose deeper subversiveness he stood firm, had maintained a general agnosticism combined with the claim to teach *arete*. The Socratic aphorism 'Virtue is knowledge' with one brilliant stroke cuts through this claim. Agnosticism is seen to be incompatible with didacticism. But though Socrates' intellectualism is defensible, particularly when seen within the context of its time, there is another element in

---

[1] Plat. *Phaed.* 69 A ff; *Laws* I 631 C.   [2] id. *Meno.* 88 C; *Laws* XII 963 A.
[3] Plat. *Prot.* 360 B; cf. Thuc. II 40.   [4] Ar. *Clouds* 94, 266, etc.
[5] Arist. *N.E.* VI 1144 b 19.   [6] Xen. *Mem.* III 9, 5.   [7] Plat. *Prot.* 345 D.

human experience, discerned by his friend Euripides,[1] and echoed in familiar words by the pagan Ovid:

> *video meliora proboque,*
> *deteriora sequor*[2]
>
> '*I see and approve the better course,*
> *while I follow the worse.*'

and the Christian Paul, 'The good that I would I do not; the evil that I would not, that I do.'[3] In fact, as Aristotle puts it, Socrates 'was mistaken in thinking that all the virtues were forms of *phronesis*, but right in saying that they cannot exist without *phronesis*',[4] or, as Bishop Butler has it, 'moral understanding includes a *practical* sense of virtue, as well as a *speculative* perception of it'.[5] In moral action the will is engaged as well as the intellect. Socrates was, of course, aware of this. He might, whimsically as was his wont, have maintained that this was still a matter of cold hard-headedness. The passage in Xenophon suggests however that he intrepreted wisdom more broadly,[6] that there was always a moral element alongside the intellectual. Democritus, interestingly, lays high value on *phronesis*; its absence leads to disaster.[7] Aristotle, in a characteristically sensible analysis, himself separated the intellectual virtues from the moral virtues.[8] Among these he distinguishes logical knowledge (*episteme*), science (*techne*), practical wisdom (*phronesis*), intelligence (*nous*), and speculative wisdom (*sophia*). Practical wisdom is different from speculative wisdom. Both are rational, but pertain to different parts of the personality. *Phronesis* deals in calculations, *sophia* in certainties. Which helps to explain why philosophers are notoriously impractical. The relationship between moral and intellectual virtue is clear; the latter can exist without the former, but not the former without the latter.[9] It was however the Socratic conception which, perhaps in the third century, passed over into Jewish thought, and

---

[1] Eur. *Med.* 1078–9; *Hipp.* 375 ff; *fr.* 840; 841 cf. Sen. *Hipp.* 177.
[2] Ov. *Met.* vii 20.   [3] Rom. VII 19.   [4] Arist. *N.E.* VI 1144 b 19.
[5] Butler, *Anal.* I v.   [6] Xen. *Mem.* III 9.   [7] Democrit. *fr.* 102; 191.
[8] Arist. *N.E.* I 1103 a 5. In *Protrept.* he treats *phronesis* Platonically.   [9] ib. VI.

influenced some later books of the Old Testament and Apocrypha.[1] In these, wisdom appears as an emanation from God, bridging the gulf between God and man. True wisdom resides in God alone. Wisdom is the master-craftsman seated beside God, the companion of God, the only-begotten of God, an effulgence of Light, author of prophecy and sobriety, understanding and righteousness, sound judgement, order, and immortality, the teacher of mankind. It is sometimes, but not invariably, identified with the Law. The chief gift of Wisdom is to discern between good and evil, that is the capacity to make right moral judgements. To the Hellenizing Jews, following Plato, Wisdom has become a theological and ethical concept. Hence 'the fear of the Lord is the beginning of wisdom' becomes almost a stock quotation,[2] and the first mark of such wisdom is to turn aside from evil.[3] This was Wisdom's zenith, but she remained too cold, aloof, and intellectual, and could not satisfy the aspirations of all men. But it is worth remembering that though St Paul regarded the pursuit of *sophia* as peculiarly Greek,[4] and therefore suspect, the great church of Byzantine Christianity was dedicated to Holy Wisdom.

Sophrosune is the most difficult of these four qualities. It has been held to be the most characteristically Greek of them all by those who exalt the Greek way of life through blinkers which focus the attention on Plato and the Parthenon and shut out the seamier side.[5] It might be more truthful to say that *sophrosune* represents the quality which the Greeks knew they ought to possess and patently did not. It does not appear in the normal catalogue of modern virtues, though in some ways it is characteristic of the British way of life (far more so than of the Greek). It is variously rendered, 'self-control', 'moderation', 'temperance', 'obedience', each appropriate but too limited. 'It is something like Temperance, Gentleness, Mercy; sometimes Innocence, never mere

[1] Job XXVIII 1–28; Prov. VIII 1–IX 6; Ecclus. XXIV 1–34; Wisdom VII 1–VIII 21.   [2] Ps. CXI 10; Job XXVIII 28; Prov. I 7; IX 10.
[3] Job XXVIII 28; Prov. VIII 13; XVI 6.   [4] 1 Cor. I 22.
[5] e.g. G. Lowes Dickinson, F. R. Earp, and even Gilbert Murray. I need not say that I am in no sense offering a dissuasive from their noble enthusiasm, from which I myself took fire.

Caution: a tempering of dominant emotions by gentler thought.'[1]
The adjective *sophron* or *saophron* is the correlative of *oloophron*.
Oloophron means 'with destructive thoughts' and is applied to
wild animals and dangerous humans. *Sophron* means 'with saving
thoughts', and Plutarch actually so paraphrases it.[2] But if it was
in origin outward-looking (and this is not certain) it soon ceased
to be. Associated with the Delphic Oracle were two familiar
precepts, γνῶθι σαῦτον and μηδὲν ἄγαν, 'know yourself' and
'eschew excess'. The first of these is a form of *phronesis*; the
second was associated throughout Greek history with *sophrosune*.
The ancient commentators noted the first literary appearance of
the idea in the *Odyssey*.

> *Be glad at heart; but this wild joy restrain;*
> *We may not rightly triumph o'er the slain.*
> *Them their vile deeds, and heaven's just wrath o'erthrew:*
> *They who of human kind no reverence knew,*
> *The good, the bad, alike, whoever came;*
> *Therefore they perish'd in their deeds of shame.*[3]

There breathes the true spirit of moderation. Henceforth it runs
through all Greek literature in some form or another. Among the
philosophers we find 'measure' as one of the stabilizing factors in
Heraclitus' philosophy of flux.[4] 'The sun will not overstep his
measure, or the Furies, ministers of justice, will find him out.'
'The universe always has been, is and will be ever-living fire,
being kindled in measure and quenched in measure.' In Pythagoras we find the injunction to be moderate in drink, food, and
sports.[5] Solon, on whom the words μηδὲν ἄγαν were later
fathered,[6] is frequent in his condemnation of excess, putting forward a doctrine of measure,[7] Theognis tells Cyrnus to emulate his
own practice of walking quietly in the middle of the road.[8] In
Pindar the philosophy is central and explicit. God is God, man

---

[1] G. Murray, *The Rise of the Greek Epic*, p. 26.
[2] Plut. *De Tranq.* 470 D. Arist. *N.E.* VI 1140 b 11 takes it as meaning 'saving
phronesis'.   [3] Hom. *Od.* 22, 411, tr. W. Sotheby; cf. 18, 125 ff.
[4] Heraclitus *fr.* 20; 94. I cannot accept G. S. Kirk's rejection of the flux doctrine.
[5] Pyth. *Golden Sayings* 32.   [6] Suid. *s.v.* Σόλων.
[7] Arist. *Ath. Pol.* 5; 12. cf. *Hdt.* I, 29–34.   [8] Theogn. 331.

is man, and the most grievous sin (*hubris*) is to aspire above the human station.

'It is right to pursue advantage with moderation; too sharp is the sting of madness arising from unattainable aspirations.'[1]

Illustrations from the dramatists will serve to show its appearance in the fifth century. The first comes from Aeschylus:[2]

> *Seek neither licence, where no laws compel,*
> *Nor slavery beneath a tyrant's rod;*
> *Where liberty and rule are balanced well*
> *Success will follow as the gift of God,*
> *Though how He will direct it none can tell.*

Then again from Euripides:[3]

> *Long life hath taught me many things, and shown*
> *That lukewarm loves for men who die are best;*
> *Weak wine of liking let them mix alone,*
> *Not love, that stings the soul within the breast;*
>
> *Happy, who wears his love-bonds lightliest,*
> *Now cherished, now away at random thrown!*
> *Grievous it is for other's grief to moan,*
> *Hard that my soul for thine should lose her rest!*
>
> *Wise ruling this of life: but yet again*
> *Perchance too rigid diet is not well;*
> *He lives not best who dreads the coming pain*
> *And shunneth each delight desirable.*
> *Flee thou extremes, this word alone is plain,*
> *Of all that God hath given to man to spell!*

It should be added that the opening words of this passage come in for some just criticism from Plutarch, who argues that hostility and anger should be under control, but friendship and love should be given, when they are given, without reservation.[4]

---

[1] Pind. *Nem.* XI 47. cf. *Ol.* I.   [2] Aesch. *Eum.* 526 ff; tr. P. Vellacott.
[3] Eur. *Hipp.* 252–66, tr. A. Lang. For other passages in Euripides see *Med.* 125–7, 635; *Hipp.* 431–2; *Phoen.* 584; *Bacch.* 641, 1150–2; *I.A.* 824; *fr.* 209, 959.
[4] Plut. *Mor.* 95 F.

When we turn to the writers whose specific concern is ethical philosophy, we find that the practical Xenophon puts *sophrosune* into the centre of his picture. We can see it in the *Memorabilia* where moral self-control (*enkrateia*) is described as the foundation of the palace of virtue,[1] or in the *Cyropaedia*, where he says that without *sophrosune* other virtues are no good.[2] This also derives from Socrates, whose self-control was of such astonishing calibre. It is an interesting reflection of the approaches of Xenophon and Plato that they should have respectively singled out *sophrosune* and *phronesis* in this way. But Plato is not solely concerned with *phronesis*, and in the *Gorgias*, in opposition to the violent amoralism of Callicles, Socrates places *sophrosune* in the centre, and claims that the man of moderation and self-control is just, brave, and pious, and has therefore the totality of goodness; he is perfectly, completely, and absolutely good.[3] This is readily explicable in the light of the particular theme of this dialogue, but it recurs in the *Republic*, where a man is advised to

'choose the middle course that avoids both extremes, for in this way he will attain the greatest possible happiness.'[4]

In his old age Plato reverted to it.

'If anyone gives too great power to anything, too large a sail to a vessel, too much food to the body, too much authority to the mind, and does not observe the mean, everything is overthrown, and in the wantonness of excess runs in the one case to disorders, and in the other to injustice, which is the child of excess.'[5]

His older contemporary Democritus often expresses an ethic surprisingly close to that of Socrates; he also praises moderation and rejects excess in either direction.[6]

In Plato's pupil Aristotle this teaching becomes systematized, and we confront his celebrated doctrine that virtue resides in a

---

[1] Xen. *Mem.* I 5, 4.   [2] id. *Cyr.* III 1, 16.
[3] Plat. *Gorg.* 507 A–C.   [4] id. *Rep.* X 619 A.
[5] id. *Laws.* III 691 C; cf. 679 B; 701 E; V 728 E; VII 729 D.
[6] Democr. *fr.* 102; 191.

relative mean.[1] Here *sophrosune* itself is only one of a list of virtues;[2] its particular field is that of pleasures (and pains). The two extremes between which it stands are licentiousness and insensitivity. But really the whole doctrine is a glorification of *sophrosune*. One or two examples will help to illustrate it. Thus courage stands in the mean between rashness and cowardice, truthfulness between boastfulness and understatement. It is to be noted that there is mutual opposition, but that the extremes are farthest apart, with the result that the brave man seems rash to the coward, and cowardly to the rash. Further the mean is not arithmetical; the brave man is closer to bravado than to cowardice. The doctrine is not always easy to apply and sometimes Aristotle is hard put to it to identify the extremes. Indeed he has to admit that in some fields the doctrine does not hold; there is no mean in adultery for example. As Cicero says, to seek a mean in vice is like jumping off a cliff and trying to stop half-way.[3] In other words virtue is in some sense absolute. Kant criticized Aristotle on the ground that moral virtue was qualitative not quantitative.

'The difference between virtue and vice cannot be sought in the degree in which certain maxims are followed, but only in the specific quality of the maxims. Hence Aristotle's principle that virtue is the mean between two vices is false.'

This does not do justice to what Aristotle actually says. He anticipates some such criticism by pointing out that the mean is in a certain sense an extreme.[4] In essence or in definition it is a mean, in value it is a peak.[5] He seems to have had some kind of picture of a target, in which the bull's-eye certainly lies between the outer ring on either side, but in score it is far more valuable. He himself uses the illustration of the middle of a circle.[6] His statement that evil belongs to the class of the infinite, good to that of the fixed bears the same implications.[7] There is one way of hitting the mark, an infinite number of missing, one centre surrounded by infinite space. Here is a parallel with the Stoic view 'omnia

[1] Arist. *N.E.* II 1106 b 36. [2] ib. II 1107 b 5. [3] Cic. *T.D.* IV 41.
[4] Arist. *N.E.* II 1107 a 23. [5] ib. II 1107 a 7.
[6] ib. II 1109 a 25. [7] ib. II 1106 b 30.

peccata paria' ('all sins are equal'). It is as though the field of
moral action were a cone. From above the vertex is a mean, from
the side it is a peak. But by this defence Aristotle deviates from
the strict doctrine of the mean as between two extremes and two
only. A second line of defence is suggested by Aristotle's point
that the mean is not an arithmetical mean, but a relative mean.[1]
Ten measures may be too much food, two too little, but this does
not mean that six is precisely right. In other words the mean may
not be strictly quantitative; its concern is with fitness rather than
numbers. But Aristotle might have developed this point differ-
ently and more convincingly, in saying that virtue is a mean, and
in a sense quantitative *in its practical application*, though not in its
theoretical aspect. Thus the diet for Milo does lie between two
and ten measures from one point of view,[2] a coat's failure to fit
may in practice be due to excess or lack of material, though ideally
only its 'fitness' need be considered. Something of this sort is
suggested in his explanation of the mean:

> 'Now with everything that is continuous and divisible it is
> possible to take either a larger or a smaller or an equal part, and
> these proportions may be relative to the object or to us.'[3]

This seems to indicate that the mean is a matter of practical
application. Unfortunately this conflicts with his statement that
virtue is a mean in essence or in definition. There is some confusion in Aristotle's mind, and the most one can say is that there
are some germs of an answer to Kant's criticism, and that Aristotle
did in some sense recognize virtue as a qualitative extreme.

Aristotle is exceedingly ingenious in his applications of this
ethical doctrine to politics. He makes it clear in the *Politics* that he
regards the ethical doctrine as demonstrated and takes it for
granted. Because virtue is a mean, it is best to belong to the
middle-class, and to have moderate possessions; and the best form
of government is neither democracy nor oligarchy but something
in between them.[4] Furthermore he extends his formula to strain-

---

[1] ib. II 1106 a 36.   [2] ib. II 1106 b 2.
[3] ib. II 1106 a 26.   [4] id. *Pol.* 1295 a 34 ff.

37

ing point when he suggests that the political wisdom of the Hellenes is due to their occupying a territorial mean between the chill northerners who possess much courage but little skill, and the Asiatics with plenty of skill but little courage.[1] One is tempted to echo the remark that even the doctrine of the mean may be intemperately pursued.

This long and minute excursus into Aristotelian philosophy has served to show why the philosophy of *sophrosune* and μηδὲν ἄγαν could not, for all its value, ultimately hold the allegiance of thoughtful people. It was bound to appear as a philosophy of compromise, a philosophy of worldly wisdom rather than of sainthood. It is—as its derivation implies—a philosophy of safety; 'medio tutissimus ibis'.[2] We see this in its appearance in the comfortable commonsensical poetry of Horace. Horace studied at Athens in his youth, and we may suppose that like young Marcus Cicero he went to the lectures of Cratippus, the leading Peripatetic of the day. At any rate the doctrine recurs throughout his writings. The first satire contains the pregnant 'est modus in rebus' ('there's a halfway house in everything').[3] This leads to the second where Tigellius appears as the type of prodigality, Fufidius of meanness—'dum vitant stulti vitia in contraria currunt' ('fools in avoiding one fault rush into the opposite').[4] A few poems later he clears himself of the charge of falling into these extremes.[5] A long poem in the second book might almost be called a sermon on the golden mean.[6] In the Epistles the doctrine is explicitly stated: 'virtus est medium vitiorum' ('virtue is a mean between vices').[7] But its most famous appearance is in the ode to Murena, where the phrase 'the golden mean' is coined of gold, the poem which A. W. Verrall saw as the key to Horace.[8]

> *You better sure shall live, not evermore*
> *Trying high seas; nor, while seas rage, you flee,*
> *Pressing too much upon ill harboured shore.*

[1] ib. 1327 b 16 ff.   [2] Ov. *Met.* II 137.   [3] Hor. *Sat.* I 1, 106.
[4] ib. I 2, 25.   [5] ib. I 6, 68.   [6] ib. II 3.   [7] id. *Ep.* I 18, 9.
[8] id. *Od.* II 10. The authorship of the translation eludes me.

The golden mean who loves, lives safely free
From filth of foresworn house; and quiet lives,
Released from Court, where envy needs must be.

The winds most oft the hugest pine tree grieves;
The stately towers come down with greater fall;
The highest hills the bolt of thunder cleaves.

Evil haps do fill with hope; good haps appal
With fear of change, the courage well prepared:
Foul winters, as they come, away they shall.

Though present times and past with evils be snared,
They shall not last; with cithern, silent Muse,
Apollo wakes; and bow, hath sometimes spared.

In hard estate, with stout show, valour use,
The same man still, in whom wisdom prevails,
In too full wind, draw in thy swelling sails.

The curious feature of this philosophy is its dominance in China. This coincidence is accidental, but is worth a passing comment. Thus

'Confucius said, "The man of true breeding is the mean in action. The man of no breeding is the reverse".'

(How Pindar would have revelled in those words!)

' "The relation of the man of true breeding to the mean in action is that, being a man of true breeding, he consistently holds to the mean. The reverse relationship of the man of no breeding is that, being what he is, he has no sense of moral caution".'

Again,

'The master said, "Perfect is the mean, and for a long time how few men have been capable of it'."

And again,

'The Master said "I know the Way is not pursued. The learned run to excess and the ignorant fall short. I know why

39

the Way is not understood. The good run to excess and the bad fall short".'[1]

This last quotation is particularly revealing. I have said that the coincidence is accidental, but it would be truer to say that it arises from something ingrained in human nature. This is in short typical middle-class philosophy. We find it in a middle-class Greek of the Roman period like Plutarch, who exalts culture because it leads to moderation,[2] in the prudential philosophy of the book of Proverbs:

'Give me neither poverty nor riches: feed me with food convenient for me, lest I be full and deny thee, and say Who is the Lord? or lest I be poor, and steal, and take the name of my God in vain',[3]

in the founders of the American constitution.[4] John Galsworthy, the middle-class novelist of the middle-class, saw it when he made one of his characters describe himself not as a Christian but as a Confucian. The philosophy of *sophrosune* has lasted as a comfort to those who do not want to go to extremes. An ultimate moral philosophy must be prepared to go to extremes. You cannot have too much goodness—though you can have a lot too much of the self-satisfaction which too often goes with it and corrupts it. The trouble is that real goodness is disquieting; so Dorothea at the beginning of *Middlemarch* is regarded as unmarriageable. The saints are difficult to live with; they upset our comfortable routines. So we plead for compromise. But we know in our heart of hearts that the truth is with them.

Andreia, the word translated 'courage', means more literally 'manliness'. In early forms of society, where the males are expected to be fighters, the predominant virtue expected of the male is bravery in the sheer physical sense, and in a society dominated by males it is an inescapable part of virtue. Later it broadens, and includes all that is meant in our popular Kiplingesque phrase by 'being a man'. But *andreia*, unlike the Latin 'virtus' which is

[1] From Tzu Ssu, Confucius' son; cf. also his grandson K'ung Chi, who wrote *The Doctrine of the Mean*.
[2] Plut. *Cor.* I i. [3] Prov. XXX 8–9. [4] Alex. Hamilton in *Federalist* No. 11.

of similar origin and up to this point underwent a similar development, never became synonymous with all virtue. The nearest approach to this is in Plato's *Menexenus* where *arete*, the generic term for virtue, is set in opposition to *anandria*, cowardice. But the *Menexenus* is a puzzle in the Platonic corpus on any view, and even if we accept it as both authentic and seriously intended, this antithesis is not to be extended outside the context of the particular dialogue. The *Laches*, one of the inconclusive early dialogues, has as its theme the attempt to define courage, which is expressly described as one part of virtue.[1] But by the time the participants have passed from example to definition, and rejected false definitions, they find that they are defining courage as 'the science of good and evil, whether past, present, or future', and this is the whole of virtue, not a part of it.[2] It follows that they have not really defined courage. A similar view is found in the *Protagoras*, where courage becomes 'wisdom in knowing what is fearful and what is not',[3] and in the *Gorgias*, where a more cautious statement suggests that some courage implies knowledge.[4] This view derives from Socrates who held, according to Xenophon, that those who know how to behave in facing dangers are brave, and those who lack this knowledge are cowards.[5] Plato was prepared to extend the use of the word to include the power to face spiritual temptation as well as physical peril.[6] This extension Aristotle will not allow except metaphorically.[7] His useful discussion isolates and rules out five spurious forms of courage—facing danger through obedience to law or public opinion; experience of the particular danger; the courage of anger; the courage of temperament; the courage of ignorance. In the *Rhetoric* he is less intransigent, and defines courage as

'the quality by reason of which men are disposed to do noble actions in times of danger, as the law commands; cowardice is its opposite.'[8]

[1] Plat. *Lach.* 190 C.   [2] ib. 199 E.   [3] id. *Prot.* 360 D.
[4] id. *Gorg.* 495 C.   [5] Xen. *Mem.* IV 6, 11.
[6] Plat. *Rep.* IV 429 C–D; *Pol.* 306 B ff; *Laws* I 633 C–D.
[7] Arist. *N.E.* III 1115 a 6 ff.   [8] id. *Rhet.* I 9, 8.

Moral Values in the Ancient World

Aristotle's authority, and the obvious fact that his definition reflected popular usage, prevented *andreia* from attaining a more exalted status. The philosopher was no longer a soldier and courage was not his prime concern. It could not be made central to moral theory; it remained on the whole the Cinderella of the virtues; and when transmitted into the Christian catalogue regained its place only when fitted out with the glass slippers of the power to resist spiritual evil.[1]

The story of the fourth of the virtues is much more tangled. *Dikaiosune* is conventionally translated 'justice', but the English word is complex in its connotation and inheritance; it weaves together the Greek strand with the Hebrew *tsedeq* (personal righteousness), and the Latin *iustitia* (in the strict sense, legality).[2] *Dikaiosune* derives ultimately from *dike*, whose appearance in Homer we have already examined.[3] The man who is *dikaios* is either the man who follows the accepted way (one is tempted to say the Tao) or the man who respects the proper claims of others. Either forms a reasonable though not a transcendent basis for morality, and the second conceives morality in some sense in terms of personal relationships. The first appearance of the noun is in Theognis.[4]

ἐν δὲ δικαιοσύνῃ συλλήβδην πᾶσ' ἀρετή ἐστιν,
πᾶς δέ τ'ἀνὴρ ἀγαθός, Κύρνε, δίκαιος ἐών.

Theognis has just said that it is better to live in poverty and piety (*eusebeon*) than to be unjustly rich (*adikos*). 'All excellence' (but the word meant 'virtue' to later readers) 'is summed up in justice; to be just is the condition of goodness.' The passage is interesting in that it links justice and piety. The thought is not so much that in obedience to the commands of the gods we must behave ourselves in this world; rather that man is involved in a society in which gods and men share, and *eusebeia* or *hosiotes*, which is right relationship to the higher powers, is essentially linked with *dikaiosune*, which is social virtue generally. Hence

[1] cf. 1 Cor. XVI 13.   [2] L. W. Grensted, *Justice*.   [3] above, p. 17.
[4] Theogn. 147. The aphorism is also attributed to Phocylides, *fr.* 14.

42

Plato is able to treat piety and justice in close combination,[1] and is able to maintain his fourfold scheme without recourse to a fifth virtue, which would be mathematically and therefore philosophically less satisfying. This was followed by the Stoics.[2] It is noteworthy that the Hermetic literature, which owes some debt to Platonic thought, defines *eusebeia* as knowledge of God, thus linking it rather with wisdom.[3] Plato makes his Protagoras, perhaps authentically, exalt justice and self-control as the two great social virtues.[4] The sophist regarded human society as artificial and conventional, but unlike some of his fellows, saw those artifices and conventions as the factors which raised man above the level of the beasts, and approved them accordingly. Thrasymachus, the spokesman for amoralism in the *Republic*, seems authentically to have based religious scepticism on moral grounds. He denies the providential government of the universe because of the absence of justice, which he describes as the greatest blessing men can enjoy.[5] Plato's own treatment is found in the *Republic*. The first book appears to be a typically Socratic dialogue. We are introduced to Cephalus who represents the 'gathered experience of a good man of the generation just passing away', and whom, as Cicero says, it would be inappropriate for Socrates to criticize. He suggests that justice is telling the truth and paying debts. These are examples (and dubious examples) not a definition, and when his son Polemarchus takes over the argument he proposes 'giving to each man his due', and defines this more specifically as 'doing good to one's friends and harming one's enemies'. Socrates has no difficulty in refuting this; he uses various arguments, but his real point is that it cannot be just to harm any man. This refutation brings Plato's Thrasymachus into the arena with a violent paradox, 'Justice is the interest of the powers that be'. He means that justice is not an absolute concept at all, but those who hold power at any time call obedience to their desires 'just' and try by the use of morality to induce submission. But Thrasymachus is not a sufficiently thorough-going amoralist; in discussion he leaves in the word a residue of moral content, and that is enough to lead

[1] Plat. *Prot.* 331 A; *Gorg.* 507 B. [2] Stob. *Ecl. Eth.* 106.
[3] *Corp. Herm.* ix 4. [4] Plat. *Prot.* 323 A. [5] Thrasymachus *fr.* 8.

43

him into self-contradiction. At this point, instead of abandoning the dialogue in *aporia*, Plato restates the case for amoralism and enters upon the constructive part of his argument. As a result of this, as we have seen, he shows that *dikaiosune* is the supreme social virtue. The ideal community would be one in which the rulers manifested wisdom, the soldiers courage, and the whole community self-control. Justice consists precisely in this condition; a state is just when each part of the community fulfils its true function and does not attempt to usurp the work of another part.[1] So it is with the human soul. The ideal personality is one in which reason rules, temper is courageous, self-control is established throughout. The just man is the man in whom these conditions fully prevail. The just man is the integrated man.

Whatever be said about the ingenuity of this analysis, it stands outside the general Greek tradition. This is not what the word would convey to the average Greek of his day. For the majority of the Greeks of the classical age—later, as we shall see, it was to change—morality is social morality and derives its sanctions from society; for Plato it derives from the eternally existing absolute principle of justice. With Aristotle the more general view prevails, subjected to an acute and thorough analysis. It is the peculiar characteristic of man to live in society, and indeed in that sort of society which was to be seen in the Greek city state.[2] Ethics thus is comprised in 'politics',[3] and the objects which political science studies are nobility and justice.[4] Justice in its universal sense means obedience to Law; if the law is defective, in so far it is not truly Law. Justice, that is to say, is the full function of man considered as a member of society, and Aristotle uses the Theognis quotation to drive this home. In its particular sense, justice comprises rules to regulate certain aspects of social behaviour. He instances distributive, remedial, and (as an afterthought) commercial justice, and is really defining what we should call 'fair dealing'. Finally, over against legalism stands equity, and it is itself part of justice. There is an interesting parallel between Aristotle's inclusion of *to epieikes* as part of *dikaiosune* and Hosea's of *chesed* as part of *tsedeq*.

[1] cf. 1 Cor. XII; also Liv. II 32.   [2] Arist. *Pol.* I 1253 a 3.
[3] id. *N.E.* I 1094 b 11.   [4] ib. I 1094 b 14.

Only Hosea brings in a personal element, while Aristotle's standard is impersonal. Into such formulations God does not enter: the God of Aristotle is too remote, and the Olympians too debased. The standard is that of Man, and Man means Man in society. Aristotle's down-to-earth commonsense analysis has had universal influence in this whole field.[1]

But Aristotle's influence was flung against the scheme of the cardinal virtues. For this there were several reasons. He disliked anything which savoured of Pythagorean number-mysticism. The unnatural artificiality of Plato's scheme could not appeal to him. The doctrine left no room for the virtue he centrally exalted, that of 'highmindedness' (there is no real English equivalent). Further his own analysis of the virtues led to a much more complex scheme, as commonsense analyses habitually will. The Epicureans similarly rejected the cardinal division, though Torquatus in the pages of Cicero is at some pains to show how all four virtues minister to pleasure.[2] Wisdom is the guide by which pleasure is attained; self-control is a means to tranquillity of mind; courage, unattractive in itself, frees us from pain of body or mind; justice secures for us that peace of mind which injustice would endanger. The Stoics however accepted it, while linking it with their own doctrine of the unity of all virtue. 'He who has one virtue has all.'[3] But as Plato has perhaps accepted a scheme from India and derived it afresh from his own psychological analysis, so the Stoics accepted it from Plato, but used a fresh analysis to demonstrate it. The desire to live according to reason, they said, takes four forms—a desire for human society, an aspiration towards truth, an ambition for prominence, and a love of propriety—and to these correspond the four virtues.[4] These definitions were apparently coined by Panaetius. Plutarch tells us that there were differences of opinion in the Stoic school about them,[5] and indeed Stobaeus has preserved a slightly different analysis, according to which all men have from Nature inclination towards

---

[1] In these paragraphs I have borrowed from my own article 'Justice and Love' in J. Ferguson (ed.) *Studies in Christian Social Commitment.*
[2] Cic. *De Fin.* II 13, 42–16, 54.   [3] D.L. VII 125; cf. Cic. *T.D.* II 14, 32.
[4] Cic. *De Off.* I 4, 13–14; *De Fin.* IV 7, 18.   [5] Plut. *De Stoic. Rep.* 7.

the discovery of one's duty, towards the control of one's impulses, towards a power of endurance, and towards equitable distribution.[1] Further they subdivided the virtues themselves—wisdom including good counsel and understanding, self-control, good discipline, and orderliness, justice, impartiality, and beneficence, and courage, determination, and vigour.[2] More complex divisions are found, whereby, for example, justice is made to include piety, and self-control to include modesty and continence.[3] But whatever the particular definition or the particular subdivision, the fourfold basis is firm.

Rhetorical eulogies from the first century B.C. are more complex. Thus Theon analyses virtue into wisdom, self-control, courage, justice, piety, nobility, and a sense of greatness.[4] But Cicero several times adverts to the doctrine, and seems to accept it as a normal part of his heritage. He professed to adhere to the Academic School, and his ethical thought inclined to the Stoics, so this is not unnatural. A typical passage comes in the *De Finibus*.[5] He is giving a constructive account of morality in criticism of Epicurus:

'Nature has engendered in man the desire to discern the truth; this is most readily apparent when we are at leisure and eager to understand even astronomical phenomena.'

This is wisdom. Next justice:

'From this starting-point we are led to the love of all truth, that is all that is trustworthy, straightforward and unchanging, and to the corresponding hatred of all that is idle, false, and deceitful, such as guile, perjury, malice, and injustice.'

Third comes courage:

'Reason further contains a noble, glorious element, fitted for ruling rather than obeying, in such a way as to look on our mortal lot as trivial and easily endurable—a lofty and exalted

[1] Stob. *Ecl. Eth.* 108. [2] D.L. VII 126; cf. also Cic. *De Off.* I 7, 20 for justice.
[3] Stob. *Ecl. Eth.* 106. [4] *Rh. Gr.* II 109 ff. [5] Cic. *De Fin.* II 14, 46–7.

element, which fears nothing, gives in to no one and is for ever unconquerable.'

Finally *sophrosune*:

'Mark these three aspects of morality. A fourth follows. It enjoys equal loveliness and is formed from the other three. To it belong order and self-control. We can see something that resembles it in physical objects, when they are beautiful in appearance, and from there we pass to moral beauty in word and deed. It derives from those three admirable qualities I have already mentioned. It shrinks from rash action, and is not so shamefaced as to harm anyone by wanton word or action. It fears to act or speak in a manner unworthy of a man.'

The whole passage is of quite remarkable interest. The fourfold division of virtue is plainly a commonplace, but its presentation is by no means commonplace. The critique is obviously Stoic, and owes something to the Stoic doctrine of the unity of all virtue. Justice derives from wisdom; courage is a part of wisdom; self-control is a product of all three. The spiritualizing of courage is notable;[1] so is its characterization as ruleworthy. It will be remembered that in Plato's *Republic* the soldiers were in fact associated with the class of guardians. In Plato *sophrosune* attaches to all parts of the state and all parts of the soul; here it derives from the other three virtues. The linking of aesthetic and moral theory at this point is remarkable and might have appealed to Plato. But the position of justice is quite unplatonic.

Cicero's concern is with the commonplaces of philosophy, and he recurs again and again to the doctrine of the four virtues, and did in fact write a book on the subject,[2] in which he subdivided wisdom into memory, insight and foresight.[3] In the *Hortensius* he argued that if there were a future life, there would be no room there for eloquence, as there would be no law-suits, nor for the virtues. The collocation and the order of the collocation are interesting. There is no room for courage where there is no toil or

[1] cf. Cic. *De Off.* I 23, 79. [2] Jer. *Comm. in Zach.* I, 2.
[3] Aug. *De Trin.* XIV 11, 14.

danger to face; for justice in a situation where one cannot covet another's possessions; for self-control in a world free from the passions; for wisdom unless we are presented with a choice between good and evil.[1] The virtues are here negatively conceived but four in number they unquestionably are. In the *De Officiis* there is a lengthy examination of the four virtues, as Jerome remarks.[2] It is based upon Panaetius, and therefore not directly illustrative of his own thought, though he uses his own examples to deck out his narrative. It is more significant that in the last book, where he has not Panaetius to guide him his thought falls promptly into the same categories.[3] Elsewhere, however, piety survives separately to form a fifth in the catalogue.[4]

In imperial Rome the doctrine, remaining current in philosophic circles, was replaced in the public eye by the new emphasis on the imperial virtues. Augustus claimed to embody a quartet of virtues also, they were, however, Courage (*virtus*), Justice (*iustitia*), Piety or Loyalty (*pietas*), and Clemency (*clementia*). These we shall examine later.[5] In the third century Plotinus, disciple of Plato, and friend of the emperor Gallienus, naturally espouses the Platonic scheme. He sees the four virtues merging into one under the command of intelligence, justice representing the direction of the soul towards intelligence, *sophrosune* the soul's intimate conversion in the same direction, and courage the perseverance of the intellect.[5] We may further note that when the pagan Julian breaks the succession of Christian rulers his panegyrist also returns to the old classification with a slightly different nomenclature, *aequitas*, *temperantia*, *fortitudo*, and *providentia*.[7]

Cicero has been the great transmitter, and it was through his influence that the doctrine of the four virtues passed to Christendom. It is not to be found in the New Testament. One passage suggests a knowledge of the pagan approach. In the letter to Titus the author suggests that we should live σωφρόνως καὶ δικαίως καὶ εὐσεβῶς, with self-control, justice, and piety.[8] The adverbs are well explained by St Bernard: 'sobrie erga nos; iuste erga proxi-

---

[1] Cic. *Hort. fr.* 12. [2] Jer. *Comm. in Zach.* 1, 2; Cic. *De Off.* I 6, 18–45, 160.
[3] Cic. *De Off.* III 33, 117–18. [4] id. *T.D.* I 26, 64.
[5] infra c. X. [6] Plot. *Enn.* 1, 2, 6 ff. [7] *Pan. Vet.* III 5. [8] Tit. II 12.

mos; pie erga Deum' ('showing self-control towards ourselves, justice to our neighbours, piety to God'). More important is the paean in praise of love in one of Paul's letters to the Church at Corinth, which ends with the triad of Christian virtues, Faith, Hope, and Love.[1] It has been reasonably suggested that the criticism of 'knowledge'[2] in the same chapter, and the earlier rejection of 'wisdom'[3] show this to be a deliberate attempt to replace the familiar pagan values, or a debased Gnostic form of them, by a new Christian triad. Dante certainly so saw it:

> *' What is it, son,' my lord began inquire,*
> *' That takes thine eyes so?' ' Those three torches*
> *there,'*
> *Said I, 'that kindle all this pole with fire.'*
>
> *And he: ' The four bright stars that shone so fair*
> *To greet thee in the dawn have dipped from view*
> *Yonder, and these have risen up where they were.'*[4]

Later he seems to hold them together:

> *Three ladies dancing in a ring there were*
> *By the right wheel; the first so red of hue*
> *She'd scarce be noted in the furnace-flare;*
>
> *The next appeared of emerald through and through,*
> *Both flesh and bone; the third of them did seem*
> *As she were formed of snowflakes fallen new;*
>
> *Now white, now red was leader to the team,*
> *And as she sang the other two likewise*
> *Or quick or slow kept measure to her theme.*
>
> *Four by the left wheel, clad in purple guise,*
> *Made festival; and she who led the ball*
> *Among them, in her forehead had three eyes.*[5]

It was in fact the Platonist Origen who first drew attention to the doctrine in Christian circles; it was Ambrose two hundred

---

[1] I Cor. XIII 13; cf. I Thess. I 3, Col. I 4–5.
[2] ib. XIII 2, 8.
[3] ib. I 19–30.
[4] Dante, *Purg.* VIII 88–93, tr. D. L. Sayers.
[5] ib. XXIX 121–32.

years later who gave it currency. The latter took it from Cicero and the Stoics, but tried to Christianize it. Wisdom is now theological: it has God as its object. Piety is thus transferred from the domain of justice to the domain of wisdom.[1] Courage is essentially the spiritual capacity to withstand temptation, though Ambrose, who disapproved of capital punishment, is too deeply imbued with the Old Testament to extend his disapproval to war, and does not exclude courage in the popular sense. Self-control is classical in its meaning, but justice is extended (as indeed it was by Cicero) to include benevolence, whose absence from the strict line of the cardinal virtues frequently disturbed Christian writers. Augustine took up the exposition where Ambrose left off, and with him the virtues are explicitly Christianized and subordinated to the Pauline triad. Courage, to Augustine, is

'love cheerfully enduring all things for the sake of God; self-control is love keeping itself entire and inviolate for God; justice is love serving God only and therefore controlling all else that is subject to man; wisdom is love discriminating between those things which assist and those things which retard its approach to God.'[2]

He characterized the virtues brilliantly—'prudentiae lumen, temperantiae decus, fortitudinis robur, iustitiae sanctitas' ('the light of wisdom, the seemliness of self-control, the might of courage, the holiness of justice'); the last is a clear Christianization. The ingenuity of his classification is reminiscent of that of Ruskin, who spoke of

'Temperance, the principle of desistance: Courage, the principle of resistance: Justice, the principle of assistance: Prudence, the principle of consistence.'[3]

The doctrine of the cardinal virtues is a valiant attempt to systematize ethical thought. But it suffered from three grave defects. In the first place it was inadequate as an analysis. Ionian philosophy dealing with the macrocosm, had sought one single

---

[1] Ambr. *De Off.* I 27. [2] Aug. *De Mor. Eccl.* 25.
[3] I owe these references to W. D. Geddes, *The Phaedo of Plato*, p. 254.

substratum whereby could be explained the manifold phenomena of experience. Once Empedocles had postulated not one root but four, and produced a physical analysis that was not simple but complex, the process could not be halted, and Anaxagoras with his homoeomeries was followed by Leucippus, Democritus, and the Atomists. Some of the moralists sought a simple, single answer to their ethical questionings, and the Christian answer when it came was single and simple, though it became overlaid with the cleverness of the professional thinkers. The doctrine of the cardinal virtues really stands to ethical philosophy as the views of Empedocles do to natural philosophy. It is half-and-half, either too diffuse or not diffuse enough. We have seen piety claiming its place, and benevolence, and both being somewhat restively subsumed under justice. Aristotle would arrogate a place to proper pride, Commodus and the Christian tradition to proper humility. Faith, hope, and love thrust themselves forward.

Secondly, the whole Greek approach, in so far as it became articulate, tended to be over-intellectualized. Language shows this; even the Homeric *aisima eidenai*. There is no real Greek word for 'to sin'; *hamartanein* means 'to miss the target'. Where we use the phrase 'take it to *heart*', the Greek said nou*thetein*. *Sophrosune* and *phronesis* are akin in derivation. It is true that this warns us not to assume too readily that words like *noein* and *phronein* have an exclusively intellectual content. It is also true that the emphasis is unmistakably intellectualist. So Sophocles can describe folly as the sister of crime.[1] In the Hellenistic Age, with the idealization of Socrates and Zeno, and Diogenes and Epicurus, it is even more marked. Nietzsche put it pungently when he said that where other nations had saints the Greeks had sages.[2]

These are principally, though not wholly, intellectual problems. But there is a more serious objection to the doctrine, because a practical one. The doctrine attempts an introspective standard of virtue. It suggests that a man should look at his own soul and discern there the lineaments of righteousness, or if he cannot do that compare the soiled and tattered images of the virtues with the pure Platonic truth. It is not my intention to minimize the value

---

[1] Soph. *fr.* 925.   [2] cf. J. C. Opstelten, *Sophocles and Greek Pessimism*, p. 202.

of such introspection. It is probably an essential part of the moral life. It is certainly an important guide in keeping us up to scratch. If it be not too Pelagian to say so, moral effort is an integral part of right living, and moral effort means the conscious attempt to live by such norms as these. But the history of Christian ethics from St Paul to Moral Rearmament testifies that to establish these or similar abstract principles as the basis of moral behaviour, is to court either despair in the failure to attain an absolute standard which is beyond the grasp of our wills or self-righteous complacency in the illusion of having attained. Worst of all is the attempt to turn love into law in this way, and to treat it as an abstract principle to be attained. Righteous behaviour at the last is a matter of personal relationships and it is not to be trapped within an abstract analysis.

IV

FRIENDSHIP[1]

FRIENDSHIP IS AN element in all society, and the subject of aphorisms from an early date. The actual Greek word *philos* appears to be in origin possessive; hence phrases like φίλον ἦτορ, φίλας ἀνὰ χεῖρας, φίλα βλέφαρα, and even φίλα εἵματα as well as παῖδα φίλην, ἀλόχους φίλας, and the like, where it is applied to parts of the body and clothing as well as wife and child.[2] In the society of the Homeric poems 'friends' means a group of people who can rely on one another. It denotes a practical, not an emotional, relationship, and represents the stage of establishing social ties similar to those existing within the family, but extending more widely. Achilles and Patroclus stand to the world of Homer somewhat as David and Jonathan to the Old Testament, but the intensity of their emotions, though it played some part in influencing the picture of friendship which later emerged, may give a misleading impression of its scope at this time. We shall obtain a more objective picture if we look at the other great model friendship, that between Theseus and Pirithous:

> *nec Lethaea valet Theseus abrumpere caro*
> *vincula Pirithoo.*[3]

'Theseus has not the power to break the chains of hell for his beloved Pirithous.'

---

[1] See E. Curtius, 'Die Freundschaft im Alterthume', *Alterthum und Gegenwart* I (1882) pp. 183–202; F. Dirlmeier, φίλος *und* φιλία *im vorhellenistischen Griechentum*, Diss. Munich, 1931; L. Dugas, *L'Amitié Antique* (Paris 1894). This last is much the fullest treatment known to me.

[2] Hom. *Il.* 3, 31; 7, 130; *Od.* 5, 493; *Il.* 2, 261; 1, 20; 4, 238, etc.

[3] Hor. *Od.* IV 7, 27–8.

This appears to have begun when Theseus caught Pirithous raiding Marathon. They entered into a mutual compact and were duty bound (as we say) to support one another on various enterprises. Or we may look at the institution of guest-friendship, and observe how Glaucus and Diomedes in the midst of battle find the ties of hospitality formerly holding their houses together stronger than the emotions of war, and actually renew them on the battle-field;[1] we may note too that Ascylus is described, a little unexpectedly, as φίλος ἀνθρώποισιν by reason of his hospitality.[2] This institution of guest-friendship was of some significance in the classical period: its unity was symbolized by the great sacrament of a common meal.

In the seventh and sixth centuries there are some traces of a new approach, and a greater individualism. Scattered maxims from the are sages of no more than passing interest and show no signs of systematic thought or exposition. Thus we have attributed to Solon, 'Do not make friends quickly, but when you have made them, be sure to keep them';[3] to Bias of Priene, 'Treat your friends as if you will one day hate them, for most men are bad' (advice which won a vigorous retort from Cicero);[4] to Anacharsis, 'It is better to have one good friend than many bad ones';[5] to Cleobulus of Lindus, 'One ought to benefit a friend so as to increase his friendship, and to transform an enemy into a friend';[6] to Periander, 'Be the same to friends in prosperity and adversity';[7] to Chilon, 'Be more ready to share in your friends' adversity than in their prosperity'.[8] These were considered useful enough to be preserved to posterity, but they do not offer anything profound in the way of social philosophy.

The first place where we can discern something deeper is among the Pythagoreans. Into the complexities of Pythagorean number-mysticism and cosmology we are happily not here called to enter; nor into the highly controversial questions of Pythagorean origins, and the provenance, date, teaching, and very existence of Pythagoras himself. But among the apophthegms attributed to the founder of the school are four that concern

---

[1] Hom. *Il*. 6, 119 ff.   [2] ib. 6, 14.   [3] D.L. I 60.   [4] D.L. I 87; Cic. *De Am*. 59.
[5] *D.L.* l 105.   [6] D.L. I 91.   [7] D.L. I 98.   [8] D.L. I 70.

friendship: μία ψυχή,[1] κοινὰ τὰ φίλων,[2] ἰσότης φιλότης,[3] and ἄρά ἐστι φίλος ἕτερος ὡς ἐγώ.[4] From the first we understand that friends come to so deep a common experience that they enjoy a common life and share in the perfect communion of a single personality—'of the twain one spirit'. The second both asserts and inculcates the principle of sharing. Nothing is private between friends; friends share all things. The third affirms in similar vein that friendship is equality. The fourth, a celebrated dictum in its Latin form, echoes the first. The friend is a second self. These precepts were put into practice within the school. The Pythagorean disciples did in fact put all their possessions into the common stock, though there is some evidence suggesting that the concept of sharing varied at different points in the history of the school, and that an arithmetical equality later gave place to a geometrical equality of proportion, justifying distinctions within the community. It was contact with the Pythagorean communities of south Italy that gave Plato the idea of the Academy, and in some sense it may be said that Pythagoras' maxims upon friendship formed the ultimate inspiration of the public school and the residential university. Plato in one of the letters speaks of the bond of friendship between students of the Academy.[5]

During the same period there is some speculation about the natural basis of friendship. The pre-Socratic philosophers based their theories of natural law upon one of two principles. Some held that like is drawn by like, and that perception, for example, is to be explained in terms of the conjunction of like and like. Thus Diogenes of Apollonia explains that smell takes place when air outside meets air of similar density inside the brain; Empedocles is constrained to postulate a fire within the eye to account for the perception of light.[6] Plato takes this up in the *Phaedo*. The body which is mutable and perishable perceives the material world

---

[1] Arist. *N.E.* IX 8, 2; *E.E.* VII 6, 7–8; *Mor. Mag.* II 11, 44; Cic. *De Am.* 81, 92; *De Off.* I 56.

[2] D.L. VIII 10; X 11; Plat. *Lys.* 207 C; Arist. *N.E.* VIII 9, 1; *E.E.* VII 2, 33–8; Ter. *Ad.* 803 f; Cic. *De Off.* I 51; Mart. II 43; Ath. I 8a; cf. Eur. *Andr.* 376. Diogenes is quoting Timaeus.

[3] D.L. VIII 10; Arist. *N.E.* VIII 5, 5; VIII 8, 5; IX 8, 2.   [4] Philo II 659.

[5] Plat. *Ep.* VI 323 B.   [6] Theophr. *De Sensu* 40; 7 cf. Democr. *fr.* 164.

which is mutable and perishable. The soul which perceives the eternal unchangeable Forms must itself be eternal and unchangeable. Later still the doctrine took on theological implications. For the Hermetists, and even, with reservations, for the Jew Philo, to know God is to be a son of God.[1] In the *Corpus Hermeticum* we read 'Unless you make yourself equal to God, you cannot apprehend God, for like is known by like'.[2] This is the celebrated ὁμοίωσις τῷ θεῷ, and in Athanasius and the Greek Fathers it becomes a part of the philosophy of the Incarnation. Goethe expresses it in a lucid line, 'Du gleichst dem Geist den du begreifst'. On the other hand stand those who, like Heraclitus, held that the basis of natural law lay in the tension of opposites, and who, like Anaxagoras, held that sense-perception arises from the meeting of opposites. It is obvious that these divergent doctrines can give rise to very different views of friendship, if they are once transferred from the universe to man, from the macrocosm to the microcosm. The one would have it that friendship is a communion of the like-minded; the other that friendship is based upon complementary qualities. Homer is sometimes quoted in support of the former view:

ὡς αἰεὶ τὸν ὁμοῖον ἄγει θεὸς ὡς τὸν ὁμοῖον.
'God always draws like to like.'[3]

Aristotle specifically links this view with the philosophy of Empedocles, and the other with Heraclitus and Euripides.[4] A further speculative element came in with the sophistic movement of the fifth and fourth centuries. The contrast between *nomos* and *phusis* which then emerged is familiar. *Phusis*, originally 'how a thing grows', is 'nature'; *nomos*, originally a dispensation, comes to mean 'convention'. They contrast the universal, unchangeable, and objective, with the particular, transitory, and subjective. The antithesis, once made, can be interpreted in two different ways. It is possible to say that conventions, having no roots in nature, are artificial restrictions with no binding force; hence the amoralism of Critias or Plato's Thrasymachus. But it is also possible to say,

[1] Philo *De Conf.* 145. [2] *C.H.* XI 20. [3] Hom. *Od.* 17, 218.
[4] Arist. *N.E.* VIII 1155 b 2; cf. *E.E.* 1235 a 4.

with Plato's Protagoras, that conventions create progress. We cannot trace this distinction as applied to friendship, but it is clear that adherents of the former view would regard the ties of friendship as not stringent, whereas those who held the latter position would tend to see in friendship a mark of civilization and exaltation.

Significantly, it is in the age when the questioning mind turns from impersonal problems to human action that the clubs which may have begun as religious associations, and which certainly continued in order to give social intercourse outside clan and family, began to take on new and sinister aspects. The clubs were called fellowships (*hetaireiai*); their members were 'fellows' or 'comrades'. It is the feminine of this word which represents the cultured *demi-mondaines* of whom Aspasia is so brilliant an example. In the middle of the fifth century these fellowships seem to have fulfilled a desire among the upper classes for intellectual and social companionship. With the darker days of the Peloponnesian War, the old values were subverted, and dissatisfaction with democratic errors grew. The fellowships, which had fulfilled the social needs of the upper classes, now became the instruments of their political discontent, and it was notorious that it was in the fellowships that the oligarchic revolutions were planned. The result was that the restored democrats banned such political associations. But the need for social intercourse remained, and the fourth century, and still more the Hellenistic Age, provide us with innumerable inscriptions, alike from Athens and the rest of Greece, testifying to the growth and number of these fellowships; in many instances the members are explicitly called *philoi*, and Aristotle several times refers to them in his discussion of friendship.[1] Such associations were natural. Family ties and conjugal affection were familiar enough in the Greek world, and we must not undervalue the position of women.[2] But, on the whole, it was

[1] e.g. Arist. *N.E.* VIII 1157 b 24, 1159 b 33, 1161 a 26, b 36, 1162 a 10; IX 1164 b 27, 33, 1165 a 29, 1171 a 15.
[2] See A. W. Gomme, *Essays on History and Literature*; H. D. F. Kitto, *The Greeks*; C. T. Seltman, *Women in Antiquity*; all of whom, however, tend to overstate their counterblast to the conventional denigration of the position of women. On the other hand L. Dugas, *L'Amitié Antique*, much understates the position.

not and could not be in the home that a man sublimated his need for intellectual and spiritual companionship. Hence friendship played a rather larger part in the life and thought of the Greeks than with us, and romantic love proportionately smaller.

The dramatists mirror their age, and it is not surprising to find in them some reflections on the nature of friendship. Aristophanes pleaded for *philia* as a political elixir to unite the Greeks.[1] Menander produced the most famous of all maxims on friendship when he said that 'Evil communications corrupt good manners', or 'Good character is corrupted by bad company'.[2] So the general maxim of tragedy is to choose good company for one's friends.[3] There is beginning to emerge, however, the later demand for self-sufficiency, characteristic of the Hellenistic Age. Thus Ajax in Sophocles' play learns to limit the scope alike of his hatred and friendship, for enemies may become friends and friends enemies.[4] One or two of Euripides' characters express the thought that friends tend to drop away from those in adversity.[5] But we have not yet reached the atomism of the later philosophic schools, and Euripides gives us three notable examples of friendship, between Orestes and Pylades, Admetus and Heracles, Theseus and Heracles. Pylades expresses well the calling of a friend to do all that his friend may need, even to dying with him.[6] Even more notable is Theseus's determination to stand by Heracles after he has killed his wife and children in mad frenzy. He stays, despite Heracles' pleas, despite the pollution involved, because 'no avenging spirit comes to harm friends from the hands of friends'.[7] This is the true spirit of friendship.

The pattern of life displayed in the tragedians is echoed in the Attic Orators, as Douglas Thomson has reminded us.[8] Isocrates has some sensible words to Demonicus on the subject of choice of friends.[9]

'Never make a friend before finding out how he has treated his former friends; expect him to show the same disposition to

[1] Ar. *Peace* 996.   [2] Also attributed to Euripides.
[3] Eur. *Or.* 627–8, 804–6; *H.F.* 1404; *fr.* 609, 1079.   [4] Soph. *Ajax* 678–82.
[5] Eur. *El.* 606–7; *H.F.* 559.   [6] Eur. *Or.* 794; *I.T.* 684–6.   [7] Eur. *H.F.* 1234.
[8] D. Thomson, *Euripides and the Attic Orators*, pp. 180–7, to whom these paragraphs are much indebted.   [9] Isoc. *Ad Demon.* 24–6.

you as he has shown to them. Do not be in a hurry to make friends; try and make your friendships lasting. It is equally bad to keep changing your companions and to be without friends. Be ready to test them, but not to your own detriment. You will do this all right if you pretend to be in need when you are actually not. Share secrets which are not real secrets with them. If it does not come off, you will not do yourself any harm; if it does, you will have a better understanding of their character. Let life's misfortunes and your friends' willingness to share in your dangers be the ground on which you try them. We test gold in the fire; we distinguish our true friends in time of misfortune. You will help your friends best if you do not wait for them to ask you but find the opportune moment to go to their aid of your own initiative. Consider it equally bad to be outdone by your enemies in doing injury and by your friends in good deeds. Include among your associates not merely those who show distress at your misfortunes, but those who show no envy your successes. There are many who sympathize with their friends in adversity but grudge them their prosperity. Remember to speak of your absent friends to those who are with you, for them to realize that absence makes the heart grow fonder of them too.'

This is a particularly interesting passage for two reasons. Firstly it is filled with commonplaces. A traditional collection of maxims about friendship has grown up, and Isocrates is drawing freely upon them.[1] Secondly, and more importantly, we see the essentially prudential nature of Greek theory about friendship. We have already seen this reflected in the institution of guest-friendship and in the general Homeric conception, and it persists through the classical age.

Elsewhere in the orators we find a similar picture to that already drawn. We find the principle of 'like to like'.[2] Hence naturally we should avoid the friendship of bad men.[3] Friendship involves

---

[1] cf. Hesiod *W.D.* 715; *Theog.* 415, 869–72; Solon *apud* D.L. l 60; Aesch. *Ag.* 832; Xen. *Mem.* II 6, 6.   [2] Lycurgus *In Leocr.* 135; cf. Dem. *In Andr.* 64.   [3] Hyperides *fr.* 210 a; cf. Isoc. *Ad Demon.* I.

the duty of beneficent action.[1] Deeper notes are struck in the still familiar refusal to abandon friends in adversity,[2] or the sense that friendship looks to something beyond the pleasure of the immediate present.[3] Again however it is a fragment of Isocrates which contains the most acute analysis.[4]

> 'True friendship seeks three things above all others—the magnetic nobility of virtue, the delight of companionship, and the compulsion of need. We must accept our friends' criticisms, enjoy their company, and help them when called upon.'

The magnetic nobility of virtue—hence it is that the whole of time will never erase the friendship of men of good character.[5]

One unique monument merits special mention; it was no doubt private and peculiar, but is none the less remarkable. It is a marble relief, at present in Copenhagen, datable to the fourth century, and it bears a dedication in clear but irregular lettering from Aristomache, Theoris, and Olympiodorus to Zeus Epiteleios Philios, his mother Philia, and his wife Agathe Tyche. The cult of Good Luck is a commonplace of this age of uncertainty; Friendship, the mother of Zeus, is without parallel. This family must have found a very deep fulfilment in personal affection. We must, I think, suppose that family affection is here referred to. But Philia is not Eros, and there is a curiously Epicurean flavour about the dedication, unfitting to the age or to the theology.

When we turn from the more popular allusions of orators and dramatists to the more esoteric treatment of the philosophers we find a systematic account of friendship in the worthy but prosy moralizings of the Xenophontic Socrates, which might almost have been taken from one of the popular orators.[6] People always speak of a friend as the mightiest of all possessions. This is no doubt almost a proverb, but it is worth thinking out the implications of the idea that a friend is a possession. Just so in the *Cyro-*

---

[1] Isaeus I 6–8, 20; Dem. *In Aristocr.* 134; Aeschines II 152; Isoc. *Ad Nicocl.* 52.
[2] Isoc. *De Pace* 21.   [3] Dem. *In Aristocr.* 134; Plato *Phaedr.* 233 B–C.
[4] Isoc. *fr.* iii 13.   [5] Isoc. *Ad Demon.* 1.   [6] Xen. *Mem.* II 4 ff.

paedia Xenophon describes trustworthy friends as the most
genuine and reliable sceptre a king can have,[1] and in the *Hiero*
laments the infrequency with which rulers enjoy it.[2] Socrates goes
on to criticize the way in which most people take more care over
the choice of other possessions than over the choice of friends.
But a good friend fills up what we lack, and co-operates with us
in all things—verbs compounded with *sun* pile upon one another.[3]
Friends are of markedly different worth. We should avoid the
self-indulgent, the extravagant, the miserly, the quarrelsome, the
selfish. Our standards should be self-control, reliability, and use-
fulness. So before choosing a friend we should examine his past
record and consult the oracle to see if the gods have anything
against him. (How calculating, how self-centred it all seems!) We
must then use all our blandishments to win them. If we would
have good friends we must be good ourselves. But all is not plain
sailing. Sometimes good men are at variance with one another;
bad men can never make true friends; and there can never be real
concord between good and bad. Still friendship exists, and exists
by nature: this is an obvious hit at sophistic theories of the con-
ventionality of friendship.[4] Friendship is the natural concomitant
of virtue; in war and peace alike we need partners and allies. Our
first aim then must be to espouse virtue. Then we will strain to
win virtuous friends as part of our own fulfilment. Socrates here
bases friendship upon *eros* and *pothos* (the love and desire which
spring from a sense of incompleteness),[5] and once again we see
how self-regarding was the Greek conception of friendship; it
springs from our needs and aspirations. But friendship, while
based on mutual affection and truthful esteem, must not degenerate into passion. We have to remember that physical homosexuality was commonly accepted in Greek aristocratic society. It was
the basis of some units of military renown, such as the Theban
Sacred Band.[6] Socrates himself felt these physical urges; his quality
is seen in the way he could keep them under control. The discourse at this point goes off at a tangent on the question how to
relieve impecunious friends. It has scarcely added depth to our

[1] id. *Cyr.* VIII 7, 13.   [2] id. *Hiero* III.   [3] cf. p. 22.
[4] See above p. 56.   [5] See c. V.   [6] Ath. XIII 561 i.

understanding, and has shown us again the link between expediency and friendship in Greek theory.

Nor does the *Lysis* of Plato, an early dialogue, which therefore probably reveals more of Socrates than Plato, help markedly towards a constructive account. As in Xenophon, there is a link between *philia* and *eros*.[1] Menexenus and Lysis are friends, and Socrates questions Menexenus upon the nature of friendship, on the grounds that he himself longs for the acquisition of friends (note that friends are an acquisition, arising from an inner aspiration). Socrates asks who is rightly given the name of friend, the subject or object of affection, and has no difficulty in tying up his examinee whichever answer he gives. This passage is important, because it establishes the point, which is not however specifically made, that friendship is a reciprocal relationship. Socrates tries a fresh tack. He examines in turn the two principal theories of attraction, 'like to like' and 'unlike to unlike', and shows that neither is adequate as a basis for friendship. There can be no true friendship between bad men. Neither can there be friendship between good men, for a good man is self-sufficient and has no need for friends—a very illuminating dictum. And it is absurd to suppose that the good would be friends of the bad. The truth must be more complex, and Socrates produces the theory that friendship may be the aspiration of that which is in itself neither good nor evil towards that which is good. Again there is the linking of *philia* with *eros*, the sense of friendship as springing from an aspiration. This theory is however again rejected, on the grounds that our need of good is pragmatically known to us by the presence of evil; the philosopher is a friend of wisdom because he knows his ignorance. It seems paradoxical to say that if evil did not exist, neither would friendship. Can the object of friendship then be an end in itself? If so, it must be a good which belongs to us but of which we are deprived. This has already been refuted, for friendship is not a 'like to like' relationship, still less a 'good to good'. In this impasse the dialogue ends. The argument is subtler than Xenophon's, though it sometimes strays too far from the world of commonsense reality. It reinforces our realization of the pru-

[1] Plat. *Lys.* 221 B; cf. *Symp.* 179 C.

dential nature of much Greek morality, and in the implicit affirmation that friendship must be reciprocal makes a fresh point of some value.

Plato never returned to the question, but Speusippus and Xenocrates both wrote treatises *On Friendship*,[1] and Simmias of Thebes was one of Socrates' associates to follow up the theme,[2] in the fourteenth of his twenty-three dialogues. Of the fourth-century philosophers however Aristotle accorded to friendship by far the most systematic treatment.

Aristotle's treatment is the fullest and most useful to be found in an ancient author, and it occupies two of the ten books of the *Nicomachean Ethics*. Burnet suggested that its importance in Aristotle's thought is due to its character as the altruistic use of *phronesis*, leading naturally on to the ultimate 'amor dei intellectualis', and thus bridging the gulf between *phronesis* and *sophia*, the practical and the theoretic life.[3] Aristotle himself gives two reasons for his treatment of it. First, friendship is a virtue itself or at least involves virtue; second, it is an indispensable requisite of life.[4] He has already spoken of the virtue of friendliness.[5] He is now far beyond any mere catalogue of virtues, and the stress here laid upon friendship is one of the most warming parts of the *Ethics*; Aristotle obviously sees it as a liberating power. The root of friendship, he suggests, is kinship. It is to be discerned in the family.[6] It extends to the whole human race and forms the cement of society. Aristotle in fact sees friendship as profoundly natural. He would have no time for Thomas Hobbes and his 'Homo homini lupus'. But there remain difficulties, and they are the difficulties which Plato has already raised. Is friendship based on likeness or opposition? And is it possible only between good men? At this point Aristotle's sturdy commonsense combined with an analytical approach to assert itself, and he puts forward the proposition that there are different kinds of friendship, based on utility, pleasure, and virtue. To some extent these are elements in friendship as well as kinds of friendship. The friendship of virtue

---

[1] D.L. IV 4; 12. [2] D.L. II 124.
[3] J. Burnet, *The Ethics of Aristotle*, pp. 344–5. [4] Arist. *N.E.* VIII 1155 a 3.
[5] ib. IV 1126 b 11. [6] cf. Xen. *Hiero* III.

is the highest, and it alone has permanence, but it does not thereby exclude the other two elements. This is a considerable advance upon any previous analysis, for it allows that there can be friendship, though not of the highest quality, where the participants are not saints. True friendship is however based on likeness. Aristotle is unusual among Greek theorists in laying some stress upon the other-regarding, altruistic aspect of friendship. In fact it is rare elsewhere in his own writings or indeed elsewhere in the *Ethics* to find this mentioned. Here he says explicitly that friendship consists rather in giving than receiving affection,[1] and in benefiting the friend for his own sake, though if there is not reciprocity it is goodwill rather than friendship.[2]

For the rest, as Ross says, 'the most interesting part of the discussion is that in which Aristotle propounds the view that friendship is based on the love of the good man for himself'.[3] There are four characteristic marks of friendship: (*a*) the promotion of another's good for his sake; (*b*) desire for another's preservation for his sake; (*c*) delight in company and similar tastes; (*d*) sharing another's joys and sorrows. The good man desires his own good and security, likes his own company and is of one mind with himself, and is acutely conscious of his own joys and sorrows. In this way Aristotle takes up Pythagoras' epigrammatic characterization of the friend as an 'alter ego' and seeks to give it a philosophical and psychological foundation. But the argument is somewhat strained, as he himself sees when he hesitates to say that a man can be said to feel friendship for himself, and he is happier in seeing selfhood as capable of extension so as to include another, as when a mother feels her child's pain as her own. Self-love is not in itself vicious, unless it is associated with irrational and base desire; there is, Aristotle suggests, a higher and ennobling self-love which is the pattern and basis of friendship. We may well remember that one of the great Christian commandments is 'Thou shalt love thy neighbour *as thyself*'.

Is friendship then necessary for happiness? Aristotle answers unequivocally 'Yes', but his reasons are a little strange. Friendship

---

[1] Arist. *N.E.* VIII 1159 a 27. [2] ib. VIII 1155 b 31.
[3] W. D. Ross, *Aristotle*, p. 231; Arist. *N.E.* IX 1166 a 1 ff.

is the greatest of external goods. It offers the noblest opportunity for the virtue of beneficence. Man needs society, and friendship provides the best sort of society. Happiness is a form of activity, and friendship with good men enables us to enter into their activity, and thereby fosters our own virtuous practices. Further, sympathy enlarges the sphere of our consciousness and hence our happiness. In conclusion, friendship is essentially a partnership—again the *sun* compounds tumble over one another—and its highest motto might be in Theognis' words, 'Learn nobility from the noble'.[1]

The most famous treatise on friendship in the ancient world came from Aristotle's pupil and successor Theophrastus. This has not survived, but it was the major source of Cicero's charming little *De Amicitia* or *Laelius*.[2] Cicero is not rigid in following his source. He is eclectic by temperament, and snaps up trifles where he can find them. Parallels with Aristotle, which are numerous, may be mediated through Theophrastus, though Cicero knew of the *Nicomachean Ethics*;[3] a quotation from Xenophon appears to be direct.[4] There is knowledge of Stoic sources, perhaps of Chrysippus,[5] and of course Cicero likes to lard his work with his usual Roman historical references. Theophrastus had gone at some length into the question whether one ought to help a friend contrary to the demands of justice, and if so on what occasions, and to what extent. He came to the view that though morality stands to expediency as gold to bronze, there can be circumstances in which a great weight of bronze surpasses in value a thin flake of gold. This whole topic Cicero dismisses cursorily.[6] In fact Theophrastus was writing as a professional philosopher for philosophers; Cicero was writing as a popular expositor for Romans. None the less with these provisos we may legitimately take the

---

[1] Theognis 35.

[2] Aul. Gell. *N.A.* I 3, 10. See also Heylbut, *De Theophrasti libris* περὶ φιλίας (Bonn, 1876), who is clear about the debt to Theophrastus but believes it to be at second hand. For the title see Cic. *De Off.* II 31, *De Am.* 5.

[3] Cic. *De Fin.* V 12. Parallels are listed in Stock's edition of the *De Amicitia*, p. 27.   [4] Cic. *De Am.* 62; Xen. *Mem.* II 4.

[5] Cic. *De Am.* 28; cf. *De N.D.* I 121; *De Am.* 45.

[6] Aul. Gell. *N.A.* I 3, 9; Cic. *De Am.* 61.

core of Cicero's argument as representing later Peripatetic doctrine. The definition he gives of friendship is 'omnium divinarum humanarumque rerum cum benevolentia et caritate consensio' ('unity of outlook on all subjects, religious and secular, combined with goodwill and affection').[1] So in one of his speeches he stresses that unity of outlook is the bond of friendship,[2] and a similar sentiment is put into the mouth of Catiline by Sallust.[3] The definition is intellectualist, as the Peripatetic tradition was intellectualist; it also bears the marks of Roman practical sense. Earlier Cicero had essayed another definition: 'Reciprocal goodwill towards the object of affection for his own sake.'[4] This also seems to derive from the Peripatetics.[5] It is in some ways a more satisfactory definition, with its emphasis on reciprocity, and its exaltation of emotion above intellect. The fact that he moved away from it may mean that in the later work he is closely following his source. True friendship is only possible to men of virtue, but virtue need not mean the perfection of Stoic saintliness. The foundation of friendship lies in nature not need; this is clear Peripatetic doctrine. We can see natural affection in the lower animals; with humans there is added the magnetic quality of virtue. We have seen Aristotle acknowledging the altruistic element in friendship. Cicero rejects altogether the notion that friendship is based on self-interest. Friendship brings benefits in its train, but they are secondary. 'Non igitur utilitatem amicitia, sed utilitas amicitiam secuta est' ('Friendship has not followed in the train of expediency, but expediency in the train of friendship').[6] Such expediencies are temporary, but the friendships are everlasting.[7] It is virtue that brings friendships into being and holds them in being.[8] Hence we should give virtue the first place in our lives, seeing that friendship depends upon it, and put friendship second to nothing else.[9] Elsewhere he is not so sure, and in one speech says that friendships are procured because they bring mutual advantages.[10] The rest of the discourse deals with practical applications of the sort which we have already noticed in Isocrates

---

[1] Cic. *De Am.* 20.   [2] id. *Pro Planc.* 5.   [3] Sall. *Cat.* 20.
[4] Cic. *De Inv.* II 166.   [5] cf. Arist. *Rhet.* II 4.   [6] Cic. *De Am.* 51.
[7] ib. 32.   [8] ib. 100.   [9] ib. 104.   [10] id. *Pro Rosc. Am.* 38, 111.

Friendship

and Xenophon, and on which it would be tedious to enlarge. Cicero's summary presentation of these strands in post-Aristotelian thought is important for two reasons. In the first place, he removes friendship from the field of self-interest, and therefore leaves it with the opportunity of emerging as a fundamental moral value. But at the same time he makes friendship depend on virtue in such a way as to prevent it being truly basic.

Theophrastus' work on friendship seems also to have been the principal source of a pleasant little treatise on the subject by Plutarch.[1] Friendship, he suggests, is essentially a relationship between two people. Where you see crowds hanging round an influential man they are no more than the flies in the kitchen. True friendship pursues three major objectives, the nobility of virtue, the delight of companionship, and the necessity of practical help. Here again we see the characteristic Peripatetic blend of an exalted intellectualism with a down-to-earth good sense. Friendship springs from similarity: this is reinforced by a typically Peripatetic reference to the animal kingdom. It follows that the man who seems to have many friends is too adaptable and therefore shallow and unstable. The fruit of friendship is co-operation, and Plutarch presents his readers with a remarkable succession of co-operative verbs:

συναγωνιᾶν, συνάχθεσθαι, συμπονεῖν, συγκινδυνεύειν, συναδικεῖσθαι, συναδοξεῖν, συναπεχθάνεσθαι, ὁμολογεῖν, ὁμοβουλεῖν, ὁμοδοξεῖν, συνομοπαθεῖν.

It is noble and noteworthy that a man will share his friend's wrongs and ill-repute and unpopularity.

One other aspect of Theophrastus' treatment of friendship merits mention. A fragment on his work on piety has been preserved to posterity by Porphyry, and a closely similar statement is to be found in Stobaeus.[2] In these passages he traces the origin of *philia* to family affection. From there its scope is gradually enlarged, first to embrace a wider group of kinsfolk, then to the political community, and so to mankind as a whole. 'Consequently

[1] Plut. *Mor.* 93 A–97 B.
[2] Porph. *De Abstin.* III 25; Stob. II 7, 13 (120 W).

67

we maintain that all mankind belongs to one family and one kin.'
There are two points to notice in this interesting analysis. The first
is the insistence that friendship is rooted in nature, and the absence
of any inclination to base it on expediency. The second is the universalism, a change of outlook which Tarn has demonstrated to
have been made possible principally by the life and thought of
Alexander the Great.

The two major strands of Hellenistic philosophy trace their
origins back to different elements in the character of Socrates. His
puritanism was inherited by Antisthenes, to whom are attributed
two aphorisms treated in the *Lysis* as mutually incompatible, that
the saint or sage is self-sufficient, and that good men are friends.[1]
Diogenes and the Cynics held an approach so similar to that of
Antisthenes that they were later represented as standing in un-
broken tradition from him, and Zeno, the founder of the Stoics,
began his philosophic life as a Cynic disciple. Cleanthes was the
only early Stoic to write a treatise on the subject of friendship,[2]
but Zeno and Chrysippus had their say. The Stoics confined
friendship (like everything else of real value) to their perfect
sages,[3] and defined it as social intercourse coupled with a common
outlook on life.[4] There are four kinds of friendship—acquaintance,
association, partnership, and hospitality, to which might be added
kinship and passionate love.[5] All this is coldly analytical. It is true
that Zeno had the warmth to describe a friend as a second self, but
this as we have seen was borrowed from Pythagoras.[6] It is true also
that the Stoics made love subservient to friendship, but this was part
of the pursuit of *apatheia* (freedom from emotional disturbance).[7]
Among the later Stoics Seneca wrote on friendship but only fragments remain. Seneca came under some Epicurean influence, and
the warmth of their friendships must have influenced him. But he
will have nothing to do with the utilitarian basis of Epicurean
ethics, and his *Letters on Ethics* contain one or two passages of great
nobility and insight, as when he suggests that we ought to wish
for friends, not so that they may comfort us, but so that we may

[1] D.L. VI 11; 12.   [2] D.L. VII 175.   [3] Stob. *Ecl.* II 601 (Gaisford).
[4] ib. II 565.   [5] ib. II 566.   [6] D.L. VII 23; cf. Philo II 659.
[7] D.L. VII 130; cf. Cic. *T.D.* IV 33, 70–34, 73.

comfort them,[1] or when he quotes with approbation Hecato's words, 'if you wish to be loved, love',[2] or when he shows that friendship is more than emotion and implies the fellowship of kindred minds,[3] or when he speaks of the communion which extends to absent friends.[4] In such passages Seneca combines the Stoic sense of duty with the Epicurean warmth of personal affection, and something deeper, which makes the petty compromises of his life seem tragic against the noble aspirations of his inner self, and explains why the Christian Tertullian could call him 'paene noster'. Dio Chrysostom, who had looked at philosophy from the outside, and is never narrow in his adherence to the tenets of a particular school, is enthusiastic in his praise of friendship.[5] His words must be seen in their political context. He is addressing Trajan, and the 'amici principis' were the emperor's advisers. None the less he is speaking as a philosopher.

'Friendship', he says, 'is the most sacred and attractive thing a ruler can have. . . . Whether in sickness or in health men must have friendship. It helps to defend wealth and relieves poverty; it adds lustre to fame and dims the glare of infamy. Nothing but friendship can minimize troubles and magnify all that is good. For what disaster is not intolerable without friendship, and what stroke of fortune does not lose its charm if friends be lacking?'

The Stoics were usually colder. Epictetus has a discourse on friendship,[6] whose sole theme is that friendship is only possible to the truly wise. Elsewhere you may see temporary demonstrations of affection, but self-interest will always prevail. Only those who have learned to identify self-interest with moral purpose can build lasting personal relationships. A few fragments from another treatise of his on friendship, in which he quoted at length from his teacher Musonius Rufus, also survive. They do not show signs of any deeper understanding.[7] Marcus Aurelius, the lonely, half-

---

[1] Sen. *Ep.* IX 8.   [2] ib. IX 6.   [3] ib. XXXV 1.
[4] ib. LV 10–1.   [5] D. Chr. 3, 86–118.   [6] Arr. *Epict.* II 22.
[7] Stob. II 8, 30; III 19, 13; 20, 60–1; IV 44, 60.

agnostic philosopher on the throne of the world, has no word upon friendship.

If the Stoics seem chill and repulsive, it was in the hands of the Epicureans that friendship became a force which might have conquered the world. Friendship had an unpromising beginning in the hands of the Hedonists. The Cyrenaics took the view that expediency is the basis of friendship,[1] and the early Hedonists denied that friendship was an end in itself.[2] Theodorus went so far as to deny that friendship exists either among fools or sages; the latter do not need it, and the former are only pursuing self-interest.[3] Traces of something deeper are to be seen in Anniceris, who in a glory of apparent inconsistency declared that love for a friend would induce a man to forgo pleasure and undergo pain.[4]

Epicurus' words on friendship have been conveniently brought together by Festugière, and are worth recording in detail.[5]

> 1. 'The noble soul occupies itself with wisdom and friendship; of these one is a mortal good, the other immortal.'[6]

That it is friendship which is immortal is shown by Cicero; it confers a blessedness comparable to that of the immortal gods.[7]

> 2. 'Of all the things which wisdom acquires to produce the blessedness of the complete life, far the greatest is the possession of friendship.'[8]

So Torquatus in Cicero's dialogue:

> 'Of all the means to blessedness that wisdom has derived none is greater, none more fruitful, none more delightful, than friendship.'[9]

> 3. 'Friendship goes dancing round the world proclaiming to us all to awake to the praises of happy life.'[10]

This enthusiastic outburst is surely one of the most attractive pronouncements ever made on the subject of friendship.

---

[1] D.L. II 91. [2] ib. 93, 96. [3] ib. 98. [4] ib. 96.
[5] A.-J. Festugière, *Epicure et ses Dieux*, p. 56. E.T. p. 36 where the versions are different from those given here. [6] Epic. *Gn. V*. 78. [7] Cic. *De Fin.* II 25, 80.
[8] Epic. *K.Δ*. 27. [9] Cic. *De Fin.* I 20, 65. [10] Epic. *Gn. V*. 52.

4. 'Friendship should always be pursued for its own sake, despite the fact that it takes its origin from the need of assistance.'[1]

5. 'What assists us in friendship is not so much the assistance which our friends give us as our confidence in that assistance.'[2]

6. 'The man who is for ever pursuing his own interest is not a friend, nor is the one who never puts together friendship and self-interest. The first barters his favours for his own benefit; the second cuts at the root of all hope for the future.'[3]

7. 'The same judgement which gives us confidence that no evil lasts for ever or even for a long time perceives also that the unshakable firmness of friendship resides above all in this limitation of the evils of life.'[4]

8. 'Excessive haste and excessive procrastination in forming the ties of friendship are equally blameworthy; but one must be prepared even to run risks in order to maintain friendship.'[5]

9. 'The wise man does not suffer more when he undergoes torture himself than when he sees his friend subjected to torture.'[6]

10. 'Let us face the loss of our friends not in lamentation, but in preserving their memory in our hearts.'[7]

It is important to have these noble and thrilling words of Epicurus before our minds, because there is no philosopher whom it is easier to misrepresent or who has been more often misrepresented. Theoretically there is no doubt that the root motive of Epicurean friendship is self-interest. The aim of life is pleasure, not carnally interpreted, but rather in the form of *ataraxia*, freedom from trouble. But however refined the pleasure, the aim is self-centred. 'Friendship has practical needs as its motive.'[8] 'Friendship cannot be divorced from pleasure and for that reason must be cultivated, because without it neither can we live in safety and

---

[1] ib. 23; cf. D.L. X 120. [2] ib. 34.
[3] ib. 39, translating with Festugière and against Usener. [4] id. K.Δ. 28.
[5] id. *Gn. V.* 28. [6] ib. 56. [7] ib. 66. [8] D.L. X 120.

without fear, nor even pleasantly.'[1] To protect yourself against external circumstances therefore it is best to attract to yourself as much as possible and avoid hostility from any.[2] In the plain reporting of an unfriendly critic this may seem a mean way of life. Lactantius says baldly, 'Epicurus says that there is no one who cares for another except for his own advantage'.[3] The statement is irrefutable but misleading. After all, even Cicero, whose theory was not egocentric, sees that without friendship there is no real pleasure in life.[4] Epicurus' theory may have been egocentric. His practice certainly was not. He may have bridged the gap along the lines of the saying, 'It is more pleasant to give than to receive'.[5] He may have taken the view that human nature being what it is the initial stimulus to friendship must be egotistic, but that it is possible to sublimate this into something higher.[6] There is some support for either view. Probably as with Anniceris, we must admit some inconsistency. The fact is that the practice of the school offered a noble example of unselfish friendship. The Epicureans were indeed a Society of Friends. In the Garden all distinctions were dropped. Adults and children, men and women, slaves and free came together in a common fellowship. Like the contemporary Bruderhof movement they withdrew from the normal life of society, not irresponsibly but in order to espouse something better. The position of Mys, a slave, in the Epicurean community, shows that these were no idle pretensions, and the warmth of Epicurus' letter—'you are a great friend of ours'[7]—conveys the same impression. The practice lasted, and centuries later Lucretius is writing of 'the pleasure of delightful friendship' for which he hopes.[8] So to the Epicurean Horace his friend Vergil or Maecenas was half himself.[9] So we read of the *contubernium* between Vergil and his friends, or between Metrodorus, Hermarchus, and Polyaenus.[10] So an anonymous Epicurean at Herculaneum advises his readers to make friends with as many people as possible.[11] As Samuel Barnett of Toynbee Hall said: 'Friendship is the channel

---

[1] Cic. *De Fin.* II 26, 82.   [2] Epic. K.Δ. 39.   [3] Lact. *Inst. Div.* III 17, 42.
[4] Cic. *Pro Planc.* 33, 80.   [5] Plut. *Contr. Ep. Beat.* 15.   [6] Epic. *Gn. V.* 23.
[7] id. *fr.* 176 U.   [8] Lucr. I 140.   [9] Hor. *Od.* I 3, 8; II 17, 5.
[10] Tac. *Dial.* 13; Sen. *Ep.* 6, 6.   [11] *Pap. Herc.* 1251 col. 22 ll. 15–21.

by which the knowledge—the joys—the faith—the hope which belong to one class may pass to all classes.' Save only for the one word 'faith', Epicurus might have written that.

Friendship at Rome demands some brief comment. Its philosophical treatment by Cicero and Seneca is derived from Greek philosophy, and has already been examined. But in political circles at Rome 'amicitia' had its own significance. It stood for an almost formalized relationship with acknowledged rights and duties; the word 'officium' is never far from a discussion of 'amicitia'. In Cicero's treatise the account of Scipio's alleged views of the limits of friendship was written with the political situation in Rome after Caesar's death firmly in mind.[1] Nothing dishonourable or unpatriotic should be done out of friendship. There are limits, but the responsibilities of friendship are stringent and when a friend's life or reputation is at stake it is legitimate to deviate from the straight and narrow path, if and only if the disgrace involved be not excessive.[2] The theoretical treatment is not without interest, but it is more interesting still to see it working out in practice. Thus Verres' successor used his power to forbid evidence being given against Verres. Cicero's comment is illuminating. 'I do not blame Metellus; he was being lenient to a friend.'[3] In Cicero's letters we have remarkable human documentation of this theme, as of so many, and Caesar and Antony appear as the orator's friends.[4] What is more he makes it clear that such friendship is true, not because it is disinterested, but precisely because it is interested. The most valuable illustration of such political friendship is to be found in an interchange of letters between Cicero and Gaius Matius,[5] the more telling because Matius seems to have been an Epicurean. Matius was a friend of Caesar, and after Caesar's murder helped to bear the expense of the games Caesar had founded in honour of the victory at Pharsalus. Those who were opposed to Caesar took offence, and Cicero had said some harsh words which grieved Matius. The grievance was conveyed to Cicero, and he wrote an affectionate letter to

---

[1] Cic. *De Am.* 33–43. [2] ib. 61.
[3] Cic. *In Verr.* II ii 68, 161; III 53, 122, etc.
[4] id. *Ad Att.* X 8 a and b. [5] id. *Ad Fam.* VI 27–8.

Matius, who replied in kind. The points which emerge particularly from the correspondence are: (*a*) the personal friendship between Cicero and Matius, of long-standing, despite political differences; (*b*) the admission of Cicero to the company of Caesar's friends after the dictator's victory; (*c*) the association of 'amicitia' with 'officium'. Matius stresses the responsibilities he owes as a friend to Caesar, and Cicero, though displeased with the act, acknowledges those responsibilities; (*d*) Cicero's setting side by side the propositions 'Friendship carries responsibilities', 'Patriotism should have priority over friendship'. It is thus clear that friendship was a semi-formal relationship with formal but ill-defined obligations, which acted to some extent across political partisanship and prevented an even wider disruption of society than actually occurred. In fact some of the great families of the Republican era, from the time of Gaius Gracchus and Livius Drusus, even graded their friends into first-class, second-class, and third-class.[1] With this in the background, we can more readily understand the way it was used under the Empire. Maecenas formally bids Horace to be in the company of his friends,[2] and the 'amici principis' become an informal council of State.[3] All informality has now gone, and in its place stands a potent and perilous political scheme.

Friendship suffered three great handicaps which stood in its way of becoming a basic moral value. In the first place, in the general Greek tradition it was founded upon pragmatical self-interest; Chase termed it 'rather harsh utilitarianism'.[4] It is true that an Aristotle or a Theophrastus might move away from this and speak of the altruism of friendship, true that an Epicurus might rise above it. The tradition was unshaken. It was not necessary to the concept, but it remained. Secondly, to the Greek friendship was a limited concept, with a defined outline. Outside lay those who were not friends and those especially who were enemies. Any attempt to extend it too far was regarded as weak-

---

[1] Sen. *De Ben.* 6, 34. [2] Hor. *Sat.* I 6, 61–2.
[3] Suet. *Tit.* 7, 2; Plin. *Pan.* 88. See now J. A. Crook, *Consilium Principis* and refs. there.
[4] A. H. Chase, *Harvard Studies in Classical Philology*, XLI (1930), pp. 186–9.

ening it; it became ὑδαρὴς φιλία in Aristotle's phrase, a 'watered-down' friendship.[1] Thirdly, friendship is a reciprocal relationship. Just as it takes two to make a quarrel, so it takes two to make friends. Greek theorists laid insufficient emphasis upon this; it is fundamental. But the basic moral attitude must be one which is independent of the response of the other person. 'God commendeth His love toward us, in that, while we were yet sinners, Christ died for us.'[2] Christian love offered something which friendship could not offer. Yet when this has been said, it is surprising that the Christian tradition has not made more of the value of friendship; it may not be basic, but it is real.[3] We are the poorer because we have not developed it. It is curious that the actual word *philia* occurs only once in the New Testament.[4] But the theological basis for it is there in the great words, 'Henceforth I call you not servants ... but I have called you friends.'[5] It is said that Christian marriage cut across the tracks and replaced the old value of friendship by the new value of marital comradeship. There is truth in this too. But a fellowship such as the Epicureans enjoyed, of men and women, rich and poor, old and young, of all nationality and any class, standing wider than the ties of blood or the passion of love, has still something to give to the world, and its basis is friendship.

[1] Arist. *Pol.* 1262 b 15.   [2] Rom. V 8.
[3] See further J. Burnaby, *Amor Dei.*   [4] Jas. IV 4.   [5] John XV 16.

V

EROS[1]

*E*ROS IS PASSION. It has none of the coolness of *philia*.
When a man is gripped by passion he seems to lose control
of himself. The very word 'passion' suggests that he is an
object, not a subject, a sufferer, not an agent. Plato, in the *Craty-
lus*, suggests that *eros* is derived from *eisrhein* ('to flow in'),
because passion enters a man from without.[2] So, just as Homer
says that sleep 'loosens the limbs',[3] Sappho, the peerless hymnod-
ist of love, follows Hesiod and Archilochus in using the same word
of Eros.[4] The famous description of the emotions of Brocheo's
lover, which fired the imagination of Catullus,[5] shows well the
overmastering power of Eros. His speech dries up, his body is on
fire, his eyes grow dim, his ears sing, sweat pours from him, his
whole person is aquiver and he is near to fainting. The power
that can do this to a man must be a mighty divinity indeed, and it
is not surprising that such a power was externalized, personified,
and sung in his own right.

> *Love comes at his hour, comes with the flowers in spring,*
> *Leaving the land of his birth,*
> *Kypros, beautiful isle. Love comes, scattering*
> *Seed for man upon earth.*[6]

So in a vase of Chachrylion at Florence Eros moves with powerful wings over the face of the waters, bearing a branching stalk of
flowers. Another vase, now in Paris, and bearing the inscription

---

[1] See further A. Nygren, *Agape and Eros* (a book to which I owe much); H.
Scholz, *Eros und Caritas*; J. Burnaby, *Amor Dei*; M. C. D'Arcy, *The Mind and
Heart of Love*. Their treatments are very different.
[2] Plat. *Crat.* 420 A.   [3] Hom. *Od.* 20, 57; 23, 343.
[4] Sapph. 137, 1; Hesiod *Theog.* 120; Archilochus 118 (Diehl).
[5] Sapph. 2; cf. Cat. 51.   [6] Theog. 1275.

'Charmides is beautiful', shows Eros as an irresistible young warrior.[1] Later and more sophisticated generations were to turn these mighty imaginings into pretty artifice. Eros is the winged infant child of Aphrodite. He is stung by a bee and his mother suggests the comparison with the arrows he fires into the hearts of men and women. The epigrammatists of all ages delight in such themes. We have no concern with them here. These are literary conceits, quite irrelevant to the life of the people and the true and deeper thoughts of anyone at all. Certainly they are irrelevant to the age wherein the first lyric poets become articulate in seeking to express and convey the manner in which Eros sweeps them out of themselves and dominates their whole being. Even in the fifth century, in the age of emergent rationalism, the dramatists sing of Eros with the same sincerity and the same power.

> *Eros, invincible in fight,*
> > *Who ragest in the flocks, Eros,*
> > *Who hauntest, tender in repose,*
> *A maiden's cheek at night;*
> *Past the deep sea thy pinion flies,*
> *Past where the hidden forest lies;*
> *And none of gods immortal may*
> *Escape thee; how shall humans, they*
> *Whose breath endureth scarce a day?*
> > *The Madman grasps his prize.*
>
> *Though man be just, by thee his mood*
> *Is warped to wrong and wrecked his life;*
> *'Tis thou, even here, has wakened strife*
> *'Tween kinsmen of one blood.*
> *All-conquering is thy spell soft-eyed*
> *That yearneth from the waiting bride;*
> *Beside the eternal laws thy will*
> *Is throned, where, irresistible*
> *And deathless, Aphrodite still*
> > *Mocketh her prisoner's pride.*[2]

---

[1] See J. E. Harrison, *Prolegomena to the Study of Greek Religion*, figs. 169, 171.
[2] Soph. *Ant.* 781 ff, tr. Gilbert Murray.

The chorus from Sophocles' *Antigone* is so familiar that we are apt to overlook the remarkable nature of its content. Whatever Sophocles is precisely getting at in the play—and Hegel has confused that issue not a little—the *Antigone* is certainly about the unwritten, eternal laws of heaven which Antigone rightly seeks to sustain and Creon wrongly to ignore. But Eros is here put alongside these eternal laws. Not a hundred lines before we have heard self-control praised as the loveliest of heaven's gifts. Now we find that Eros is more glorious, and assuredly more powerful, than self-control. And his power is strictly amoral. This is no guide as to how men should live—except in affirming that we ignore the power of Eros at our peril. And this is not Euripides, but Sophocles!

The other great choric hymn to Eros comes indeed from Euripides: its purport is the same. Elsewhere Euripides calls Eros a tyrant over gods and men alike.[1] Here in the *Hippolytus* the women of Troezen meditate upon the way in which Eros has driven their mistress to the point of distraction.

> *O Love, immortal Power,*
> *Love, dropping desire like dew on yearning eyes,*
> *Love, whose triumphant arms*
> *Ravish the conquered soul with sweetest ecstasy!*
> *Come not in cruelty,*
> *Never with ruthless violence invade my life!*
> *Fiery stroke of star or sun*
> *Is less to fear than Aphrodite's dart*
> *Which flies from the hand of Love, child of Zeus,*
> *To madden a mortal heart.*
>
> *In vain by Alpheus' banks,*
> *In vain at the Pythian shrine shall sacrifice multiply,*
> *And the blood of bulls pour forth,*
> *Toll from the pastures of Greece to Apollo and Artemis;*
> *While Eros, Master of man,*
> *Who holds Aphrodite's key*

---

[1] Eur. *fr.* 132 (Nauck).

To her chamber of sweet delight,—
Him in our prayers we slight;
Love, whose coming has brought, since the world began,
Death and calamity![1]

This passage of Euripides is of considerable importance. It is extremely unlikely that Euripides took his personifications seriously. They were part of the traditional inheritance of tragedy and in any case of great dramatic convenience. But it is certain that he took seriously the powers represented by his personifications. Euripides has been lopped or stretched to fit the Procrustean bed of many systems. The most convincing view still seems to be that Euripides is a preacher, and that the message of the *Hippolytus* is that Passion and Purity are both powers in human living, and to hand our lives over to one and attempt to eschew the other is to court disaster. In just the same way the theme of the *Bacchae* is a recognition of the real power of religious ecstasy, the more striking because coming from one who had been notoriously sceptical about orthodox religiosity. These powers are amoral, as Sophocles too had seen. Eros uses ruthless violence and brings death and calamity. But they are real. For the moment, progress with this conception can go no further. Two possible lines of development suggest themselves. On the one hand Eros, instead of being amoral, might be seen as a moral power, or at least as a force which in its ultimate direction leads to right ends, whatever aberrations may be seen at lower levels, or possibly as itself amoral, but an instrument of immense value if controlled for moral purposes. Any of these suggests that Eros is not an ultimate power, but subjected to an end higher than itself. On the other hand Eros may be restored from the macrocosm to the microcosm, and removed from the pantheon of Olympus to the palaces of the human soul. If we are right in supposing that the anthropomorphic divinities are in Euripides no more than dramatic convention, the first step to this has already been taken. Along these lines development would be psychological, not theological, and Eros would become an impulse, an energy, a vitality, which may run wild, if left to itself, but may be

---

[1] Eur. *Hipp.* 525 ff, tr. Philip Vellacott. Cf. also *Tro.* 841 ff.

disciplined and directed to right ends. It is perhaps in this sense we are to understand one of the fragments which appears to say that Eros is the chief teacher of virtue in general and wisdom in particular.[1] But history does not always conform with logic, and the genius of Plato to some extent wrested the pattern into a new shape.

Before we turn to examine this however we must look at another aspect of the earlier Greek conception of Eros. It is natural that the lyrical and dramatic poets should be concerned with the power of passion on the minds and lives of men and women. But the power of Eros is wider than this. Eros is the great urge by which the year renews its life. This is the Eros who, in Sophocles' words, rages in the flocks, the god of the year's fertility, and in thinking of him we are thinking of one of the most primitive and deep-rooted of human religious aspirations. This power of fertility appears under many different guises, often as a goddess, Cybele or Aphrodite or Demeter or Persephone, sometimes as a god, like Dionysus or the Roman Mars. In this capacity Eros was worshipped at Thespiae: he was regarded as a fructifying power alike among flocks and humans. Here he was originally represented by a crude stone: a more refined but less profound age added all the delicacy of statuary. At Phlya, where the mysteries were reputed to be older than those of Eleusis, the cult of Eros was fused with that of the Earth Mother.[2] At Athens he had an altar at the entrance of the Academy, but more important was the sanctuary of Eros and Aphrodite on the north slope of the Acropolis. The nature of the phallic offerings thence disinterred show clearly his capacity as a spring daemon. Besides this we know of his worship at Sparta, Samos, Parion, Megara, Elis, Aegina, and Crete, to mention only those who are named by Pausanias and Athenaeus.[3] An important inscription from Smyrna speaks of Heavenly Eros, associated with Heavenly Aphrodite.[4]

Some attempt to see intellectually the cosmic significance of

[1] Eur. *fr.* 897.

[2] See J. E. Harrison, *Prolegomena to the Study of Greek Religion*, c. XII.

[3] Paus. I, 30, 1; 43, 6; 3, 26, 3; 6, 24, 5; 7, 26, 3; 9, 27, 1; Ath. XIII 561; cf. Plut. *Amat.* I.

[4] *C.I.G.* 3156; cf. Farnell, *Cults of the Greek States*, V, 476–7.

this is to be found in Hesiod. The *Theogony* is the first piece of conscious, systematic, religious writing in Greece. In it the Boeotian poet brings together the myths, legends, and traditions about the gods and tries to weave them into a coherent and acceptable whole. The resulting system, incorporating as it does the Homeric traditions, became the basis of orthodox Greek mythology. First of all, says Hesiod, Chaos came into being. Chaos is a gaping void. Most primitive cosmologies deal with the forcing apart of earth and heaven, which are united together; the gap between them is Chaos. In Hesiod's picture Chaos comes into being without any explicit process of forcing apart. Then Earth, Tartarus (the Underworld) and Eros emerge. These simply come into being. There is no process of procreation yet. Eros is thus one of the primeval powers. Plato too lets him be described as the oldest of the gods:[1] Eros in Hesiod is the most handsome of the gods, and rules over the minds and counsel of all gods and all men without exception.[2] This priority of Eros is remarkable. It is one of the points at which Hesiod transforms Homer. He elevates Love into a cosmic principle. The reason for this is no doubt twofold. It springs in part from his sense of the all-powerful nature of Love. But more, it expresses the realization that there can be no process of procreation until Love is at work, and procreation is the natural explanation of the emergence of new beings. Henceforth there is a continuous chain of being. The emergence of these four primeval powers is accepted without explanation. But even so Jaeger is right in pointing the contrast with Hebrew ideas.[3] The Greek gods are stationed within the world, being descended from earth and heaven by the power of Eros, who himself belongs within the world. The Hebraic conception is of a process creative not procreative, and external not internal. To the Greek, Eros may overpower the human heart from outside, but as a cosmic power he is wholly within the natural order.

It is here that the Orphics are important.[4] The extent and significance of the Orphic movement is controversial, its history

[1] Plat. *Symp.* 178 B.   [2] Hes. *Theog.* 120 ff.
[3] W. Jaeger, *Theology of the Early Greek Philosophers*, p. 16.
[4] See W. K. C. Guthrie, *Orpheus and Greek Religion*; I. M. Linforth, *The Arts of Orpheus*.

speculative, and the accounts of its beliefs late. But we can safely say that there was such a movement, that it was a mystical religion and that it came into prominence in the sixth and fifth centuries B.C. For our purpose there are two factors of primal importance. The first is the position of Eros (sometimes called Phanes, 'The Shiner') arising from the primal egg formed in the pure aether by Time: the cosmogony is not quite that of Hesiod. He is thus the first of the great gods, and the principle of generation by which the other gods come into being. Eros is at the heart of the universe. The second factor is that the religion is a religion of aspiration. According to the myth, Dionysus was killed and eaten by the evil Titans. Zeus crushed them with his thunderbolt. From the dead god's heart, which was saved, was created a new Dionysus, the god of the mysteries. From the Titans' ashes sprang the race of men. Man is thus part Titan, part god, that is part body, part spirit. Man's aspiration, his yearning desire, is to realize the divinity which is within him, and to hear the words 'Happy and blessed one, thou art become god instead of mortal'.

The mythologists follow Hesiod. Acusilaus also declares Eros to be the oldest of the gods.[1] Pherecydes appears to have held that Zeus transformed himself into Eros in order to ensure the unity of the world.[2] From the mythologists this cosmic conception of Love passed to the philosophers.[3] It recurs curiously in Parmenides, though naturally in the Way of Opinion, not the Way of Knowledge. In the true, unchanging, uniform world of Parmenides' reality there was no room for arbitrary and independent impulse. But the Way of Opinion appears to be intended as a system which will 'work' provided the framework is limited enough, rather as Newtonian mechanical principles will explain adequately most terrestrial phenomena, though they are invalid for the behaviour of minute particles at one end of a scale or for certain astronomical phenomena at the other. In the centre of Parmenides' world of opinion sits the goddess Necessity, and Eros is the first of the gods

[1] Plat. *Symp.* 178 B.

[2] Proclus *In Tim.* 32 C. In Max. Tyr. 4, 4 Eros stands between Zas (=Zeus) and Chthonie cf. Ar. *Birds* 1737; Kirk-Raven, *The Presocr. Phils.* p. 61.

[3] W. Jaeger, *Theology of the Early Greek Philosophers*; O. Gigon, *Der Ursprung der griech. Phil.*

she creates.[1] Parmenides does not seem to have tried to moralize Eros; his readers have to introduce such moralizing for themselves, if they are that way minded.[2] But Empedocles did. He accepted and extended the idea of Love as a cosmic principle. In Empedocles Love is the power of union and harmony which seeks to bring the elements out of which the universe is compounded into a single coherent homogeneous whole. Strife on the contrary seeks to break up the universe into isolated, independent, and homogeneous entities. Although the process is in a sense almost mechanically inevitable—there is a cycle from the state of complete union to the state of complete disunion and back—there are at the same time distinct moral implications in the process. Strife is dread, Love is joyous. There is an almost Zoroastrian conception of the struggle between the two. But Empedocles has seen the difficulty of moralizing Eros, and chooses instead to name his principle *Philotes*, which is cooler and more dispassionate, and more closely akin to *Philia*. But the nature of the development may be seen in later comments on one of the most famous fragments of Empedocles.[3] This description of *Philotes* Plutarch the Platonist claims for Eros, Clement the Christian for *Agape*.[4] The insights are deepening.

This philosophical conception of the place of Eros in the universe is reflected in the more philosophical of the dramatists. A fragment of Aeschylus' *Danaids* runs:

'Love moves the pure Heaven to wed the Earth; and Love takes hold on Earth to join in marriage. And the rain, dropping from the husband Heaven impregnates Earth, and she brings forth for men pasture for flocks, and corn, the life of men.'[5]

Euripides prefers to speak of Aphrodite in this connection, though he uses the verb *eran*; for his Eros is more personal and less cosmological.[6]

Socrates took this up in his own way out of his own introspection. In the pages of Xenophon he calls himself at one point

---

[1] Parm. *fr.* 13. [2] Plat. *Symp.* 195 C. [3] Emp. *fr.* 17.
[4] Plut. *Am.* 756 D; *Fac. Lun.* 926; Clem. *Strom.* V 15.
[5] Aesch. *fr.* 44. [6] Eur. *fr.* 839, 898.

erotikos, at another an initiate of Eros.[1] Indeed he says that he cannot remember the time when he was not in love with someone or other. Plato naturally records this, and in the Academic *Theages* Socrates is made to say that the only science he really knows inside out is the science of love, a poor thing but his own,[2] and in the *Symposium* his declaration of his devotion to Eros is authentically Socratic.[3] But Plato goes far beyond his master.

'The Eros of Socrates is not that mystical emotion which Plato paints in the highly imaginative mythical discourse in the *Phaedrus*. If less exalted and poetical, it was more unequivocally pure. It was not the beauty of Alcibiades, but his splendid mental endowments, his great capacity for good or for evil, which excited the admiration and the solicitude of Socrates. οἱ εὐεργετοῦντες μᾶλλον φιλοῦσι τῶν εὐεργετουμένων is the deep and true remark of Aristotle; and it was the memory of what he had done and suffered for his brilliant but erring friend which warmed the heart of Socrates towards Alcibiades, and prompted him to even greater efforts on his behalf. This affection was not diminished by the grievous faults in the character of its object, and would have remained equally strong had Alcibiades been as ugly as a Satyr. For an attachment like this φιλία seemed and was too cold a word. Socrates could find no other name for it than ἔρως, and he represented himself as the ἐραστής of Alcibiades accordingly.'[4]

No doubt there was a strong element of Socrates' characteristic whimsicality in his profession of being a votary of Eros, but equally certainly it represented a psychological actuality.

This then was Plato's heritage, on one side what was really a psychological analysis leading to the identification of an overmastering power of passion independent and perhaps beyond the control of man, on the other a cosmic principle of union. It was from these starting-points that he evolved the philosophy of Eros which appears in the *Symposium* and the *Phaedrus*. But before we turn to Plato's remarkable exaltation of Eros we may usefully see

[1] Xen. *Mem.* II 6, 28; *Symp.* VIII 1. [2] [Plat.] *Theages* 128 B.
[3] Plat. *Symp.* 212 B. [4] W. H. Thompson, *Plato's Phaedrus*, p. 153.

what Eros meant to a group of typical Athenian intellectuals who
consorted with Socrates. At the dinner-party which Plato purports to record in the *Symposium* each of the guests makes a speech
in praise of Eros. These speeches are presumably inventions of
Plato's: he was only eleven at the dramatic date of the dialogue. In
any case they are sifted through his brain, and so designed as to
illuminate by anticipation or contrast points which later emerge
in the speech of Socrates. But in the nature of the case they do not
represent Plato's position, and we may therefore take them as
typical cultured approaches to the theme. The findings of drama
and philosophy, and the presuppositions of mythology are in the
background, but we are reminded that Love in its most natural
sense is a relation between persons—not 'characters' or 'principles'. This relation is part physical part spiritual, and to the
Greek aristocrat of the fifth or fourth century it was exemplified
more clearly homosexually than heterosexually. Heterosexual love
introduces the complicating factor of procreation; homosexual
love has no such essential third-party relationship.

The first speaker, Phaedrus, treats of love in its obvious meaning. He quotes Hesiod, Acusilaus, and Parmenides on the primacy
of Eros, and goes on to speak of the power of love to induce a
sense of honour and a spirit of sacrifice, and illustrates his thesis by
examples from mythology, in which heterosexual love has its say
in the person of Alcestis, though homosexuality is uppermost in
his mind. Pausanias takes up the theme on much the same level,
but introduces a useful and significant distinction between base
and noble love. The former is merely sensual, it has no spiritual or
intellectual content; it is directed towards women and young lads.
Noble love is male and adult, and it imposes standards of moral,
intellectual and spiritual excellence, which make it socially and
individually desirable. The course of Pausanias' address contains
some useful sociological material upon the official attitude to
homosexual love in different parts of the Greek world. Some of
the comments are superficial, but it is stated that tyrannies dis-
courage the practice because they know that it breeds nobility of
character. The important thing in these two speeches is the
attempt to give to Eros a moral content. A philosophy of life

whose central affirmations are divorced from morality cannot satisfy.

The next speaker is the pompous and pedantic Eryximachus; Aristophanes, who was to speak next, is afflicted with an unfortunate hiccough. Eryximachus accepts the distinction between the love that is noble and the love that is base. But he sees it operative not merely in human relationships but throughout the whole of life. Medicine, music, and all other such activities have as their object the creation of concord. It is the energizing vitality of Eros which enables such activities at all. The base Eros will lead to discord, the good and noble Eros to harmonious contentment. Eryximachus' speech is strained, but he takes a step where the others have failed, in exalting Eros as a cosmic principle. We are not merely concerned with physical desire, however ennobling that may be.

Aristophanes is now ready. His whole approach is quite different. Where Eryximachus has been staid and dull, Aristophanes is brimming over with sparkling wit. It is he who calls Eros *philanthropos*. Originally, he suggests, there were three sexes, male, female, and hermaphrodite, springing from sun, earth, and moon respectively. These primitive beings were double-humans with two of each organ where we have one, and four where we have two. To prevent their challenge to his power Zeus bisected them, and produced the human race as we know it—after some structural modifications. A human being is incomplete, and yearns for his partner, of the opposite sex if he be a moon-man, of the same sex if born of earth or sun. Love is the power which urges us towards a partnership which will draw as near to the satisfactions of our original state as anything can. This is a delightful fantasy. It is noteworthy that Aristophanes, against the logical tenor of his thesis, plainly regards the love of man for man as quite different from either of the other two. The sun is greater than the earth or moon, but that hardly prepares us for his scorn of heterosexual or Lesbian love. The new factor in Aristophanes' treatment, when we have set aside the trimmings, is his sense that love springs from need.

The last speaker before Socrates is Agathon, the tragedian. His speech is a careful construction, ordered, and analysed, a little artificial, and lacking Aristophanes' exuberance, but not without distinct quality. He is not afraid of contradicting tradition and asserting that Eros is the youngest of the gods. Nothing but good comes from him; his gifts are peace and friendship. He is supreme in beauty and in goodness—in right-doing, for he works by consent not violence, in self-control, for love masters all pleasures in courage, for Ares, god of courage, succumbed to love. Being of this nature himself he creates these qualities in others (Agathon drops for a moment into verse).

> *Peace among men, and calm upon the sea,*
> *Rest for the winds from strife, and sleep in sorrow.*

'It is Love', he goes on in a splendid peroratory panegyric, 'who empties us of the spirit of estrangement and fills us with the spirit of kinship; who makes possible such mutual intercourse as this, who presides over festivals, dances, sacrifices, who bestows good-humour and banishes surliness; whose gift is the gift of goodwill and never ill-will. He is easily entreated and of great kindness; contemplated by the wise, admired by the gods; coveted by men who possess him not, the treasure of those who are blessed by his possession; father of Daintiness, Delicacy, Voluptuousness, all Graces, Longing, and Desire; careful of the happiness of good men, careless of the fate of bad; in toil, in fear, in desire, in speech the best pilot, soldier, comrade, saviour; author of order in heaven and earth; loveliest and best of all leaders of song, whom it behoves every man to follow singing his praise, and bearing his part in that melody wherewith he casts a spell over the minds of all gods and all men.'[1]

Agathon's command of language is superior to his command of thought, as Socrates has no difficulty in showing. But the moral exaltation of Eros which is his central theme, and his identifying the object of Eros with beauty plays some part in what follows.

What has gone before is the attempt to present the raw material on which Plato is working. He has to explain and justify the desire for procreation, the fellowship which is expressed in homosexual

[1] Tr. W. Hamilton.

relations, the pursuit of beauty, the sense of man's incompleteness. He has to present this explanation in terms of cosmic force and moral principle. The presentation, put into the mouth of Socrates, is deliberately not attributed to him, but to the otherwise unknown woman Diotima. Eros is a daemon, a spiritual power intermediate between men and gods, not wholly beautiful and good or he would not need to pursue a beauty and goodness which he possessed, not wholly ugly and evil, or he would not desire to do so. Eros is in fact the aspiration of the soul towards that true, perfect, and absolute beauty and goodness which is the culminating point of Plato's metaphysical thought. At the elementary levels this expresses itself in the desire to attain a sort of immortality through procreation, physically through the conjunction of bodies or spiritually through that conjunction of minds which may lead to wisdom and virtue and renown. The pilgrim along the spiritual road will start by worshipping physical beauty in a single individual, he will go on to honour beauty wherever he sees it in honouring all beautiful things, till he learns to see the beauty apart from the individual objects in which it manifests itself.

'He who has been instructed thus far in the science of Love, and has been led to see beautiful things in their due order and rank, when he comes towards the end of his discipline, will suddenly catch sight of a wondrous thing, beautiful with the absolute Beauty; and this, Socrates, is the aim and end of all those earlier labours; he will see a Beauty eternal, not growing or decaying, not waxing or waning, nor will it be fair here and foul there, nor depending on time or circumstance or place, as if fair to some and foul to others; nor shall Beauty appear to him in the likeness of a face or hand, nor embodied in any sort of form whatever, whether of heaven or of earth; but Beauty absolute, separate, simple, and everlasting; which lending of its virtue to all beautiful things that we see born to decay, itself suffers neither increase nor diminution, nor any other change.

'When a man proceeding onwards from terrestrial things by the right way of loving, once comes to sight of that Beauty, he is not far from his goal. And this is the right way wherein he should go or be guided in his love; he should begin by loving earthly things for the sake of the absolute loveliness, ascending to that as it were by degrees or steps, from the first to the second, and thence to all fair forms; and from fair forms to fair conduct, and from fair conduct to fair principles, until from fair principles he finally arrives at the ultimate principle of all, and learns what absolute Beauty is.

'This life, my dear Socrates,' said Diotima, 'if any life at all is worth living, is the life that a man should live, in the contemplation of absolute Beauty: the which, when once you beheld it, would not appear to you to be after the manner of gold or garments or beautiful persons, whose sight now so ravishes you, that you and many others consorting with your lovers forget even to eat and drink, if only you may look at them and live near them. But what if a man's eyes were awake to the sight of the true Beauty, the divine Beauty, pure, clear, and unalloyed, not clogged with the pollutions of mortality, the many colours and varieties of human life? What if he should hold converse with the true Beauty, simple and divine?

'O think you,' she said, 'that it would be an ignoble life for a man to be ever looking thither and with his proper faculty contemplating the absolute Beauty, and to be living in its presence? Are you not rather convinced that he who thus sees Beauty as only it can be seen, will be specially fortuned? And that, since he is in contact not with images but with realities, he will give birth not to images but to very Truth itself? And being thus the parent and nurse of true virtue it will be his lot to become a friend of God, and, so far as any man can be, immortal and absolute.'[1]

Plato's love is essentially non-physical. In this sense and only in this sense has our term 'Platonic love' the slightest justification. (Cervantes speaks of the *amores platónicos* of Don Quixote for Dulcinea). It is not an absence of physical attachment but its sublimation. The stories of Socrates are pointless unless he felt strong physical urges over which he had still stronger control. The

[1] Tr. Robert Bridges.

desire for physical intercourse between two people of the same sex is sublimated into a passion for common study. The impulse may be fixed on objects other than the human body, just as we may speak of love of one's country (which is not the same as love of one's fellow-countrymen), love of honour ('I could not love thee, dear, so much, Loved I not honour more'), or love of God. Indeed, Plato's point is that the love which seems to be directed towards a body is in fact an aspiration towards something higher and greater, and if that is realized it can be realigned towards its true object. At the level of personal relationships Grube writes well:

> 'He knew that affection for boys and men, friendship, which can be satisfied and be a source of great delight with the minimum of physical contact. Teaching always remained for him a communion between master and pupil, research always a common quest between friends. He knew that man cannot stand alone, that he needs sympathy from, and interchange of ideas with, congenial minds.'

And on the intellectual quest itself Victor Gollancz in his Repton lectures remarks usefully:

> 'Plato excites us, above all, by his intellectual passion. . . . It was with the search for something fixed, something absolute that Plato fell in love, and so he fell in love with thought as its instrument. "Fell in love" is just: he rejoiced, like an ἐραστής, in intellectual effort.'

In this field Plato is the profoundest thinker, apart from Freud, that Europe has known.

We have seen in the *Symposium* the ascent of the soul. The *Phaedrus* shows the other process.[1]

> 'He who is not fresh from initiation, or who has been corrupted, is not quickly led hence to beauty itself that is yonder. He directs his gaze to what is called beautiful here below, so that he does not revere what he sees but surrenders himself to pleasure. . . . But the initiate, he who gazed at length upon the

[1] Plat. *Phaedr.* 250 E ff.

things above, when he sees some divine face, a fair imitation of beauty, or a body of fine appearance, at first he shivers and some of the fears he felt above creep upon him, then he looks and reveres it as a god, and he would offer sacrifice to his darling as to the statue of a god, did he not fear to be thought quite mad. And as he looks he ceases to shiver, and perspires from unaccustomed warmth. For as his eyes absorb the stream of beauty, the roots of his wings'—the soul in the *Phaedrus* is depicted as winged—'become warmed and refreshed, the hardness that sealed the wings away and blocked their growth is melted, and as nourishment flows upon them, the tips swell and start to grow, in his whole soul. For the whole soul was winged once. Then the whole soul of him whose wings begin to grow seethes and throbs with an itching and irritation such as is felt in the gums at the growing of the teeth, for as it grows wings it seethes and irritates and itches. And as it looks upon the beauty of the boy and particles come flowing thence upon it, which is called desire, it is warmed and refreshed, it is relieved of its pain and rejoices. But whenever it is alone and in need, the lips of the passages where the wing is pushing through dry and close and shut off the growth, and the wing, imprisoned with desire, pulses like an artery, pressing its way out so that the whole soul, goaded this way and that, is crazed with pain, yet rejoices in the memory of the beauty it has seen. Frenzied by the anxiety of both feelings together and the perplexity of its strange plight, maddened by sleepless nights and restless days, it is driven by desire to where it thinks it will see him who is beautiful. While looking on him desire now freed opens the closed barriers; the soul finds rest from stings and pains, and culls the sweet pleasure of the moment. Thence it will not willingly depart. Nothing is more precious than the beautiful beloved. Mother, brother, friends are all forgotten, fortune lost through neglect is of no account. Law and manners, in which it formerly took pride, are all despised and it is ready to be a slave, and to sleep as near to the object of desire as one allows it. And besides revering the beautiful one it finds in him the only healer of its greatest travail. This is the state that men call love.'

Here, told somewhat whimsically, we see the way in which the vision of the ultimate beauty leads the soul to kindle with love for earthly beauties. The philosophy is essentially the same. Love, like prophecy and poetry, is a species of madness. That is to say, the lover is taken by his love out of himself; he is in the grip of a power greater than himself, and that power, like Apollo and the Muses, is divine. All love springs ultimately from the same source; it is the aspiration towards the highest beauty.

> *From fairest creatures we desire increase,*
> *That thereby beauty's rose might never die.*

Even if this remains on the merely physical level it is good, though not as good as it might be. But if Eros brings the lover and the loved out of a merely physical companionship into an intellectual companionship and the common quest of philosophy, then their lives are filled with true harmony and bliss.

Because of its great importance both intrinsically and historically, we must try here to sum up what Eros meant to Plato. Eros represents a need or aspiration of the soul, visible in all life, but especially in humans. This is the aspiration towards beauty, but it is not to be divorced from the aspiration towards wisdom and goodness, for they are all aspects of the same process—spiritual growth. The highest ideal for human relationships is to share in the common aspiration, each stimulating the other. This relation may start from physical attraction, for such attraction is part of the aspiration towards beauty, but if it is healthily directed it will soon transcend it. It is perhaps worth observing that there appears to be a not wholly legitimate leap in Plato's thought from the love which is directed by two individuals towards one another, to the love which is directed by them conjointly but independently towards the same outside object. The transition from the first to the second is not wholly explained, and it is not easy to see on Plato's premisses why the second should form a bond between the lovers in the same way as the first. Such criticisms do not destroy the grandeur of Plato's scheme. It offers a purposive direction for life and a healthy basis for human relations in terms of a power which is cosmic in scope and yet relevant to the human heart.

We can imagine from the *Symposium*, which contains six discourses on the subject of Eros, and the *Phaedrus*, which contains three, that such theorizings were not uncommon in the fourth century. Certainly sculpture and vase-painting mark out the mid-fourth century as, in Webster's words, 'particularly the time of Eros'.[1] Praxiteles portrayed him subtly and spiritually in a famous statue.[2] On several bronze reliefs he appears, sometimes with Psyche. Two vases in New York show him as sharing in a Dionysiac procession. The comedians discuss how he should be properly represented, and Alexis seems to know Plato's dialogue on the subject.[3] But by the end of the century the theme is debased, and the Erotes who play with Alexander's armour in Aetion's picture of his marriage with Roxane anticipate the *putti* of the Renaissance.[4] Plato's was not the only literary treatment of Eros. We have an essay on the same theme which purports to come from the pen of Demosthenes, and may actually do so. It is not in itself of any great interest, but one aspect of the treatment merits comment. This is the assertion that the mortal object of Eros arouses immortal longings.[5] This is part of Diotima's theme in the *Symposium*, and is mentioned here to show that Plato is not the only person to try to link the normal affections of love with something deeper and more abiding. More interesting is the use of the word *pothos* ('longing'). *Pothos* is yearning for that which is not present, and is contrasted with *himeros*, a passionate attachment to that which is before one's eyes.[6] Both are associated with Eros, and indeed in Aphrodite's temple at Megara Scopas, the celebrated fourth-century sculptor, had statues of all three powers.[7] In Aeschylus Pothos is the son of Aphrodite;[8] he is associated with her in Trygaeus' prayer in honour of peace in Aristophanes' comedy.[9] He stands with Wisdom, Ambrosia, Quietude, and the

[1] T. B. L. Webster, *Art and Literature in Fourth Century Athens*, pp. 103 ff.
[2] Ath. XIII 591 a.   [3] Alexis *fr.* 20; Aristophon *fr.* 11 K; Eubulus *fr.* 41.
[4] Lucian, *Herod.* 4.   [5] Dem. *Erot.* 11.
[6] Plat. *Crat.* 420 A; Arist. *N.E.* IV 1167 a 6.   [7] Paus. 1, 43, 6.
[8] Aesch. *Suppl.* 1039.   [9] Ar. *Peace* 455.

Graces among the presiding deities of Cloud-cuckoo-land;[1] this is the war-weary escapist's dream of the leisures of love. Sometimes he is associated with Dionysus, both in literature and art.[2] At its lowest this is the common association of women and wine; on a higher plane it is the acknowledgement of two transcendent, overmastering powers. *Pothos* may be used of a multitude of objects, of the beloved man or woman,[3] of food and drink,[4] of long life,[5] of imported luxury goods,[6] of a wanderer's homeland.[7] But there are two examples of its use which call for special comment. Gorgias uses the word to describe the immortal element in man.[8] No doubt it is this passage which Demosthenes has in mind. Even more interesting is its recurrence throughout the story of Alexander. He has a *pothos* to cross the Ister, to go to the citadel of Gordium, to found Alexandria, to visit Zeus Ammon, to take Aornos, to see the land the Nysaeans had linked with Dionysus, to sail down the Euphrates and Tigris, to see the gymnosophists, to know about the Caspian.[9] Alexander acted on impulse, and it is that impulse which is represented by *pothos*. The picture of him sighing for fresh worlds to conquer is quite unhistorical. But the *pothos* it implies is authentic. It well expresses one aspect of Eros, expresses indeed with the greatest possible poignancy the keenness of its aspiration.

> *Ah, but a man's reach should exceed his grasp,*
> *Or what's a heaven for?*

It may be that the accident of its close association with Alexander accounts for the fact that it never attained a wider usage for more metaphysical longings and aspirations.

Overtly the philosophy of Alexander's tutor Aristotle has comparatively little to say about Eros, but implicitly the motif is there. Only, where Plato had seen in Eros predominantly the yearning

---

[1] id. *Birds* 1320.
[2] Eur. *Bacch.* 414; Beazley, *Attic Red Figure Vases* 801, 1; 835, 9.
[3] e.g. Eur. *I.A.* 431, 555, 1304, 1410; Theocr. II 150, VIII 58; Ap. Rh. III 33, 86, 752.   [4] Ap. Rh. IV 619.   [5] Soph. *O.T.* 518.   [6] Theocr. X 9.
[7] Ap. Rh. III 262; Arr. IV 27, 6.   [8] Sauppe, *Or. Att.* II 130.
[9] Arr. I 3, 5; II 3, 1; III 1, 5; 3, 1; IV 28, 4; V 2, 5; VII 1, 1; 2, 2; 16, 2.

and striving of the individual soul, Aristotle is more concerned with a metaphysical interpretation of a physical analysis.

'Platonic love as modified by Aristotle,' says Scholz, 'is thus a striving after that which is worth striving after, and is so conceived that the existence of this love is claimed, not only for individuals with souls in our sense of the term, but for all the elements of the cosmos.'[1]

Aristotle's analysis of the physical world statically into matter and form, dynamically into potentiality and actuality, is coherent with a philosophy whereby matter yearns or strives to become form. Aristotle does not exactly say this, but some Aristotelians have spoken in such terms as the 'drive towards form'. The whole conception of the ladder of being extending from Pure Form at the highest, which is God, to Pure Matter at the lowest, whose existence we must infer in order to complete Aristotle's scheme, has been mightily influential in the philosophy of aspiration. But Aristotle goes further, and explicitly uses Eros as the analogy of the force (not, *pace* some critics, as the force itself) which moves the universe. At the outside of the universe sits God, himself unmoved. How then can he be the first Cause of Motion if he is unmoved? Aristotle, with a fine disregard for the fact that he has sarcastically rejected Plato's use of 'inane poetical metaphors' in philosophical speculation, says that he moves the universe, himself unmoved, as the beloved, however indifferent, moves the lover; we think inevitably of Beatrice and Dante. κινεῖ ὡς ἐρώμενον.[2] Cornford once said wisely that 'the idea of aspiration' was a common feature of the philosophies of Socrates, Plato, and Aristotle.

Among the later austerities of the Stoics it is sometimes forgotten that in his younger days Zeno took Eros as the presiding deity of his ideal commonwealth, the god of Friendship and Freedom, the provider of Concord (though nothing else), the greatest contributor to the city's safety.[3] This is curious, and it is hard to say

---

[1] H. Scholz, *Eros und Caritas*, p. 16, quoted by A. Nygren, *Agape and Eros*, E. tr., p. 183.　　　　　　　　　　　　[2] Arist. *Met.* XII 1072 b 3.
[3] Ath. XIII 561 C. The word for Concord is *homonoia*. See c. VII.

from where it derives. Zeno was in general hostile to Plato and critical of the *Republic*, but it may be right to associate this with Plato's Aphrodite Urania or his Eros *philanthropotatos*. Alternatively Tarn may be right in tracing it to Aristotle's First Cause, it may even go back to Pherecydes and Zeus' transformation of himself into Eros for the sake of concord and friendship. Whatever its origin it is frustrating not to know more of what Zeno was driving at. Zeno's *Republic*, written 'while still under the tail of the dog', that is under Cynic influence, is a book which we would give much to possess.

The Stoics soon learned other ways. And in general the philosophies of the Hellenistic age had little room for Eros. The dominant concept of the time, as we shall see, was *autarkeia*, self-sufficiency. Eros was too disquieting an influence to admit. The Stoics sought *apatheia*, a freedom from emotional disturbance. In such a system Eros, however, spiritualized, could have no prime place. Chrysippus wrote on the subject in a rationalizing approach. In general the Stoics made it subserve friendship, removed it from a gift of the gods to make it a human affection, and defined it as an effort towards the making of friends which is occasioned by the visual appearance of beauty.[1] This is altogether too cold; it could not possibly form the basis of a way of life. It may be these Stoic ideas which underly an interesting papyrus fragment of an Alexandrian work, which describes love as the stabilizer of friendship.[2] We would be more inclined to reverse the rôles. The very Platonists turned Sceptic and sought imperturbability. This is a very different world from the excited ecstasy of the *Symposium* and the *Phaedrus*. As for the Epicureans, the best commentary on their attitude is the almost cynical assault on sexual love in the fourth book of Lucretius, a passage that some find too bitter to be amusing. It is true that Epicurus is quoted as speaking of the desirability of a love (*eros*) of true philosophy, but it seems doubtful at best whether the citation is accurate.[3] His famous characterization of love as an impetuous desire for sexual union associated with frenzy

[1] D.L. VII 130; Von Arnim *S.V.F.* III 716; Cic. *T.D.* IV 72.
[2] *P. Grenf.* I 14.
[3] Usener, *Epicurea*, 457; Porph. *Ad Marcell*, 31.

and distress accords with Lucretius and no doubt represents the normal attitude of the school.[1]

Plutarch has an interesting and important treatment of love, which he chooses to portray in a sort of Platonic dialogue, with reminiscences of the *Phaedrus* and the *Symposium*. His view of love is broadly Platonic, but it is in some ways more exalted. He will not allow the element of need to enter in, and calls Love not *daimon* but *theos*. Furthermore, he has a proper sense of the place of love in marriage. Dugas, who ignores the evidence of the monuments which show the existence of conjugal affection, and thus underestimates the position of women, actually says that 'Plutarch reasserts for women the right of love'.[2] Certainly the right was challenged. 'It is not proper for respectable ladies to feel or be the object of passion', says one of the characters in the dialogue. Plutarch asserts that true marriage is rooted and grounded in love, and such love between man and woman is the highest, even the only true form of love. Plutarch distinguishes, however, between Aphrodite and Eros, between physical and spiritual attachment. The second arises from the first, but not inevitably. True spiritual love is the most exalting of human experiences. It transforms cowards into heroes, illiterates into poets, misers into philanthropists, misanthropes into good companions. And it is the key to the divine life; it is love which can pierce the clouds which veil the eternal Beauty. Derivative and second-hand Plutarch's thinking may be, but it becomes a part of himself, and though it did not affect the main development of ancient thought it remains a fascinating record of the outlook of a thoughtful and sensitive gentleman.

It is with Plotinus and the neo-Platonists that Eros comes back into its philosophic own. Here we return to the Platonic teaching in its fullness.

'The natural love which the Soul feels proves that the Good is there; this is why paintings and myths make Psyche' (i.e. the Soul) 'the bride of Eros. Because the Soul is different from God,

[1] Usener, *Epicurea*, 483; C. Bailey, *The Greek Atomists and Epicurus*, 520–1.
[2] L. Dugas, *L'Amitié Antique*, 146.

and yet springs from him, she loves him of necessity; when she is yonder, she has the heavenly love, when she is here below, the vulgar. For yonder dwells the heavenly Aphrodite, but here she is vulgarized and corrupted, and every soul is Aphrodite. This is figured in the allegory of the birthday of Aphrodite, and Eros who was born with her. Hence it is natural for the Soul to love God and to desire union with him, as the daughter of a noble father feels a noble love. But when, descending to the world of generation, the Soul, deceived by the false promises of a lover, exchanges its divine love for a mortal love, it is separated from its father and submits to indignities; but afterwards it is ashamed of these disorders and purifies itself and returns to its father and is happy. Let him who has not had this experience consider how blessed a thing it is in earthly love to obtain that which one most desires, although the objects of earthly loves are mortal and injurious, and loves of shadows, which change and pass, since these are not the things which we truly love, nor are they our good, nor what we seek. But yonder is the true object of our love, which it is possible to grasp and to live with and truly to possess, since no envelope of flesh separates us from it.'[1]

Love is thus, as in Plato,[2] 'an activity of the Soul desiring the Good'. Eros is a spirit, intermediate between God and man, a *daimon*. Or rather more than one, since there are different powers corresponding to the different stages of spiritual development. The Universal soul has a Love 'which is its eye, and is born of the desire which it has' for the One.[3] Love of physical beauty with Plotinus and with Plato is the first step to a higher and purer love. 'Human Love', writes Dr Inge, 'is the sacrament of the union of Souls Yonder.' 'First step' is just. Plotinus himself speaks of the people who have begun to climb the ladder—the lover of wisdom, the man of culture, and lover:[4] they represent intellect, the fine arts, and love. Elsewhere, with a slight variation there are three upward paths—practical activity, intellectual conjunction and 'desire' (the word is *orexis*).[5] The highest form of love is of course

---

[1] Plot. *Enn.* 6, 9, 9, tr. W. R. Inge altd.
[2] ib. 3, 5, 4.   [3] ib. 3, 5, 3.   [4] ib. 1, 3, 1.   [5] ib. 4, 3, 8.

wholly independent of material things. At the very highest Plotinus commits himself to an assertion for him surprising. Like Plutarch, he calls Eros not *daimon* (spirit) but *theos*. True, he qualifies this in his later examination.[1] Eros is a hypostasis, associated with the Heavenly Aphrodite who is herself justly called not *daimon* but *theos*, and the paradox remains. Furthermore, as Inge says,

> 'If the vision of the Godhead is reserved for the "spirit in love", it follows from the principles of this philosophy that God is love; for we can only see what we are.'[2]

That this is right is seen in Plotinus' explicit assertion about God.

> 'He is worthy to be loved, and is Love as well, that is Love of himself, inasmuch as he is beautiful only from himself and in himself.'[3]

This is an astonishing statement. I cannot help thinking that Plotinus knew the familiar Christian affirmation and was deliberately formulating a counterblast in terms of Eros. But it leads him into philosophical difficulties, for Eros is essentially an aspiration and can hardly be predicated of Him who is all in all, or put at the centre of the universe wherein He manifests Himself, and this is not really solved by making it an aspiration towards Himself. Yet Plotinus' God does condescend—'the higher cares for the lower and adorns it';[4] only according to Plotinus' philosophy he scarcely ought to. At any rate Plotinus' disciples were not wholly satisfied with his presentation of the spiritual categories. Porphyry sees four fundamental stages in our relations with the divine—Faith, Truth, Love, and Hope. We must have faith that salvation comes only from turning to God, we must press on to know the truth about Him, we must love what we come to know, and in this love we must sustain our spirit with high hopes about life.[5] The ablest of the neo-Platonists, Proclus, essayed a more stringent analysis. He transforms Eros till it comes close to the Christian idea of love, for he dares to speak of Eros as coming down.

[1] ib. 3, 5, 2; 3, 5, 6. [2] W. R. Inge, *The Philosophy of Plotinus*, II, 232.
[3] Plot. *Enn.* 6, 8, 15. [4] Plot. *Enn.* 4, 8, 8. [5] Porph. *Ad Marc.* 24.

'Eros comes from above, from the sphere of the intelligible to the material universe, turning everything towards the beauty that is divine.'[1]

For

'from what source could love come among men if it were not first among the gods? Everything good, everything saving that is found in human souls has its determinate cause from the gods.'[2]

Eros thus acts as a kind of unifying factor in the universe, and whereas Plotinus played with the idea of each soul having its individual eros, thus fragmenting the universal conception, Proclus, in a figure of measureless influence, saw them all bound together in a single Chain of Love (ἡ ἐρωτικὴ σειρά).[3] So to his analysis. There are three attributes which make up the essence of Divine things, and are constitutive of all the higher categories—Goodness, Wisdom, and Beauty; and there are three auxiliary principles, secondary in importance to these, but extending through all the divine orders—Faith, Truth, and Love.[4] Elsewhere he elaborates this. Goodness, Wisdom, and Beauty, besides being constitutive attributes of the Divine nature, are active principles. When they are actively engaged, they take the form of these secondary principles, Faith, Truth, and Love, respectively.

'Faith gives all things a solid foundation in the Good. Truth reveals knowledge in all real existences. Love leads all things to the nature of the Beautiful.'[5]

I do not think that this is what Plotinus meant by saying that God is Eros, but it is a noble attempt to give clear significance to his words. But its outcome is to make Eros an element in man's aesthetic, not his moral aspiration, and thus to prevent its becoming a basis for a universal philosophy of life.

This vitiated the attempt which was made to Christianize it. 'John called God Love, and I do not think that anybody can be

---

[1] Procl. *In Alc.* 2, pp. 141 f.   [2] ib. p. 150.   [3] ib. pp. 82–6.
[4] id. *Theol. Plat.* 1, 1.   [5] id. *In Alc.* 2, p. 141.

censured for calling Him Eros', wrote Origen.[1] He went on: 'In fact, I remember that one of the saints, named Ignatius, said with reference to Christ, "My Eros is crucified".' This is a curious comment, for Ignatius, who did at times show an almost mystical devotion to Jesus,[2] in this passage is not referring to Christ, but his own sensual nature,[3] and is taking up Paul's words that 'they that are of Christ Jesus have crucified the flesh with the passions and lusts thereof'.[4] Origen however had his own purposes. He wanted to interpret the sensual language of the *Song of Songs* as a mystical allegory of the relation between Christ the Bridegroom and his Church. More generally he wanted to leave room for the integration of his own Platonic philosophy with the language of scripture. He was followed in this by Pseudo-Dionysius, who discussed the propriety of Eros as a name of God at some length,[5] and it passed from there into the language of mystical piety. As applied to God it lost, except in some of the extremer mystics, its sense of aspiration, of incompleteness. As applied to man it represented well his need of God and enabled many noble spirits to sublimate their sexual energy in the deeper devotions of religion. But in itself it remained amoral. In its inmost nature it was the love that gets not the love that gives, and it could hardly be acceptable as an universal approach.

[1] Origen, *Prol. in Cant.* 3 ff.   [2] Ign. *Rom.* 7, 3.
[3] ib. 7, 2.   [4] Gal. V 24.   [5] [Dion.] *De Div. Nom.* 4, 10–2.

VI

PHILANTHROPIA[1]

THE FIRST SERIOUS attempt to estimate the force of the word *philanthropia* is to be found in Diogenes Laertius.[2] It is an analysis attributed to Plato in a document falsely attributed to Aristotle. Its origin is quite uncertain, except that we can reasonably say that it dates from the Hellenistic age.[3] The word literally means 'love of mankind'. According to Diogenes it may take three forms, a readiness to meet and greet people personally, charity to the needy, and generous hospitality, arising apparently from an enjoyment alike of good food and social intercourse. This reads almost like the aims and objects of a Rotary Club. A far more acute division was made by Thomas Magister in about A.D. 1310.[4] He says that *philanthropia* has two meanings. Strictly it refers to an attitude of goodwill from superior to inferior such as God may show to man, or a monarch or anyone else in a position of authority to a subject or subordinate. But it has the wider connotation of friendship and a loving disposition of one individual towards another. This, so far as it goes, is excellent. It picks out and states the basic meaning of the word and the supreme point of interest in its history. And the Christian writer also sees that the word came to be linked both with the supreme pagan social virtue of friendship and with the supreme Christian social virtue of *agape*.

The original meaning of *philanthropia* is clearly care shown by the gods for mankind. The word is not metrically adapted to epic, and the idea is alien to Homer's thought. Hence its catastrophic

---

[1] See S. Lorenz, *De progressu actionis* φιλανθρωπίας, Diss, Leipzig. 1914; De Ruiter in *Mnem.* lix, 1931, p. 271. My own studies have generally confirmed and to some extent elaborated their conclusions.　　　　[2] D.L. III 98.
[3] Rose, *Aristoteles Pseudepigraphus*, 679 ff.　　　　[4] Thom. Mag. 896.

first appearance is in Aeschylus' *Prometheus Vinctus*, where the Titan is taunted for his love of mankind which has outrun all bounds.[1] He has given man fire, and from that gift, as the argument of the play reminds us, has come all science and all industry. It would be hard to exaggerate the importance of this twice-repeated epithet. A new conception of the higher powers is breaking through, and from that will spring a new insight into the responsibility of a man to his neighbour. For the moment the gods condemn Prometheus for his act. The poet to some extent shares that judgement. Prometheus is not just the innocent and gallant victim of a brutal and licentious tyrant. But neither is he a justly condemned villain whose punishment matches the inherent viciousness of his practices. In Zeus' first dominion, there was no place for *philanthropia*. Prometheus is a rebel against such an order and is wrong to be so; he is a disruptive influence in society. But a new order is coming which will enshrine a new set of values, and in this new society *philanthropia* will be the order of the day. Prometheus is, so to say, the reformer born before his time.

Whether this was in Aeschylus' mind or not, this is certainly what happened. Before the end of the century Hermes, who in Aeschylus defends the ordinances of Zeus against the rebel, is described by Aristophanes as 'of all the gods the greatest lover of mankind and the greatest giver of gifts'.[2] Plato applies the word to Eros in the *Symposium* and more remarkably to the one god of the *Laws*, of whom it is also later said that if a man realizes the ignorance of his words about the gods, then God Himself of His grace will give him aid.[3] In a fragment of Philemon peace is called φιλάνθρωπος θεός.[4] Plutarch, whom Hirzel calls 'the apostle of *philanthropia*', repeatedly applies it to the gods. They are εὐεργετικοὶ καὶ φιλάνθρωποι, their work is φιλάνθρωπον καὶ κηδεμονικὸν καὶ ὠφελιμόν.[5] He uses it of Apollo's gift.[6] It is especially applied to the three popular divinities, Prometheus, by Xenophon for example and Lucian, Heracles, signally by Isocrates, and Asclepius,

---

[1] Aesch. *P.V.* 11, 28. Epicharmus *fr.* 274 must be about the same time.
[2] Ar. *Peace* 392. [3] Plat. *Symp.* 189 D; *Laws* IV 713 D; X 905 C. [4] Kock II 71.
[5] Plut. *De Stoic. Rep.* 1051 E; *De Comm. Nat.* 1075 E; cf. *V. Numae* 4; *De Gen. Soc.* 593 A. [6] id. *De Pyth. Or.* 402 A.

by Aelian.[1] It is notable that it does not apply to any of the
Olympians, with the exception of Hermes, and Hermes held a
peculiar position among the Olympians as a popular deity, a cun-
ning trickster, and the 'go-between' of gods and men. We may
observe with interest one exception which does not affect the
argument. An epigraph of the late third century A.D. tells of a
slave who was cured of illness 'divino Martis amore'. The
Olympians were too aloof; they were the gods of the old order,
and in affection, if not in reverence, they were being displaced by
other divinities with a more personal interest in mankind. What
is more, the quality of *philanthropia* is manifested in the giving of
gifts. Prometheus is the giver of fire. Aristophanes explicitly links
the two ideas. Philemon has no sooner described Peace as a lover
of men than he lists her gifts—weddings and festivals, friends and
relations, health and wealth, food and drink, and a general good
time. Friday's child, runs the old saw, is loving and giving. These
gods were children of Friday.

The first extension of meaning appears sufficiently obvious.
The eastern potentate stood to his subjects as a god. In any case
there was an obvious parallel between the demeanour of gods
towards men and that of kings towards their subjects, and *philanthropia* came to be extolled as a kingly virtue. Xenophon uses it
of Agesilaus, and repeatedly of Cyrus; it comprises the ideas of
philein, eunoein, euergetein—friendliness, a favourable disposition,
and the actual conferring of benefits.[2] Isocrates applies it to
Evagoras and Antipater, and sets it as an ideal, together with
eunoia and *praiotes*—a favourable disposition and leniency—before
Philip and Alexander.[3] Plutarch and Diodorus also use it of
Alexander, the former recording it as an injunction laid by Philip
upon him.[4] Polybius speaks of kingly duties as the conferring of
material benefits combined with *philanthropia*.[5] In the *Epistula
Aristeae* it so appears associated once with *agapesis*—affection—
and once with a sort of sweet reasonableness.[6] That this attribu-

[1] Xen. *Mem.* IV 3, 5-7; Luc. *De Sacr.* 6; Isoc. *Phil.* V 116; Ael. *N.A.* IX 33.
[2] Xen. *Ages.* I 22; *Cyr.* I 2, 1; 4, 1; IV 2, 10; VIII 2, 1; 4, 7; 7, 25.
[3] Isoc. *Evag.* II 11; 15; IX 43; *Antip.* IV 9; *Alex.* V 2; *Phil.* V 114; 16.
[4] Plut. *Mor.* 330 A; D.S. XVIII 2, 2; 4, 1, 3, 9; Plut. *De Fort. Al.* 333 F; *Reg.
et Imp. Apoph.* 178 B.   [5] Polyb. V 11, 16.   [6] *Ep. Arist.* 265; 290.

tion to monarchy has become formal is evidenced by its appearance several times in the books of the Maccabees.[1] Later under Rome it became part of the titular nomenclature of the emperor. Dio describes Hadrian as φιλανθρωπότατα ἄρξας.[2] Aristides speaks of Marcus Aurelius' φιλανθρωπίαν καὶ προνοίαν (the latter his forethought or providence, another typically imperial phrase; the linking of the two ideas dates back to Xenophon).[3] Julian is addressed in an inscription as θειότατος καὶ μέγιστος καὶ φιλανθρωπότατος βασιλεύς ('king most godlike, most mighty and most beneficent to mankind'); here the link with divinity is explicit.[4] Septimius Severus and Caracalla are φιλανθρωπότατοι Αὐτοκράτορες ('absolute rulers of the highest beneficence to mankind'.)[5] In the papyri of the second and third centuries ἡ σὴ φιλανθρωπία and later σοῦ ἡ φιλανθρωπία become purely formal titles, and as such are used by Athanasius.[6] From all these came a further extension. That which was applied to monarchs might also be applied to rulers who were not monarchs. Thus Isocrates lays down *philanthropia* as an ideal for the democracy at Athens;[7] it is applied to the Roman senate in a passage whose reference I have mislaid; it is used in an inscription of the relations of the state of Thespiae with a group of workers,[8] and again of interstate relations between Delphi and Sardes.[9] Hence it comes in the Hellenistic age actually to mean an alliance, friendly relations or conditions of peace. Again Plutarch uses it often of the heroes of his biographies,[10] of Solon, of Cleomenes, and it came to be attributed to any benefactor of the state, with the result that *ta philanthrope* means benefactions, liturgies, and even taxes; there are over six hundred examples of this use in inscriptions.

The important thing to notice about all these usages is that though they have the common factor of gifts and of service to the community, they also have a common element of condescension, like the Latin *clementia*. This is the point of Socrates' words to

[1] 2 Macc. IX 27; XIII 23; XIV 9; 3 Macc. III.
[2] D.C. 69. 2.   [3] Aristides, εἰς βασ. 14; Xen. *Mem.* IV 3.
[4] O. Kern, *Die Inschriften von Magnesia am Mäander*, 201[2]; Ditt. *SIG.* 906 B.
[5] *P. Oxy.* IV 705, 21.   [6] Athan. II 792 B; cf. *P. Fay* 20[16].   [7] Isoc. *Paneg.* 29.
[8] Ditt. 693.   [9] Collitz 2645.   [10] Plut. *Solon* 2; *Cleom.* 32 etc.

Euthyphro: 'I am *afraid* that people may think it due to *philanthropia* that I speak freely to everyone without pay.'[1] This most interesting passage shows clearly that *philanthropia* was not considered a desirable accoutrement of the ordinary citizen. The word 'benefactor' (*euergetes*) acquired a similar flavour in Hellenistic times through its court usage, and even Jesus speaks of this with a tinge of sarcasm.[2] If *philanthropia* could have rid itself of this element of condescension it would have become a word of immense moral power. Some such development was imminent in the fourth century. There was in circulation a famous Hippocratic precept: 'Where there is *philanthropia* there is *philotechnia*'— 'Where there is love of mankind, there is love of medical science.' This is very close to the Christian *agape*. Aristotle's thought, though with a colder science, was moving in the same direction. He speaks of the natural ties which bind an animal to other creatures of its own kind, and used *philanthropia* to denote this trait in man.[3] Tarn, in upholding his Alexander-ideal, has tried to confine Aristotle's use of the word to the natural bond between Greek and Greek, but linguistics are surely against him. At any rate later, as we shall see, it came to be used in the full sense of 'humanitas', and represents perhaps the highest ideal the pre-Christian world knew. And it was certainly from Aristotle that its philosophical use derives.

Before we follow this trail, however, it is well to remind ourselves that linguistic history is a complex and ravelled business, and side by side with these extensions of the basic idea of *philanthropia* were extensions of its literal application. *Philanthropia* means ' love of man', and it was used widely and variously of the more or less domesticated animals, of the goat,[4] the horse,[5] the dog,[6] the dolphin,[7] the jackal[8] (by both Aristotle and Aelian), the fawn,[9] and even one of Aesop's bears![10] Further it was extended to those arts and activities which bring profit and pleasure to mankind, to agriculture, to music, to wine and the wine-bowl, to the care of

[1] Plut. *Euthyphr.* 3 D.   [2] Luke XXII 25.   [3] Arist. N.E. VIII 1155 a 18.
[4] Longus 4, 10.   [5] Poll. I 195; Xen. *De re eq.* II 3.
[6] Poll. I 195; Xen. *De re eq.* III 9; VI 25.
[7] Plut. *Mor.* 162; 984 C; Luc. *Dial. Mar.* 8, 1.
[8] Arist. 630 A 9; Ael. I 7.   [9] Plut. *Sert.* 11.   [10] Aes. *H.* 69.

the body.[1] It was used botanically as the name of a clinging burr, which we learn from Pliny was also called Aparine.[2] And, if we may trust the reading, it was used by Aeschines with reference to homosexual practices.[3] These developments are unfruitful. They are peripheral not central. The significant usages of the word lie elsewhere.

The most curious stage in the word's history lay in the second half of the fourth century. At that time *philanthropia*, having been a comparatively rare word with a comparatively specialized meaning, suddenly surged into prominence on the lips of men. It occurs not once in Lysias or in the majority of the Attic orators. In its three forms (noun, adjective, and adverb) it occurs seventy times in Demosthenes, and begins to have the most general application to man in relation to his fellows. It is associated with *dikaiosune* (right social relationships),[4] with *sungnome* and *eleos* (fellow-feeling; pity),[5] with *metrios* and *demotikos* (moderate; democratic),[6] with *charis* (charm, grace),[7] with *aidesis* (a sense of propriety).[8] It is used of a man who wishes to prevail among the citizens by authority.[9] It is almost defined as meaning one who by speech and act shows himself genial, kindly, and friendly to his fellows.[10] Words are *philanthropoi* when calculated to rouse pleasure or pity.[11] The calumniator and pretender wear the guise of *philanthropia*.[12] And these citations are not from Demosthenes alone, but from Aeschines, Aristotle, and Isocrates, and by the end of the century may be paralleled from many inscriptions. Yet in reading the impressive testimony of these passages it is important to realize that this *philanthropia* is in general exercised over a limited field. Though he has overstated his case, Tarn has helpfully reminded us of the dangers of looking too widely and too early for a sense of universal brotherhood. Heracles possessed

---

[1] Xen. *Oec.* XV 4; Plut. 50 C; 132 D; 158 C; 810 B; 1135 D.
[2] Diosc. 3, 104; cf. Plin. 27, 5 § 15; 24, 19.
[3] Aeschines I 171.   [4] Dem. VI 1; VII 31; XLIV 8.
[5] Dem. XXI 148, 185; XXV 81. Arist. *Poet.* 1452 b 38; 1453 a 2; 1456 a 21.
[6] Dem. XXIV 24; cf. Aeschines III 57; Arist. *Ath. Pol.* XVI 8.
[7] Dem. XXI 148.   [8] Dem. XXI 43.   [9] Dem. XVIII 268.
[10] Dem. XXIV 24; XXI 128; Isoc. XV 131.
[11] Aeschines II 15; Dem. XXI 75; *Prooem.* XXIII.   [12] Arist. *De Virt.* 1251 b 2.

philanthropia indeed, but in practice his beneficent acts were directed towards the Greeks. This 'love of men' finds its actual outlet in application to relative, friends, fellow-citizens, or allies. Two passages of Demosthenes[1] make it clear that *philanthropia* is something practised between fellow-citizens, exercised in the assemblies for themselves and their allies, shown among neighbours. So an inscription of the fourth century reads φιλανθρώπως ἔχει πρὸς πάντας τοὺς ἐν τοι δήμοι οἰκοῦντας 'he is well-well-disposed to all those who live within the community of the people'.[2] So too in the difficult passage in Aristotle's *Poetics* it is actually *philanthropon* that a bad man should fall.[3] But after the fourth century *philanthropia* is commonly used in the sense of 'humanitas', of a genuine love of mankind. The change, as Tarn has shown, was due to the vision and work of Alexander, and we need not doubt that there was a significant change at this point, even if we think that Tarn has unduly minimized some possible anticipations of it. To Aristotle the barbarian and slave were classed together as scarcely human. To Alexander the good man was the only Greek, and the bad man the only barbarian.[4] Whatever we make of Aristotle's use of *philanthropia*, whether we suppose that his biology and his ethics were at variance, or whether we think that we have to interpret the biology in the light of the ethics, Theophrastus, writing after Alexander's revolution, is explicit in his interpretation of his master: 'So we assert that all men are in fact kin to one another. We have a common *philanthropia*.'[5] Henceforth it is taken up by Stoics and Cynics,[6] and Plutarch can direct it even towards enemies, and coins the word *sunanthropeuein* ('to have a common feeling of humanity'), reminiscently of Antigone.[7] Philo can watch the sun kindling the moon, and the moon giving freely her light, and can see therein a lesson of right behaviour and *philanthropia*; the sun and moon of course shine impartially on all men. And the later Pythagoreans describe their master as a kind of beneficent power, supreme in his

[1] Dem. VIII 33; XXV 89. [2] Ditt. 720. [3] Arist. *Poet.* 1453 a 2.
[4] Arr. VII 11, 9. [5] Porphyry, *De Abst.* III 25; Stob. II 7, 13.
[6] D. Chr. VIII 5; IX 1; Arr. *Epict.* IV 8; 32 etc.
[7] Plut. 799 C; 823 B; cf. Soph. *Ant.* 523.

love of mankind, and claim to take from him the teaching that men must themselves practise *philanthropia* and love their fellows.[1]

Before we follow the story of the Christianization of the word we must return to the fourth century and seek the reason for this extraordinary upsurge in its usage at that period. Suessius suggested that it was introduced by Gorgias and popularized by Isocrates. But as there is no real evidence of its association with Gorgias and only twelve instances of the stem in any of its forms in Isocrates this seems highly doubtful. Mühl and Mewaldt both imply that it was a revival. Mühl derives it from Empedocles and the Pythagoreans, who held there was a fellowship between gods, men, and animals, in that all exist by breathing in air,[2] and equates the *philia* which Theophrastus accepted as *philanthropia* with the *philotes* which provided Empedocles' principle of union. Mewaldt takes it from Antiphon, who declared there was no distinction between Greek and barbarian because both breathe through their noses.[3] Tarn has criticized these pretensions, and in any case they throw no light on the peculiar history of the word *philanthropia*. Epicurus was alive to the value of words in rejecting *philanthropia* because of its theistic associations and using *philia* instead, and the history of the two terms cannot be assumed to be identical. I should like to suggest that there were two chief factors in its growing use. The first was the popularization during the fourth century of the *philanthropoi theoi*, Heracles and Asclepius. This can be exemplified from the history of Cynicism. Antisthenes, Diogenes, and Crates all identified their work with that of Heracles.[4] Asclepius only reached Athens in about 420, and thereafter achieved enormous prominence. The growth in their popularity would popularize the ideas and vocabulary associated with the gods, and would coincide with the actual increase in the word's usage during the middle of the fourth century. The other factor was its application to Philip and Alexander, which gave it an importance in the political propaganda of the period. We have seen how Isocrates used it of both, and how it was an injunction

[1] Iambl. *Vit. Pyth.* VI 30.　　　　[2] Sext. Emp. *Adv. Math.* IV 1.
[3] *P. Oxy.* 1364, ll. 275–99.　　　　[4] D.L. VI 12–13; 71.

which Philip laid on his heir. It is possible that its use by Demosthenes is a deliberate counterblast to this. 'Here are men seeking help. Philip sets himself up as their helper. I say that we can help each other.' Hence its association with law, as opposed to the monarch's arbitrary will, with social justice, and with the democratic words *demotikos, metrios, koinos* (democratic, moderate, sharing). Its prominence in propaganda would easily bring it into widespread use.

As the Jews succumbed to Hellenization under the Successors the concept was taken up by Jewish writers, and began to play some part in Graeco-Jewish thought, that strange and fascinating borderland between two civilizations. In the book of Wisdom, for example, we read that 'Wisdom is a loving spirit'. The word is *philanthropon*, and it recurs in the long catalogue of the virtues of Wisdom.[1] We have already noted its occurrence elsewhere in the Apocrypha. It is a favourite word of Philo who several times applies it to the Law.[2] These attributions in Jewish thought to Wisdom and to the Law are of peculiar interest. At this stage there is a tendency for God to become remote, and Wisdom and the Law to stand as His representatives, His vicegerents, before men. In other words, when allowance has been made for the very substantial differences of outlook and atmosphere, there is a legitimate parallel between the position of Wisdom and the Law in Jewish thought at this period, and that of the non-Olympian divinities among the Greeks of the fifth and fourth centuries. Philo however went further. He in fact wrote a treatise *On the love of mankind* which appears to have been among his more influential works. In it he systematically graded mankind into groups from fellow-countrymen close at hand to foreigners far away, and the word used for the loving relationship is that which is to be central for Christianity—*agapan*. A passage in Josephus[3] suggests that this is a classical passage in Jewish apologetics, for there the same picture of concentric circles is drawn, with fellow-Israelites in the centre, proselytes, and resident aliens next, then enemies, slaves, animals, plants through to the whole creation.

[1] Wisdom I 6; VII 22.   [2] Philo V 32, 105, 118, 131, 287.
[3] Jos. *c. Apion.* II 209 (28 ff).

But ultimately more significant than this is the use of *philanthropia* by Christian writers. It is rare in the New Testament, occurring twice in Acts in the sense of 'humanus',[1] and once, gloriously, in Titus: ἡ χρηστότης καὶ ἡ φιλανθρωπία ἐπεφάνη τοῦ Σωτῆρος ἡμῶν Θεοῦ ('the kindness and love of God our Saviour toward man appeared').[2] The passage has sometimes been taken as confirmation of Paul's familiarity with Greek literature. But it may derive directly or indirectly from Philo, whose association of *philanthropia* with *agape* would commend him to the Christian writer. But this dramatic appearance, almost as tremendously catastrophic as the original Aeschylean passage, is equally barren of immediate fruit. Perhaps both were too tremendous for immediate imitation. On this occasion it seems to have been more than a century (unless one dates Titus very late) before the word is taken up by Christian writers. Now it appears in Theophilus.[3] At creation, God endowed man with freedom and the possibility of self-determination. What man lost through disobedience God gives through *philanthropia*. Man brought death through disobedience; he can have eternal life through obedience. The passage is worth noting; it is a characteristically accurate usage by a sensitive Greek: the classical elements of condescension and of giving are meticulously preserved. Clement of Alexandria is more explicit still;[4] he identifies the major example of God's love of mankind with the Incarnation. From Clement it passes to Origen, and he was perhaps the chief cause of its growing use in Christendom. He in fact rarely uses *agape* and much prefers *philanthropia*. It is true that in controversial works, such as his answer to Celsus, he may have been influenced by the need to use a vocabulary which non-Christians could readily understand; it is probable also that his own affection for Greek studies led him to revert to the classical word rather than accept the usurping innovation. Whatever the cause, it is to *philanthropia* that he turns. 'It was through Jesus' love of mankind that He emptied Himself' we read, and the passage may be amply paralleled.[5] God is the God who loves man; Christ dies because of His love for man. After the time of Origen

[1] Acts XXVII 3; XXVIII 2. [2] Titus III 4. [3] Theoph. *Ad Autolyc.* II 27.
[4] Clem. Al. *Paed.* I 8, 62. [5] *C. Cels.* IV 15, 17; VI 15, etc.

the word and the idea become a commonplace of Greek Christianity. They occur repeatedly in Eusebius and Theodoretus.[1] In Gregory of Nyssa's *Oratio catechetica magna*[2] we read, 'If love of mankind be a characteristic of the Divine nature, here is the reason for which you are in search, here is the cause of the presence of God among men.' Or again in his exposition of the Song of Songs he uses *philanthropia* freely to represent the love of God.[3] Even later in Maximus Confessor we read that Christ was God, but through His love of mankind became man.[4] It is noteworthy how the word finds its peculiar appositeness in reference to God's self-giving. Here are preserved its primary elements—condescension and giving. It is not surprising that it recurs in the pages of Athanasius, and especially in his early *De Incarnatione Verbi*, like a kind of *leit-motif*. Our sin called out the *philanthropia* of the Logos; for our salvation *philanthropeusaato*; we were called into being by the presence and *philanthropia* of the Logos; He came through His father's goodness and love of mankind.[5] The association with goodness (*agathotes*) is frequent. It is important to add that *philanthropos* in Athanasius can also represent a quality shown by man to man, and is found linked with *praios* (gentle).[6] Similarly in the Liturgy of Basil and Chrysostom *philanthropia* is almost a refrain. There is a splendid example of a Christian prayer preserved in papyrus, beginning ὁ Θεὸς ὁ παντοκράτωρ ὁ ἅγιος ὁ ἀληθινὸς φιλάνθρωπος καὶ δημιουργός.[7] God is characterized as almighty, holy, true, gracious to man, creator. It would in short appear that *philanthropia* became regarded as a peculiar attribute of the Christian God. This is interestingly confirmed by Julian's work 'Against the Galileans', where he uses the word four times, once with bitter sarcasm of the Christian God ('I suppose his *philanthropia* will eventually reach us too'), twice in the sense of 'humane' challengingly of the Romans, and once defiantly of Zeus for his gift of divination. Man was distraught, ὁ δὴ φιλάνθρωπος ἡμῶν δεσπότης καὶ πάτηρ Ζεὺς ἐννοήσας ('Our lord and father

---

[1] Eus. IV 64, 5; 139, 27; Theod. 75, 21; 278, 7 etc.

[2] *Or. Cat. Magn.* 15.   [3] e.g. *Hom.* X 988.   [4] *Lib. Asceticus* 10.

[5] Athan. *De Inc. V.* I 3; IV 2, 3, 5; VIII 4; *C. Ar.* III 67.

[6] Athan. *De fuga* 7.   [7] *P. Oxy.* VI 925[2].

Zeus in *his* love of mankind took note of this . . .'). It is no more
than a coincidence, but an interesting one, to find Julian himself
described as 'monarch most divine, most mighty, and most
gracious to mankind.'[1] An important inscription, pertaining either
to Julian or to Severus Alexander, celebrates the emperor's remis-
sion of the *aurum coronarium*; his purpose is not to enrich himself,
but to extend his empire φιλανθρωπίᾳ καὶ εὐεργεσίαις,[2] by
grace to mankind and beneficial acts.

It was natural that this rebirth in the religious use of the word
should lead to a recrudescence in its secular use as applied to the
Byzantine Emperors. The duties and responsibilities of these
emperors were religiously ordered. Their position was hieratically
conceived. In a Christian civilization they could not be deified.
But beatified they frequently were, and in life their persons were
sacrosanct, and if not divine at least god-like. In life they were
God's viceregents and after death they sat to bear joint rule with
the Son of God. It is not surprising that the formal oath which the
emperor came at some unknown period to take upon his accession included the obligation to show *philanthropia* towards his
subjects. And the writers who treat of the ideal demeanour of the
emperor constantly stress the requirement that he shall be filled
with this love of mankind. We find this in the notable oration
which Themistius delivered on this specific theme before Constantius at Ancyra in 347. *Philanthropia* is the touchstone of a
ruler's character: it is the stamp which placed on other virtues
gives them a new imperial dignity: it is a quality one may safely
attribute to God—but also man may share it with God. We find
it in Synesius, who links it with *eusebeia*; the task of a monarch is
to honour God and love man.[3] We find it again in Agapetus, in
George of Pisidia and elsewhere. But political developments at
Byzantium did not allow the counter-offensive of a less autocratic
interpretation of the word. 'Democracy' in the Eastern empire
meant revolution, anarchy, and chaos.[4] There was no possibility of

---

[1] O. Kern, *Die Inschriften von Magnesia am Mäander*, 201[2]; Dittenberger, *S.I.G.*
906 B; see above p. 105.

[2] Grenfell–Hunt–Hogarth, *Fayoum Towns and their Papyri*, p. 116, No. 20.

[3] N. H. Baynes, *Byzantine Studies*, pp. 55 ff.

[4] See e.g. Eus. *Triacont.* 3; Basil, *Longer Rules*, 45.

a word that was so closely associated with the overlord being extended to the normal relations of citizen with citizen.

Philanthropia came very close to satisfying the moral aspirations of the ancient world; in its highest usages it is very close to *agape*. And we may well ask why it proved ultimately unsatisfying. To understand this we have to reassert the nature of the quest. The quest was to find a practical ideal for human living that was at once religious and ethical. Religion divorced from ethics quite properly falls into contempt; ethical systems that are not founded on religion have never proved convincing to the majority of mankind. This means that the search is for an attitude of man towards his neighbour, and towards his God, which springs directly from the relationship of God to man. *Philanthropia*, the love of man, plainly cannot express the attitude of man to God, but that alone would not have stultified its triumph. In other regards it seems at first sight to have everything to offer. Why then did it fail?

The reason is to be found in a complex of historical accidents. In the first place *philanthropia*, though the form and root of the word do not in any sense imply it, came, as I have already stressed, to contain an element of condescension which it never wholly lost. It started by meaning the love of mankind which may be exercised by non-human beings, and it caught the imagination as applied to the gods, in a way in which it did not as applied to beings who were regarded as sub-human. This meant that its first human application was to rulers who stood in contrast to their subjects rather than to normal men in relation to their fellows and equals. The association with gifts and giving confirmed this; a gift is naturally conceived as passing from a being of superior endowment to one of inferior endowment. When the Christians revived the word the same tale is told, and its association with the hierarchical structure of the Byzantine court effectively prevented its wider extension.

Secondly it happened that the person most clearly responsible for its use in Christendom was Origen, and many of the writers who use it most widely, Athanasius, Gregory, and Maximus for example, are Origenist in tradition. But this very fact made its use suspect elsewhere, and especially in Western Christendom. Indeed Augustine, who moulded the thought of Western Christendom more than any other individual, finds the whole idea, in whatever expression, difficult to accept. For him love implies need, and as God has no need the whole conception of God's love towards man is to him hard of comprehension. Hence in his commentary on St John's Gospel he has no comment to make on the celebrated verse 'God so loved the world'.[1] The association in Origen of the revival of the classical terminology and theological trends which were regarded as heretical is not wholly accidental, for it is precisely his tendency to base his thinking upon pagan antecedents that is so often called in question. But it did mean that his language and his thought were regarded with suspicion even where they were genuinely fruitful.

Thirdly, we have to deal with the coalescence of Greece and Rome into a single, uneasily unified civilization. That the differences continued to cut deep is shown in the subsequent division of Church and State. But it is a healthy historical tradition which regards the two as manifesting essentially a single culture. No concept could satisfactorily dominate the Graeco-Roman world which could not find adequate expression both in Greek and Latin. The genius of the two languages is quite different, and the delicate meanings that are possible in Greek through combinations of the form *philanthropia* are not so readily to be found in Latin. There is no Latin equivalent of *philanthropia*, and the possible circumlocutions such as *amor generis humani* are intolerably clumsy in repetition and in any case lose the subtle ambiguity of the Greek. It follows that the Latin writers had to make do with other words, which inevitably represented different and more limited concepts, none of which offered the hope of becoming the ground of a universal ethic. On the one hand there were words like *clementia* and *misericordia*, in both of which the element of condescension was inescapable. They might well be the virtues of an emperor, and Seneca holds *clementia* before Nero as homiletically as Isocrates sets *philanthropia* before Philip, or Themistius before Constantius. But they can hardly apply to the ordinary man in

[1] Later he came to a deeper veiw cf. *De Trin.* 8; *Hom.* 7 *in Ep. Ioh.*

his ordinary relations. On the other hand there was *humanitas*. This might well be the virtue of an ordinary man. It had a long and noble tradition well represented by Terence's celebrated words 'Homo sum; humani nil a me alienum puto'[1] ('I am a human being, and reckon all that affects man affects me'). The elder Pliny indeed praised Rome for having given *humanitas* to mankind.[2] It is a favourite word of Cicero, for whom it unites the ideal of culture and kindliness, *paideia* and *philanthropia*. Thus on the one side it is linked with learning, knowledge, literary studies and education.[3] In the *De Oratore* Crassus argues that the ideal orator must possess *humanitas*, by which he means knowledge of the humane studies. Antonius, who opposes him, experiences an overnight conversion. 'The night has educated you and made you a man', comments Crassus, and Antonius himself signalizes his conversion by suggesting that to neglect Greek studies is to abjure humanity and turn oneself into a wild animal.[4] On the other side *humanitas* is linked with *clementia* and *mansuetudo* (lenience), and set against *severitas* (sternness).[5] It is Atticus's *humanitas* which gives Cicero the hope of getting matters through without too much unpleasantness; Appius's *humanitas* which gives him confidence of the latter's help.[6] *Humanitas* is in fact that which makes a man a man. To a liberal of Cicero's background this was his capacity for intellectual activity, combined with his ability to exercise moral control over his actions. The Greeks and Romans regarded these as part of the same process, governed by the same organ of personality, but they distinguished their fruits. It must be added that the part played by *humanitas* in moulding the mind of Rome has been somewhat exaggerated because of its prominence in Cicero. Cicero was out of favour in the early principate; even the gentle Vergil pillories him under the figure of Drances.[7] It is principally in Ciceronian circles that the idea is to the fore, in the younger Pliny for ex-

---

[1] Ter. *H.T.* I 1, 25.
[2] Plin. *N.H.* 3, 39.
[3] Cic. *Pro. Arch.* 3; *De Or.* 2, 18, 74; 2, 37, 154; 3, 24, 94.
[4] id. *De Or.* 2, 10, 40; 2, 36, 153.
[5] id. *Q.F.* 1, 1, 21; 1, 1, 25; *Ad Fam.* 13, 65, 1.
[6] id. *Ad Att.* 1, 17, 4; *Ad Fam.* 3, 2, 1.
[7] Verg. *Aen.* 11, 340–1. See F. Olivier, *Deux Etudes sur Virgile* (Lausanne, 1930).

ample.[1] *Humanitas* as it emerged could not satisfy the moral aspirations of the ancient world, and that for several reasons. The emphasis on culture made it the prerogative of an aristocratic few, though Cicero can apply it to a slave.[2] Its association with Cicero and the rather different Augustan emphasis prevented it from becoming a central theme of imperial propaganda. It was not readily to be associated with *gravitas*; it is a matter of somewhat surprised congratulation that Atticus has achieved *humanitas* without losing *gravitas*.[3] Further, it could hardly be applied to God, even to the Christian God, and it is significant that its later derivatives have come to be used of ethical systems which have no religious foundation.[4]

[1] Plin. *Ep.* 8, 24, 2, etc.   [2] Cic. *Ad Att.* 7, 7, 7.   [3] id. *De Leg.* 3, 1.
[4] For a fuller treatment of *humanitas* see Reitzenstein, *Werden und Weser der Humanität in Altertum*; Schneidewin, *Antike Humanität*.

VII

HOMONOIA[1]

HOMONOIA MEANS LITERALLY 'like-mindedness' though it is better translated 'unity of purpose', and its history is linked both with that of *philia* and that of *philanthropia*. It represents the social aspect of both. Wider than *philia*, which is essentially applied to personal relations, less condescending than *philanthropia*, it stands as one of the highest aspirations of the Greek world. But it was never exactly a moral concept, seeing that by its nature it could be applied only to a group of people. An individual could not practise 'like-mindedness' though *homonoia* might proceed from an attitude of mind held in common by a group of individuals—generally *philia*.

Probably in origin it denoted the natural unity of the family, but just as Aristotle saw the natural unit of the family expanding into a congregation of families or village, and so into a congregation of villages or state, and as we have seen his successor Theophrastus widening the scope of *philia* from family to clan and thence to state, so *homonoia* came to be extended to like-mindedness in a political community, and this in turn came to be its principal meaning. The city-state (*polis*) seemed to the Greek of the fourth century to be rooted in nature, and Aristotle, as so often, was expressing the common sense of his age when he said so; this is the real meaning of the much-quoted 'Man is a political animal.'[2] But the city-state was riven by discord, which the Greeks called *stasis*. Already Solon and Theognis had expressed

---

[1] See H. Kramer, *Quid valeat* ὁμόνοια *in litteris Graecis*; Eiliv Skard, *Euergetes—Concordia*; Zwicker, 'Homonoia' in *P.W.* 2266; H. Fuchs, *Augustin und d. antike Friedensgedanke*, 96 ff; W. W. Tarn, *Alexander the Great*, II, appendix 25. My debt to Tarn throughout this chapter is marked and obvious, though I differ from him in a number of details.   [2] Arist. *Pol.* 1253 a 3.

their apprehension of this.[1] The reflective period which inevitably followed the triumphs and disasters of the fifth century emphasized in the light of even more bitter experience the need for like-mindedness. '*Homonoia*', says Socrates, addressing Hippias in the pages of Xenophon,[2]

'is generally agreed to be the greatest blessing a state can have. Cabinets and leading citizens regularly tell the people *to achieve unity of purpose*. Everywhere in Greece there exists a law that the people must swear *to pursue the same ends in common purpose*; everywhere they take this oath. I don't believe the purpose of this is merely to ensure that they vote for the same dramatic companies, approve the same musicians, exalt the same writers, and have the same tastes: it is to ensure that they obey the law. It is where the people uphold the law that a state achieves strength and prosperity. But without *homonoia* no state and indeed no family could be in a healthy condition.'

One may doubt whether Hippias, who had seen beyond the law of the state which might be tyrannical, to the unwritten laws of nature,[3] really needed this homily, but as typical of the general reflections of the period it has its significance. Thus Democritus, whose aphorisms at times, as we have noted, bear a striking resemblance to those recorded of Socrates, says that neither war nor any major enterprise is possible for a state unless *homonoia* exists as a starting-point.[4] This is an important passage, for it shows *homonoia* not merely within the state but confined to it. It extends no wider. Similarly, to Plato *philia* and *homonoia* are the two qualities demanded of a citizen,[5] and the results of the activities of the true statesman.[6] The first letter of Demosthenes is an appeal for internal unity.[7] The inscriptions are full of appeals to the principle.[8] In all these instances the concord appealed to is internal concord.

What is more, despite the moralizings of Socrates, the *homonoia* thus conceived was largely negative. It consisted in the absence of

---

[1] Theog. 781; Solon 3, 19 (Diehl).   [2] Xen. *Mem.* IV 4, 16.
[3] Plat. *Prot.* 337 D–E.   [4] Democr. 250.   [5] Plat. *Alc.* 126 E.
[6] id. *Polit.* 311 C.   [7] Dem. *Ep.* 15.   [8] e.g. OGIS 237.

stasis. 'You would all agree', says Lysias in one of his speeches in almost identical words to those of Socrates, 'that *homonoia* is the greatest blessing a state can have, and *stasis* is the origin of all our troubles.'[1] This is understandable to anyone who reflects what *stasis* meant to the Greek world. At the end of a long life Isocrates summed it up:

> '*stasis*, murder, unmerited exile, confiscation, maltreatment of women and children, revolution, debt cancellation, redistribution of land and other intolerable disasters.'[2]

A bourgeois view perhaps, but including much that is disastrous by any standards. We can see it still better in the caustic pages of Thucydides' account of the revolution at Corcyra, the more caustic because of its objectivity.[3] He describes in unforgettable narrative and brilliant analysis

> 'all the acts of retaliation commited by men who have shaken off self-control and dedicated themselves to unscrupulous ambition.'

The account is familiar and accessible and does not require elaboration here. It remains one of the most masterly analyses of human depravity, and should be compulsory reading for all intending politicians. *Homonoia* meant freedom from all this. The word has not yet acquired in any marked degree a positive significance.

The next stage was in fact quantitative rather than qualitative. Expediential politicians in the fifth century, confronted with situations of emergency, had seen the advantages of a unity of purpose and action which extended beyond a state to a group of states. This was patently true during the Persian Wars and those states which Medized were regarded in some sense as betraying the common unity. Similarly Hermocrates, the Syracusan statesman, presented with the prospect of Athenian aggression, appealed successfully to the factious states of Sicily to lay aside their quarrels in their own interest. He does not speak of *homonoia*,

---

[1] Lys. XVIII 17.   [2] Isoc. *Panath.* 259; cf. *Antid.* 127.   [3] Thuc. III 80–4.

but he does describe their divided condition as *stasis*.[1] It seems that it was Gorgias who, in his famous speech at Olympia, first applied the word *homonoia* to this wider conception.[2] A leader of the British peace movement in the 1930s had a cook and housemaid at loggerheads with one another, and this brought from his wife the remark, 'E——, this can't go on; we've got a peace-meeting in the drawing-room and war in the kitchen.' Gorgias' home was suffering from internal *stasis* at the time, and this made his words less effective than they should have been. For the moment they fell on deaf ears, though it appears that other sophists echoed them.[3] One of these was no doubt Antiphon. But though he wrote a treatise on *homonoia* he does not seem to have exalted it into a political principle. Nobody made a decisive attempt to take up Gorgias' words. Yet they were not forgotten.

Isocrates was in many ways Gorgias' natural successor. He saw three things about *homonoia*. The first, as we have seen, was that *homonoia* is a necessary constituent of the healthy state.

'Would we be satisfied with (*a*) political security; (*b*) economic prosperity; (*c*) internal unity of purpose (*homonoia*); (*d*) externally a good name? Personally I believe that if we had these our country would enjoy the perfection of happiness.'[4]

It follows that it is the ruler's job, where a state is monarchically governed, to foster *homonoia*, and he said as much to Nicocles;[5] it is notable that domestic and political concord are here coupled together. Secondly, Isocrates argued that Greece had no future except as a single entity. This means that war between Greek states is to be regarded as *stasis*, and that *homonoia* is to be extended to the whole Greek race. At this point Isocrates laid hold of a curious feature of human psychology—that it is apparently easier to unite against an enemy than for a common end. The U.S.A. and the U.S.S.R. united more easily against Nazi Germany than when this danger was removed; a cynic might suppose that the easiest way to obtain peace on earth might be to invent an invasion from Mars. After all, this was the lesson of the Persian

[1] Thuc. IV 61. [2] Plut. *Mor.* 144 B–C.
[3] Isoc. *Paneg.* 3; cf. Thrasymachus *fr. I*. [4] id. *De Pace* 19. [5] id. *Nicocl.* 41.

Wars and of the statesmanship of Hermocrates. So Isocrates: 'I have come to advocate war against Persia, unity of purpose amongst the Greeks.'[1] And again, 'We shall have to find unity of purpose and exercise true goodwill towards ourselves.'[2] But Isocrates' ideal, though it was in advance of the general thinking of his day, was still pathetically limited, as we may see if we reflect upon the fervour with which he advocated race-purity within the state.[3] Thirdly, as the years passed, and Isocrates' appeal to the Greeks met with little response, his thinking progressed further, and he looked for an individual to produce *homonoia* in the Greek world. He toyed with one or two possible champions before finally fixing his choice upon Philip of Macedon. It is at this point that *homonoia* becomes linked with *philanthropia*. Hitherto *homonoia* has been regarded as the natural product of a society in which the citizens practise *philia*. Now it is to be imposed upon the citizens by a ruler whose own motive is *philanthropia*.[4] It is thus evident that *homonoia*, though expanded and extended by Isocrates, is not really a moral concept. It is still essentially negative, and it is a condition of society, but not one which springs from the free action of individual citizens.

Isocrates passed his lesson on to his pupils, and Python of Byzantium (though the story is also told of his fellow-citizen Leon) was concerned both to allay civil strife within Byzantium and to support the unifying policy of Philip against the disruptive influence of Athens. To this end he found a neat parable in his own fatness.

'Gentlemen,' he said, 'you see my build. But I've actually got a wife much fatter than I am. When we're of one mind, any old bed does for us. If we quarrel, the whole house isn't big enough.'[5]

The monuments of this time show some reflection of these ideas. Cephisodotus' familiar representation of Peace holding the infant Wealth may have been sculpted to celebrate the peace-treaty of 373; if so it was unduly optimistic. Theopompus'

---

[1] id. *Paneg.* 3.   [2] ib. 174.   [3] id. *De Pace* 89.
[4] id. *Philippus* 114.   [5] Ath. XII 550 f, but cf. Suidas s.v. Λέων.

comedy *Peace* dates from the same time. Further, at this period painters link the gods in unfamiliar pairings—Apollo and Dionysus, Apollo and Heracles, Dionysus and Hephaestus, Dionysus and Aphrodite. In the pictures the gods welcome one another, or take food and drink together. As Webster well says, 'the painters represent *homonoia* in heaven to symbolize the *homonoia* which is so much desired on earth'.[1]

The definition of *homonoia* in positive terms we owe to Aristotle, though in his concept of its extent he is a retrogression from Isocrates. He treats it under the general heading of friendship,[2] and in giving it a clear positive content he differentiates it from *homodoxia*, or agreement of opinion. Plato in the *Republic*[3] subsumed *homonoia* under *sophrosune*, defining it as the harmony of the naturally better and the naturally worse over the question which shall rule, whether in a state or an individual; he later speaks of this more properly as agreement of opinion. His language suggests that there is another deeper unity. Aristotle seeks to define this deeper unity, and, as we have said, subsumes it under friendship. *Homonoia*, he says, is a political concept. It comprises (*a*) unanimity between citizens about their common interests; (*b*) agreement on policy; (*c*) united action. *Homonoia* is the social and political expression of friendship, and it is active. But there is unlikely to be any real unity of purpose except between men who are trying to do what is right. There may be honour among thieves, but it is very limited and soon breaks up. Consequently unity of purpose must be linked with morality. This is both a noble attempt to moralize the conception and a demonstration that it is not in itself a basic moral value, or it would not need linking with morality.

Once with Isocrates you have extended *homonoia* from family to state, and from state of group to states, united geographically or ethnically, there is no logical reason for stopping there rather than extending it to embrace all mankind. As we have seen, following W. W. Tarn, it was Alexander who took this decisive

[1] T. B. L. Webster, *Art and Literature in Fourth Century Athens*, p. 16.
[2] Arist. *N.E.* VIII 1155 a 24; IX 1167 a 23 ff.
[3] Plat. *Rep.* IV 432 A, 433 C; cf. I 352 A.

step, and who took it explicitly. He started from a background which combined the thinking of Isocrates and Aristotle. He had followed Philip in uniting Greece in common purpose against Persia. He had absorbed from his tutor the idea that the Greek was a superior being, the 'barbarian' or non-Greek inferior by nature; he had also perhaps accepted Aristotle's positive outlook. As he swept across Asia he came on soldiers he could respect like Memnon, and administrators he could trust like Ada or Mazaeus, and in the hard school of experience he changed his views. Here Tarn is certainly right. It may be that one or two earlier Greeks had anticipated his discovery of the brotherhood of man; but it was not from them that he learned it. It is not necessary to go in detail into Tarn's argument nor his refutation of his critics. There are four key-passages[1] in which we can see that Alexander had in fact taken this step, and Tarn has successfully shown that they can be traced back to authentic eye-witness accounts of the banquet at Opis, and that the step represented more than an attempt to fuse together Greeks and Persians. It is true that this last was part of Alexander's policy. He came to trust Persians with administration, to admit them into his army, to marry Roxane and Barsine himself and encourage mixed marriages generally. It is possible that he began with a more limited objective, and came later to the wider vision. It is equally possible that the initial shock of finding Persians who were as able and as good as Greeks startled him into some deeper thinking, and that the policy of fusion was only part of the wider vision almost from the first. Certainly it appears that, as early as his visit to Egypt, he expressed approval of the sentiment that God was king of all men, but felt himself drawn to a conclusion springing from a deeper insight into truth, namely that God was the common father of all mankind, making the best men peculiarly his own.[2] Hence his verdict that the good man is the true Greek and the bad man the true barbarian[3] (a clear transcending of Aristotle's teaching). For

---

[1] Plut. *Alex.* 27; Arrian VII 11, 8–9; Eratosthenes *apud* Strabo 1, 4, 9, and Plut. *De Alex. Fort.* 329 B; 330 E.

[2] Plut. *Alex.* 27.

[3] Plut. *De Alex. Fort.* 329 B; cf. Strabo 1, 4, 9.

'he believed that he had a mission from God to bring general harmony and to be the reconciler of the world . . . bringing ingredients from everywhere into a single unity, mixing men's lives and customs, marriages and habits, as in a loving-cup.'

This is an astonishing passage, and, as Tarn points out, the phrase 'reconciler of the world' is extraordinary, the more extraordinary because (as he does not point out and as his version of the passage obscures) the whole emphasis here is not on reconciling men, but their practices throughout the world. It is on the whole easier to reconcile an individual polygamist with an individual mono-gamist, than it is to reconcile polygamy with monogamy. But all this must be based on the scene at Opis. There were seated there Macedonians, Persians, Greeks, and Magi, and representatives of other peoples both from inside and outside his dominion. On the table stood a great bowl of wine. At the sound of the trumpet all those sitting round the table drew wine from the same bowl, and poured a libation, presumably 'to God'. Then Alexander offered prayer, and the keynotes of the prayer, which is recorded both by Arrian from Ptolemy and by Plutarch from Erastosthenes[1] are *homonoia* and partnership—'for all men', adds Plutarch. Alexan-der in short believed in the brotherhood of mankind under the fatherhood of God. He believed himself to be divinely sent to exercise a ministry of reconciliation throughout the world. In practice this meant the extension of *homonoia* till its scope was universal.

Behind Zeno lay Alexander; before Alexander lay Zeno; and Alexander's vision was transmuted philosophically into Stoic universalism. But the Stoics were pantheists and fatalists.

> *And, spite of pride, in erring reason's spite,*
> *One truth is clear—Whatever is, is right.*[2]

To the Stoics *homonoia* already existed. It is to be seen in the uni-verse, said Zeno,[3] and later the example of the heavenly bodies was used in demonstration of the fact.[4] Sometimes instead of

---

[1] Arrian VII 11, 9; Plut. *De Alex. Fort.* 330 E.   [2] Pope, *Essay on Man*, I, 293–4.
[3] Von Arnim, *S.V.F.* I 263.   [4] D. Chr. XL 35 ff.

speaking of *homonoia* they spoke of harmony, in a word which they may have borrowed from Heraclitus (where it perhaps meant something different), and which Alexander had used of his mission. Thus Cleanthes:

> *In thine eyes*
> *The unloved is lovely, who did'st harmonize*
> *Things evil with things good, that there should be*
> *One Word through all things everlastingly.*[1]

Posidonius uses the same conception. But it is in terms of *homonoia* that Chrysippus makes his great affirmation 'God is homonoia'.[2] Plainly a view of such universal scope has social implications and it is not surprising to find Zeno in his early ideal commonwealth exalting Eros (as we have seen) as the god who helps to make the state secure, because Eros is the god of *philia* and *homonoia*. So too in Iambulus' Utopia, which was written in the latter half of the third century, and which, though not exclusively Stoic, contains Stoic elements, the citizens prize *homonoia* above all things.[3] And Utopias apart, in general Stoic thought, which divides mankind rigidly into 'worthy' and 'unworthy', the worthy are regarded as enjoying *homonoia* with one another.[4] Zeno himself spoke of it,[5] and it was subsequently defined as ἐπιστήμη κοινῶν ἀγαθῶν, an understanding of the general good.[6] A later Stoic, Musonius, quotes with evident approval the doctrine that a ruler should promote *homonoia*.[7]

Meantime the idea was equally prominent outside Stoic circles. Alexander's empire might break up, but the monarchs who ruled its fragmented parts were his successors, and within the limits which history imposed upon them stood in the same tradition. The position—an age of decadence and of autocracy, in which education and speculation had passed into the hands of people who no longer exercised any direct political responsibility—prompted innumerable treatises on kingship,[8] which have fortunately not

---

[1] Cleanthes, *Hymn to Zeus*, tr. J. Adam.   [2] Von Arnim, *S.V.F.* II 1076.
[3] D.S. II 58.   [4] Stob. II 7, 11 b.   [5] Von Arnim, *S.V.F.* I 61.
[6] ib. III 160.   [7] Stob. IV 7, 67.
[8] E. R. Goodenough, *The Political Philosophy of Hellenistic Kingship*, Yale Class. Studies I, 1928, p. 55.

survived, for they would have been intolerable in the mass. We
have fragments of two of them, an anonymous author who writes
under the name of Ecphantus, and an otherwise unknown
thinker named Diotogenes. The first of these propounds the view
that there is an analogy between the king's function in the state
and the operations of God in the universe. A state would fall apart
without the bonds of fellowship (*philia*) and partnership. These
correspond on earth to the *homonoia* of the universe (he is thinking
of the ordered constellations of heaven). It is therefore the king's
function to promote these things.[1] Diotogenes writes in very
similar terms, except that he uses the concept of harmony instead
of *homonoia*;[2] we have already seen the two linked in the mind of
Alexander. That such ideas were widespread in the Hellenistic
Age we cannot doubt, and Musonius in the early days of the
Roman empire refers back to them; the king is 'living law'
(words which Diotogenes actually quotes from Aristotle),[3] his
job is to effect ordered government and *homonoia* and to avert
lawlessness and *stasis*, holding the same paternal relationship to
his subjects that God does to mankind.[4]

There are various records of the worship of Homonoia in
different parts of the Greek world during the Hellenistic Age and
earlier. As early as the fifth century a coin of Metapontum bears a
female head with the inscription Ὁμόνοια.[5] This may represent a
cult title of Demeter. Sometimes the goddess is the divinity of
domestic felicity. This is clear in Chariton's account of the temple
at Miletus; it was there that bridegrooms met their brides.[6] But
this is by no means the only motive. A shrine on the island of
Thynias in the Black Sea occasions a description by Apollonius of
how the Argonauts pledged there their unity in common purpose.[7] A quite clear reference to internal politics is given by inscriptions pertaining to shrines at Cos and Iasos,[8] the first of these
dates from the second century B.C. In Thera too the cult was
political, and seems to have been taken over by the state;[9] this is

[1] Stob. IV 7, 64.   [2] ib. 61.   [3] ib. 61; cf. Arist. *Pol.* III 1284 a 13.   [4] ib. 67.
[5] *B.M. Cat.* Italy, p. 244; Head, *Hist. Numm.* p. 62.   [6] Chariton, *Erot.* III 2.
[7] Ap. Rh. II 718.   [8] Paton and Hicks 61, cf. 401; Hicks, *Gr. Inscr. B.M.* 443.
[9] *C.I.G.* Ins. xii Fasc. iii Suppl. 1336.

also a second-century inscription. One or two cults relate to agreement between more than one state; they are mostly late. It was to be expected that some worship of Homonoia would be found at Olympia, the one place where quarrels were laid firmly aside, and Pausanias tells us of an altar there;[1] an altar with a fragmentary inscription was in fact found.[2] Similarly at Lebadeia Homonoia had her high priest, for there the Greeks united in the mysteries of Trophonius.[3] An inscription of the first century A.D., found, a little curiously, at Thebes, reads: 'Homonoia of Athens and Thespiae', and no doubt accompanied a statue.[4] Other dedications relate to Issos, Priene, Cyzicus, and Tralles.[5] The cult was evidently widespread.

Not the least interesting of Alexander's successors was Cleopatra of Egypt. The older history books, steeped in Roman propaganda, fail to do her justice; a more judicious estimate has emerged in comparatively recent times. The woman whom to generations of Egyptians it was enough to call 'the queen', whom a seventh-century Coptic bishop praised as 'the most illustrious and wise among women', 'great in herself and in her achievements and in courage and strength', who could hold her own in talking philosophy with Cicero, and who had the business acumen and technical knowledge to run a wool-mill—she is not to be written off as if she were a Hollywood film actress. Rather we do well to remember Tarn's eloquent words 'Rome, who had never condescended to fear any nation or people, did in her time fear two human beings; one was Hannibal, and the other was a woman'.[6] Cleopatra was by no means just a tool of Mark Antony; it would be truer to say that Antony was the instrument of Cleopatra's ambitions. Cleopatra had a vision; how far it was a genuine aspiration and how far a propaganda façade it is impossible now to discern. She was to cast Rome down from heaven to earth, then raise her from earth to heaven, inaugurate a golden age for Asia and Europe alike, and end feud, war, and bloodshed.

---

[1] Paus. V 14, 9.
[2] *Ath. Mitth.* 1878, 226.
[3] *C.I.G.* Sept. 3426.
[4] ib. 1784.
[5] Michel 1203; 1 Priene III, I, 148; *Ath. Mitth.* 6, 130; Appian, *Mithr.* 23.
[6] *C.A.H.* X, p. III.

'Tranquil peace shall foot it over all the Asian land, and Europe then shall be happy, a fruitful clime many a long year, strongly established, that knows no storm or hail, bearing all things, both birds and beasts that go upon the earth. . . . For from the starry heaven will all fair order and righteousness come upon men, and therewith Concord (*homonoia*) with temperance that is for mortals beyond all riches, love and faith and friendship among strangers, and afar will flee from men in those days poverty and murder and baneful strife and bitter wranglings and nocturnal theft and every evil.'[1]

Cleopatra and Antony are to make real Alexander's vision of a world-wide empire in which the nations are mixed as in a loving-cup. In this prophecy four things require notice. Firstly, *homonoia* is central and crucial; secondly, it is universal and inclusive; thirdly, it is the creation of a monarch; fourthly, though it retains its negative connotation, it has also positive moral content, being associated with 'love and faith and friendship'. There is here an overt contradiction. A monarch can impose unity, but he can hardly impose love and faith and friendship. Such contradictions have seldom worried either prophets or propagandists.

But Cleopatra lost, and the destiny of the world passed to Rome. The Latin for *homonoia* was *concordia*. Later Roman tradition, imbued with Greek speculation, connected the idea with the origins of the city and the great kings Romulus or Numa.[2] Tradition also placed the founding of the first temple to Concordia early in the fourth century; the person responsible being M. Furius Camillus, and the occasion the settlement of a class-dispute between patricians and plebeians.[3] Another was dedicated by Cn. Flavius late in the fourth century. The evidence about this is conflicting. The Samnite war was over, the Aequi were defeated, and peace was made with a number of other peoples. It might seem that the occasion was a peace celebration. Pliny however

[1] *Orac. Sibyll.* III 350–61, 367–80. For a full treatment see W. W. Tarn in *J.R.S.* XXII 1932, 135 ff.

[2] D.H. II 3; Plut. *Numa* 20.

[3] Ov. *Fasti* I 639 ff. Momigliano doubts the authenticity of the tradition. 'Camillus and Concord' *C.Q.* XXXVI (1942) 111–20.

tells us that Flavius, a man of humble birth, but ability and eloquence, vowed the shrine if he succeeded in mediating between
the upper classes and the common people. The curious fact is that
he seems to have dedicated the shrine without effecting the reconciliation, and this was ironically itself the cause of some internal
ill-feeling, since the aristocracy disputed the right of a mere curule
aedile to take such an action.[1] This shrine was dedicated *in Grae-
costasi* and *in area Vulcani*. This may suggest the direct influence of
the Greek *homonoia*. In 216 L. Manlius dedicated a temple of Concord on the citadel, to celebrate the quelling of a mutiny. This
was no doubt the shrine which Tiberius later rededicated.[2] A
fourth dates from the repression of the Gracchi, and was conse-
crated by Opimius.[3] It is thus evident that in general *concordia*
meant to the Romans of the republic what *homonoia* meant to the
Greeks of the early fourth century, the absence of party-strife, and
class-conflict. The story of Flavius is exceptional enough in many
ways to suggest that he may have been a visionary before his time,
at least with the perspicacity of a Gorgias. The senate met in one
of these temples,[4] a fact which shows the general sense that *concordia* was an internal political aspiration. One interesting example
will suffice. About the year 55 B.C. Paullus Lepidus struck a coin
which celebrates the agreement of the triumvirs at Luca with the
inscription CONCORDIA. Towards the end of the Republic, as is
well known, Cicero made the central plank of his political plat-
form the *concordia ordinum*, that is to say, a unity of common purpose and action between aristocracy and the bourgeoisie. He
achieved this momentarily in face of the common danger from
the revolutionary Catiline (a pattern we have seen emerging
before). It is interesting, in view of Tarn's association of *homonoia*
with the line of kingship, that he was accused of aspiring to kingship. But even in his later thought he looked to a monarch to
bring about this concord, though he called him *rector* rather than
the ill-omened name *rex*. Practically, he seems to have realized

[1] Liv. 9, 46, 6; Plin. *N.H.* XXXIII 1, 6, 19.
[2] Liv. 22, 33, 7 and cf. H. F. Rebert and H. Marceau, 'The Temple of Concord in the Roman Forum' *Mem. Amer. Acad. Rom.* V (1925) 53.
[3] Aug. *De C.D.* 3, 25; Cic. *Pro Sest.* 140; App. *Bell. Civ.* 1, 26, 120; Plut. *V.C. Gracchi* 17. [4] Cic. *Phil.* II 8, 19; Sall. *Cat.* 46, 4.

shortly after his consulate that the rôle was not to be his. Instead he cast himself for Polonius, a part which he was not ill-fitted to play, and toyed with first Pompey and then young Octavian for the central office, rejecting Caesar and Antony.

He was right about Octavian, though that implacable young man had no use for Cicero beyond the immediate present. When he achieved dominion under the more familiar appellation of Augustus, he did indeed appear as the reconciler of the world; to the east he was certainly in the line of Hellenistic kings; in the west he appears as the inaugurator of the golden age.[1] Tiberius, fulfilling a vow he had taken earlier, on succeeding him summed up his achievement as emperor by dedicating a temple to Concordia Augusta.[2] Augustus in short had produced *homonoia* and this *homonoia* was patently not confined to one city, one people, or one race. It was the immeasurable majesty of the Roman peace, of which Pliny speaks, and which even the Christian apologists laud.[3] Henceforth in one form or another concord forms an essential theme of imperial propaganda. Sometimes, like *homonoia* in its early stages, it means no more than connubial bliss. Sometimes it is clearly political. Its commonest appearance is in the phrase CONCORDIA AVGVSTA, but Galba had on his coins CONCORDIA PROVINCIARVM; Vitellius actually took, or proposed to take, CONCORDIA as a surname, somewhat optimistically.[4] By and large it is a fair appraisal of the Roman achievement. A larger area of the inhabited globe had a longer era of virtually untroubled peace than at any other time in the history of the world (the only possible exception being the Chinese empire). Further, whatever the motives which prompted Caracalla's action, from A.D. 212 every free provincial became a Roman citizen. The aspiration was realized. But the concord thus achieved was imposed and paternalistic. It originated in the policy of the sovereign rather than the will of the people. It is a social grace rather than a moral value. Its association lies with *philanthropia* rather than *philia*.

[1] cf. Verg. *Aen.* VI 791-4.
[2] Suet. *Tib.* 20; D.C. LV 8, 9; LVI 25; Ov. *Fast.* I, 641.
[3] Plin. *N.H.* XIV 2; XXVII 3; cf. Orig. *C. Cels.* 2, 30; Prud. *Adv. Symm.* I, 287; 2, 582; *De Cor.* 2, 413.   [4] Suet. *Vit.* 15, 4.

This shows well enough why *homonoia* could not fulfil the moral gropings of the ancient world. In the first place it depends upon the consensus of more than one person; indeed upon the united consensus of society. A genuine moral value must be expressible in and through society, but it must also reflect an attitude of mind which can be adopted by the individual in despite of society—*Athanasius contra mundum*. In the second place, by the accidents of history, like *philanthropia* it acquired an element of condescension, a value imposed from above rather than rising from the inner springs of personality. But it was a noble vision and it played its part in shaping the thought of the ancient world.

VIII

THE TRIUMPH OF AUTARCY[1]

To understand how the doctrine of 'autarcy'—'self-sufficiency' or 'independence'—came to grip the Greek world we have to glance for a moment at the physical environment which the Greeks enjoyed. To reduce morals to geography is absurd. To ignore the effect of climate upon character and thought is equally absurd, and there is something in the air of Greece which makes for sharp outline, something precise and cutting. Consider the difference between a Greek temple and a Gothic cathedral. A Gothic cathedral has grown across the centuries. It may have changed its style of building in the middle, not once but two or three times. Additions and extensions may have been brought to it. Yet in its own atmosphere it remains a dynamic unity. The unity of a Greek temple is quite different. It is single, whole and complete, and any change of style or later extension is unthinkable without the effect being spoiled. The Greek temple is *autarkes*. Similarly, the Greeks were the first people to make statues which were complete in themselves, designed to be seen from all sides, and not parts of an architectural complex. A Greek tragedy is complete in itself, and Aristotle says so. Anyone who tries to remove a scene, let us say the Hecuba-Helen debate in *The Trojan Women*, which is not very successful in itself, will soon find that he has spoiled the balance of the whole. The epigram, that 'dwarfish whole', is in some ways the most typical product of Greek art.

Furthermore, Greece is a land of mountain barriers.

'The obstacles to easy travel within the Greek mainland are

---

[1] See A. N. M. Rich, 'The Cynic Conception of αὐτάρκεια' *Mnem.* (1956), pp. 23–9, an article which came into my hands too late to use fully.

even greater than a mere glance at the map, showing its high relief, would suggest.'[1]

It follows that the natural political institution of Greece lay within a single plain or river-valley in some isolation from its neighbours. 'That peculiar institution, the Greek city-state, had its roots in the geographic conformation of the Greek lands.'[2] The life of the average Greek was irrevocably bound up with one or other of these natural units. He lived in it, and depended on it. He bore a greater or lesser responsibility for its government; in Athens where the oligarchy characteristic of all Greek states had been extended to include all free citizens, the share was considerable. His conventional religion was wrapped up with his political loyalty, as the position of Athene at Athens reminds us. It bounded his horizon. It is true, as Ehrenberg has said, that there was a sort of natural unity round the shores of the Aegean,[3] but historically it never came to much. At Olympia open hostilities were laid aside, but even there the competitors were striving for the glory of their particular state; a glance at Pindar's odes makes that clear enough. That unscrupulous and opportunist politician Demosthenes knows well the appeal a narrow patriotism will make to his hearers, and even Isocrates, who had a far deeper vision of the needs of the Greek world, shows in the *Panathenaicus* that his thinking is rooted and grounded in the concept of the city-state. This is certainly true of Plato and Aristotle. The greatest of metaphysicians and the greatest of scientists are equally blind to the political future of the world in which they live. History has never perpetrated greater dramatic irony than in making Aristotle the tutor of Alexander. If neither philosophers nor politicians could rise above the city-state, it is not surprising if it was the whole world to the man in the street. It follows that when the city-state broke, he broke. By the end of the fifth century the writing was already on the wall. Few states had escaped a period of *stasis*. The great war between Athens and Sparta had shattered the buoyant optimism and expansive extravagance of the mid-century. This

---

[1] M. Cary, *Geographic Background of Greek and Roman History*, p. 47.
[2] ib. p. 52.   [3] V. Ehrenberg, *Aspects of the Ancient World*, p. 34.

was true, so far as our records permit us to judge, throughout Greece. It was certainly true of Athens, and Athens was factually what Pericles' proud boast claimed for her, 'the school of Greece'. Nearly all the ideas which affected the Greek world found their way through Athens, and it is with her cultural heritage that we associate men like Protagoras of Abdera, Gorgias of Leontini, Hippias of Elis, Aristotle of Stagira, Zeno of Citium, Epicurus of Samos.

The collapse of the city-state was inescapable. In the event the fallen fragments were integrated into massive empires governed from without. After Alexander's death a few pathetic attempts were made to reassert independence, by Phocion at Athens or Cleomenes at Sparta, and there were some interesting experiments in federalism. On the whole, people felt themselves in the grip of world powers which they could not control or even affect. Their civic independence and their responsibility were alike gone, swept out on the ebbing tide of destiny. Athenian degeneracy may be seen in the fulsome flattery with which they welcomed Demetrius, declaring that he was the only true god, all the others being asleep or away or non-existent, and offering him the Parthenon as his private residence.[1] It was this world in which the cult of Tyche, Fortune, spread so widely. Purpose had gone out of life, and Chance ruled.

Meantime parallel psychological and educational changes were taking place. We have seen already how the age of colonization encouraged a new individualism and led to the conscious formulation of a philosophy of co-operation which had hitherto been taken for granted.[2] The development of democratic government in Athens and elsewhere intensified the individualism. The growth of individualism in the fifth century can be seen vividly reflected in the history of tragic drama. At the beginning of the century, if we may still accept the *Suppliants* as representative, the play is about the chorus. By the end of the century the chorus has become little more than a purveyor of musical interludes. It must be remembered that democracy at Athens meant (*a*) direct government by an assembly in which all citizens might attend,

[1] Ath. VI 253 C; D.S. XX 100. [2] *supra*, p. 22.

speak, and vote; (*b*) executive action by officers chosen, with very few exceptions, by lot from the whole citizen body.[1] As Glover told his American audience in no uncertain terms, no Greek would ever have called America democratic—or Britain for the matter of that. This individualism is one of the criticisms which the 'Old Oligarch' brings against Athenian democracy. *Quot homines tot sententiae* is no maxim for a state whose survival may depend upon *homonoia*. But the individualism was there, and the appropriate education came to meet the demand. Cicero said that Socrates brought philosophy down from heaven and planted her upon earth—a flowery way of saying that he turned his attention from astronomy to ethics. That achievement may more properly be laid at the door of the sophists, though Socrates had his share in it; indeed Aristophanes and Aeschines call Socrates a sophist. They directed men's thoughts, in a phrase used by Democritus and later by Aristotle, from the macrocosm to the microcosm, from the universe to man. People demanded to get on in life. The sophists offered courses to enable this. They called their subject *arete* (the conventional 'virtue' but really 'excellence' or 'success'). In the conditions of the fifth century this meant an emphasis on rhetoric, for eloquence in the assembly was the condition of power, and eloquence in the law-courts the condition of security (a lawyer might write your speech, but he would not deliver it). In the hands of scrupulous teachers this might not do much harm, and Protagoras, Gorgias, Thrasymachus, Hippias, and Prodicus made genuine contributions to the study of language and logic. In the hands of an Euthydemus or a Dionysodorus it was a dangerous toy. It was so easy for the process of making a weaker argument appear stronger to degenerate into a facility for making an immoral argument appear convincing. The sophists have an honourable place in the history of Greek education, but it is undeniable that they helped to foster that individualism which they emerged to serve. Their influence went on through the fourth century, as the polemical writings of Plato and Isocrates remind us. Those whom they attack by name may have lain hidden

[1] See W. Headlam, *Election by Lot*; T. R. Glover, *Democracy in the Ancient World*.

under their Via Flaminia, but the abuses are real and contemporary. Then at the end of the century the new political situation affected the period of military training, which was reduced to one year, and the training was given in Athens instead of the Piraeus barracks or the frontier forts. This freed the young men for liberal education, and it was to serve them that the Stoic school began.[1]

Individuals in the Hellenistic world were thus left crying: 'What must I do to be saved?' 'Where shall security be found?' The two dominant philosophies each had their own answer. Epicureanism said,

'The end of life is tranquillity. Public life can only destroy tranquillity. Live in retirement, in the seclusion of the Garden, in the delights of friendship.'

Stoicism said,

'The events of life are determined, unalterable and good. What is not determined is the response of your mind. Practise non-attachment, and the world cannot touch you. Say

I am the master of my fate
I am the captain of my soul.'[2]

'Since you can't have what you want, best want what you can have', says a character in Terence, in the mood of the times. The philosophies of the Hellenistic Age, for all their nobility, were essentially philosophies of escape, and the principal means of escape lay in the cultivation of autarcy.

The noun does not seem to antedate the fourth century, as indeed one might suspect. Who coined it is uncertain. Its appearance in the letters attributed to Hippocrates is almost certainly of later date.[3] The sophist Hippias practised a sort of autarcy without apparently using the word. He appeared at Olympia with everything about him 'home-made', including a papyrus-roll containing one of his own poems. But this is the autarcy of pride, not that

[1] W. S. Ferguson, *Hellenistic Athens*, pp. 128–9.
[2] W. E. Henley, *Invictus*.   [3] Hippocrates, *Ep.* 17, 35–7.

of insecurity, of expansion not contraction. The word appears in Democritus[1] with clear philosophical implications. 'Service overseas teaches self-sufficiency; a ration of bread and a straw mattress are the pleasantest remedies for hunger and weariness.' The imposed hardships of a mercenary soldier's life may discipline the soul. In other fragmentary quotations the precarious gifts of chance are contrasted with the self-sufficiency which comes from nature and from *sophrosune*.[2] If the word was in fact coined by Democritus it is the more interesting to find it occurring in Plato. In the *Philebus* he uses it of the supreme Good.[3] At first he is curiously loath to use even the adjective, which had been current for about a century. In the *Lysis* in writing of the good man he speaks of him being 'sufficient unto himself' (ἱκανὸς αὑτῷ).[4] A similar though more complicated circumlocution appears in a similar context in the *Menexenus*.[5] In the *Republic* the doctrine recurs, this time with the word. It is true that no one is economically self-sufficient; that is the basis of society as a natural organism.[6] But, so far as anyone may, the good man has in himself all the resources for a good life (μάλιστα αὐτὸς αὑτῷ αὐτάρκης πρὸς τὸ εὖ ζῆν—the intensification of the phrase is remarkable even for Plato).[7] It looks then as if the word came into philosophical currency in the 390s. This was the period in which mercenary service developed rapidly as an occupation for the demobilized troops of the Peloponnesian War, and Xenophon's *Anabasis* is one account of such service. It was the period also in which this was a natural psychological response to the march of history.

There were historical grounds for the doctrine's appeal. But its spread was given a considerable fillip by the personality and outlook of Socrates. Socrates' life had been a triumph of independence (I need not spend time to refute the jaundiced view which would see him as the aristocracy's boot-licker). He had refused to co-operate in the unjust practises of either the left wing or the right. His hardihood in campaigning at Potidaea or Delium became legendary.[8] His courage in face of death is a recurrent

---

[1] Democr. 246.   [2] id. 176, 210.   [3] Plat. *Phileb.* 67 A of 20 E.
[4] id. *Lys.* 215 A.   [5] id. *Menex.* 247 E.   [6] id. *Rep.* II 369 B.   [7] ib. III 387 D.
[8] id. *Symp.* 219 E–221 B.

theme with his admirers,[1] and to a generation from whom the very suggestion of a life after death drew an exclamation of startled surprise,[2] this was the supreme example of independence. His attitude to others invited the same interpretation. He criticized the sophists because, being themselves agnostics, they yet professed to teach. He rejected any suggestion that he was a teacher. He offered, with his tongue in his cheek no doubt (this is the meaning of Socratic 'irony'), a far more radical agnosticism than theirs. When the Delphic Oracle replied to Chaerephon that Socrates was the wisest man in Greece, Socrates, who, like Bernard Shaw, put a bold face before the world and was humble at heart, was genuinely puzzled. So began the search for a wiser man than he, and the exposure, by ruthless logic, of the pretensions of those who professed wisdom—the Socratic elenchus. So came the paradoxical conclusion that the Oracle was right, for no one knew anything, but at least he knew that he knew nothing. Much of this was whimsical, but behind the whimsy was a steely resolve that slipshod thinking and ignorance masquerading as knowledge should not sit unchallenged on the throne. The Socratic elenchus had its positive side too. This is to be seen in his claim to follow his mother's profession of midwife.[3] Teaching was not possible; the professed teachers were ignorant, and he did not make their exalted claims. What he could do was to enable people to give birth to the thoughts that were in them. This was linked with his favourite doctrine of Recollection or Reminiscence. Knowledge cannot be imparted or acquired. All knowledge is recollection of something which has been experienced before birth. We need not now go into the questions this raises; the problem of how knowledge can be acquired is as cogent before birth as after. What it means for us here is that the individual is self-sufficient. He has within himself the seeds of his future development.

That this is genuinely Socratic is clear. The *Lysis* and *Mene-xenus* are early dialogues written when Plato was concerned to do little more than record his master's approach to life; he had scarcely begun that process of interpretation which led him

---

[1] e.g. id. *Apol.* 41 C ff; *Phaedo* passim.   [2] id. *Rep.* X 608 D.
[3] Plat. *Theaet.* 149 A ff; Plut. *Quaest. Plat.* 1.

steadily away from Socrates' ethical approach into advanced
metaphysics. The passage in the *Republic* also is, as Adam comments, 'full of Socratic colouring'.[1] This is confirmed by Xenophon, who may have been limited in his understanding of
Socrates, but lacked the genius to impose a philosophical interpretation upon him. It appears likely that the first two chapters of
the *Memorabilia* were written in the late 390s as an answer to
Polycrates' attack on Socrates, and the remainder was an expansion of and commentary on his own defence of Socrates, being
added some five or ten years later. The new vocabulary was open
to him, and he uses it in his remarks about Socrates.

> 'He lived on very little and was supremely *independent*; he
> had perfect self-mastery in all kinds of pleasures.'[2] 'He worked
> to enable his associates to be *independent* in the work each was
> fitted for.'[3] 'His wisdom was such that he was unerring in his
> judgement of good and evil; he was *independent* in his know-
> ledge of them and needed no prompting.'[4]

This derived from Socrates. But it became an integral part of
Plato's own thinking. That self-sufficiency is the mark of the good
man he seems to have accepted unquestioningly, but it was he
who gave it metaphysical and theological implications. Thus at
the end of the *Philebus* he declares that neither mind nor pleasure
is the absolute good in that each lacks self-sufficiency.[5] In other
words, self-sufficiency is the mark of the *summum bonum*. This he
has effectively stated near the beginning of the dialogue.[6] In the
Timaeus he applies it to the Universe.

> 'It was created by design so as to supply its own sustenance
> by its own wasting, and to have all its action and passion in
> itself and by itself; for its artificer thought that if it were self-
> sufficing it would be better than if it stood in need of things
> from without.'[7]

It is further applied to the divine shepherds of the *Politicus* in their

---

[1] J. Adam, *The Republic of Plato*, ad loc. [2] Xen. *Mem.* I 2, 14. [3] ib. IV 7, 1.
[4] ib. IV 8, 11. [5] Plat. *Phileb.* 67 A. [6] ib. 20 D. [7] id. *Tim.* 33 C–D.

relations with the animals under their care;[1] each has the full resources for his task. This last is a passage of particular interest for the absence of self-sufficiency leads to war (Plato argued this in the *Republic* and implied it in the *Phaedo*) and autarcy thus takes the place of *homonoia* in avoiding conflict. Elsewhere, where the language is different, the ideal is the same. Take, for instance, the great description of Absolute Beauty in the *Symposium*,

> 'a Beauty eternal, not growing or decaying, waxing or waning; nor will it be fair here and foul there, nor depending on time or circumstance or place, as if fair to some and foul to others; nor shall beauty appear to him in the likeness of a face or hand, nor embodied in any sort of form whatever whether of heaven or earth; but Beauty absolute, separate, simple and everlasting.'[2]

Beauty absolute is certainly *autarkes*, and the same, which is said of subsidiary divinities, must also be admitted of the Divine Artificer, who surely does not make the world because of any need of his own. Plato, in other words, gave the ethical postulate its metaphysical and religious grounds.

Aristotle, for all his metaphysical divagations, remained Plato's pupil. The coping-stone of his metaphysical system is God, who is pure Form, and who sits in eternal self-contemplation—since contemplation is the highest activity, and the object of his contemplation must be the highest possible—himself unmoved, moving the universe as the spectacle of the beloved moves the lover.[3] With this ultimate vision it is not surprising if his ethical system exalts the idea of self-sufficiency. In an interesting passage of the *Rhetoric*,[4] summarizing characteristically the views of others, he accepted the following possible definitions of happiness (a) prosperity combined with virtue; (b) self-sufficiency (*autarkeia zoes*); (c) the life that combines pleasure and security; (d) plenitude of possessions in the form of animals and slaves with effective control. Almost everyone, he says, admits that happiness consists in one or more of these. It is not quite clear what self-sufficiency here means. The natural interpretation of the words

---

[1] id. *Polit.* 271 D.   [2] id. *Symp.* 211 A; tr. Robert Bridges.
[3] Arist. *Met.* XII 1072 b 3 ff; 1074 b 15 ff.   [4] id. *Rhet.* I 1360 b 15.

would suggest economic independence, but this would seem to
be the fourth of his definitions, and what follows makes it much
more likely that he is envisaging a general ideal of independence,
including economic independence (Aristotle is too down-to-
earth to omit that), but transcending it. He goes on to identify
the parts of happiness as good birth, numerous and good friends,
wealth, numerous and good progeny, and a prosperous old age.
In addition a man should be healthy, handsome, strong, of fine
physique, athletic, well spoken of, honoured, lucky, and virtuous.
A man who possessed these personal blessings of mind and body
and the external blessings of birth, friends and the like, combined
with position and fortune (for security's sake), would be *autar-
kestatos*, supremely self-sufficient. It is worth noting that the
occurrence of *autarkes* in superlative form shows that it is being
used loosely. It is really as much of a solecism to say 'most self-
sufficient' as to say 'rather unique'. A thing is either unique or it
is not, and a person is either self-sufficient or he is not. This shows
the chimerical nature of the ideal. We are not self-sufficient, and
Plato and Aristotle knew it and said it. We are born into society,
we have strongly gregarious elements in our nature, and we are
dependent upon society. As Shaw once pungently put it:

'Rousseau said that Man is born free. Rousseau was wrong.
No government of a civilized state can possibly regard its citizens as born free. On the contrary, it must regard them as born
in debt, and as necessarily incurring fresh debt every day they
live, and its most pressing duty is to hold them to that debt and
to see that they pay it. Not until it is paid can any freedom
begin for the individual. When he cannot walk a hundred
yards without using such a very expensive manufactured
article as a street, care must be taken that he produces his share
of the cost. When he has paid scot and lot his leisure begins, and
with it his liberty. He can then say boldly "Having given unto
Caesar the things that are Caesar's I shall now, under no tute-
lage or compulsion except that of my conscience, give to God
the things that are God's". That is the only possible basis for
civil liberty.'

A Greek would sacrcely have written in those terms, least of all
Aristotle, to whom the non-Greek world was designed by a providential Nature to give to the aristocracy of Greeks that leisure
which would enable them to fulfil the true destiny of man. But
even in Aristotle's own terms, our mutual dependence was a cold
and obvious fact, and the approach to independence could never
be more than asymptotic.

The same ambiguity extends to the *Ethics* and led one scholar
to make a distinction between two different meanings of *autarkes*,
as sufficient, and as sufficient and independent.[1] Aristotle, the suggestion goes, fluctuated from one to the other, and what he was
really saying is that his supreme good lacks nothing in its end,
though it may lack something in the means of its achievement.
Aristotle is certainly not as clear as he might be, but it is better
to say that he is speaking loosely rather than that he is confusing
two specific meanings. A typical passage appears in the first book.[2]
He is arguing that happiness is the supreme good.

'The same conclusion seems further to follow from the self-
sufficiency of happiness; it is generally agreed that the supreme
good is self-sufficiency. By self-sufficiency I am not suggesting
that an individual is self-sufficient, living a life of isolation; we
must include his parents, children and wife and his friends and
fellow-countrymen generally, since man is naturally a social
being. But we must accept some limit; if we extend it to pro-
genitors and progeny and friends' friends the list will never end.
This requires further consideration; for the moment we define
self-sufficiency as that which, all else apart, makes a man's life
desirable and free from wants. I believe that this is happiness.
. . . Happiness then is shown to be complete and self-sufficient;
it is the ultimate aim of all our activity.'

The confusion is already evident, and it is not long before he is
saying that happiness requires external prosperity, which is outside a man's control.[3] The political implications of his reservations
do not escape him. Plato had seen the state emerging from the

[1] J. Léonard, *Le bonheur chez Aristote*.
[2] Arist. *N.E.* I 1097 b 7 ff.   [3] ib. 1099 b 1–8.

fact that individuals are not self-sufficient. Aristotle commits himself to the paradox that they come together in partnership so as to be self-sufficient.[1] In the last book he returns to the consideration of happiness, and involves himself in the same contradictions. Here he is identifying the perfection of happiness with the contemplative life and justifying his identification.

'What we mean by self-sufficiency attaches itself to the contemplative life above all. Of course the philosopher, like the saint or anyone else, needs the necessities of life. But even if these are in adequate supply the saint, the hero, and the others need people on whom to practise and people with whom to work. The philosopher can actually contemplate on his own, the more effectively the better philosopher he is. No doubt he works better as one of a team, but even so he is supremely self-sufficient.'[2]

The qualifications and the recurrence of the superlative are to be noted. A little later he intensifies the qualifications.

'Man's nature is not self-sufficient for the activity of contemplation; he needs bodily health, food and other requirements. Still, even if blessedness is not possible without external goods, you must not think that a man will require many or great possessions if he is going to be happy. Neither self-sufficiency nor moral action demands super-abundance.'[3]

The crown of the virtues in Aristotle's scheme is *megalopsuchia*,[4] a word for which we have no real English equivalent. It means literally 'greatness of soul'. 'Dignity' is Joachim's suggestion; Peters renders it 'highmindedness'. It consists in a sort of loftiness of outlook which we cannot help regarding as Pharisaical and priggish. Nothing but the best is good enough for its possessor; to be honoured is his chief concern, but even that is a triviality to him, and he does not pursue cheap popularity. Virtue he will possess, for without it he would not really be honoured, but it must regretfully be admitted that it seems rather like a means to

[1] ib. V 1134 a 27.   [2] ib. X 1177 a 28 ff.   [3] ib. 1178 a 34.
[4] ib. IV 1123 a 34–1125 a 35; cf. Heraclides Pont. in Ath. XII 512 a.

an end. He has learned that it is more blessed to give than to receive, seeing that to give is the mark of superiority, to receive of inferiority. He never displays or feels either admiration or jealousy. He walks slowly and speaks deliberately, and does not speak evil, even of his enemies, except when he wants to be purposely insulting. And—'he likes to own things that are beautiful and useless rather than things which are useful and economical, for this is typical of a man of independence'. It is a strange ideal. The one thing which should be said of it by contrast with the general Hellenistic approach to autarcy is that it is positive rather than negative. Aristotle does seem to see a character of this kind as desirable in itself; he admires it. The Hellenistic Age sought autarcy to protect itself against the slings and arrows of outrageous fortune.

The negative conception of autarcy is to be seen most clearly among the Cynics.[1] Cynicism was not really philosophy; it was a way of life, almost a religion. Later tradition traced their origin back to Socrates through a quite unhistorical association between Antisthenes and Diogenes. Their real founder was Diogenes of Sinope, who was expelled from his home town during some political reprisals associated with a financial crisis. His father, a financial officer, had been responsible for putting bad coinage out of circulation, and the son took upon him the mission to put bad moral coinage out of circulation.[2] In this the parallel with Socrates is clear, and Plato is recorded as calling him 'Socrates gone mad.'[3] He fulfilled his mission by teaching and example; the latter included the deliberate flouting of conventions which won him a reputation for shamelessness and an ascetism of the sort which Antisthenes had indeed practised, but which Diogenes learned neither from Socrates (who had remarked 'How many things I can do without!'), nor Antisthenes, but from observing a mouse.[4] Diogenes lived through the years from about 340 to 320 as an itinerant preacher, without citizenship, without home (except for his celebrated tub, or rather jar), and without possessions (except for scrip and staff). Even cup and bowl he threw

---

[1] See in general D. R. Dudley, *A History of Cynicism.*   [2] D.L. VI 20.
[3] ib. VI 54; Ael. *V.H.* XIV 33.   [4] ib. VI 22.

away after seeing a child manage without them.[1] Living in an age
of breakdown, having himself experienced disaster, he preached
a gospel of non-attachment which became the Cynic prescription of salvation. Plato and Aristotle had limited their ideal of
autarcy by the need for social and political ties. After his exile
Diogenes refused to associate himself with a single city. He
divided his time between Sparta and Athens like the Great King
moving from his summer to his winter residence. He is often
spoken of as residing at Corinth. 'Naturally Diogenes goes to
Corinth,' wrote Wilamowitz, 'the Capuchin belongs in the city
of sin.'[2] We have records of him meeting Aristippus at Syracuse,
visiting Megara, Myndus, Olympia, Aegina, Crete, and elsewhere. He showed sympathy with the moral struggles of Greek
and barbarian, Persians, Medes, Syrians, Macedonians, Athenians,
Spartans. He had praise alike for Agesilaus and Epaminondas.
Julian says that he refused initiation into the mysteries because it
meant committing himself to Athenian citizenship and would
gladly have entered the temple had it not meant subjecting himself to a single set of laws and constitution.[3] Here there is a contrast with Socrates, who accepted the privileges and responsibilities of citizenship even to death, and the later attribution of
Cynic cosmopolitanism to Socrates must be fictitious.[4] But he is
in contrast also with the cosmopolitanism of the Stoics. When he
declared that he was *cosmopolites*, a citizen of the world, (and in
Lucian's skit said he came from 'everywhere') his concept was
negative rather than positive. He meant that he was free of air
and sky, and untrammelled by the ties of particular citizenship.[5]
He was 'as free as a bird, unconstrained by law, undisturbed by
politicians'.[6] His follower Crates described himself as a citizen of
Diogenes.[7]

The Cynic aim then was autarcy, and the means to this were
two, *askesis* and *ponos*. The former, from which we derive our
word 'ascetic', denotes training, practice, discipline. The latter

---

[1] ib. VI 37.   [2] Wilamowitz, *Aristoteles und Athen*, II 24.
[3] Jul. VII 239 A–C.   [4] Arr. *Epict.* I 9, 1; Plut. *De Exil.* 5; Cic. *T.D.* V 108.
[5] D.L. VI 38, 63, 72; Arr. *Epict.* III 20, 47; Lucian *V.A.* 8.
[6] Max. Tyr. XXXVI 5.   [7] D.L. VI 93.

covers toil, labour, and hardship; Heracles with his labours was the typical Cynic saint. In Diogenes' mind the two were linked. He used to affirm that training was of two kinds, mental and physical. By the latter through constant exercise perceptions are formed which procure freedom of action for deeds of virtue. The one half of the training is incomplete without the other, good health and strength being equally important physically and mentally. He used to provide demonstrations of how easy it was to find virtue from physical exercise. We can see how in manual and other crafts craftsmen achieve extraordinary dexterity through practice. A musician or athlete gets to the top of his profession by continuous work in that particular field. If only they had transferred their discipline to the mind as well, they would never labour in vain. Nothing in life can succeed without disciplined training, he would say; disciplined training can overcome every obstacle. Men in their madness choose to be miserable. Instead of useless labours, they should pursue those labours nature recommends and so live in happiness.[1] There was nothing very new in the cult of *askesis* and *ponos*. It had for centuries been the practice at Sparta, and Diogenes, in common with most moralists, shows some admiration for the Spartan system.[2] His older contemporary Isocrates, whose life was almost over by the time Diogenes was forced to abandon Sinope for the mainland of Greece, and who must be accounted one of the great educationalists of antiquity, repeatedly stressed both.[3] What was new was the intensity of the training. 'In summer he used to roll over in the scorching sand, in winter to embrace the snow-covered statues, using every means of self-discipline.'[4] What was new also was the motive.

> *Therefore, since the world has still*
> *Much good, but much less good than ill,*
> *And while the sun and moon endure*
> *Luck's a chance, but trouble's sure,*

[1] ib. VI 70–1. [2] ib. VI 27, 59.
[3] Isoc. *Demon.* passim; *Pax* 36, 44; *Busiris* 18, 22; *Helen* 11, 16, 23 ff; 36, 52, 57; *Evag.* 45, 80; *Nicocl.* 64 etc. [4] D.L. VI 23; cf. D. Chr. VI 8.

I'd face it as a wise man would,
And train for ill and not for good.[1]

The Cynic training was directed to securing immunity from the
worst that circumstance could bring—exile, exposure, captivity,
poverty. 'He used to say that all the curses of the tragedies had
heaped upon his head. He certainly was

A homeless exile, to his country dead,
A wanderer who begs his daily bread.

But he claimed to confront fortune with courage, convention
with nature, suffering with reason.'[2] The result was autarcy.

It is not needful to follow the ideal as the Cynics upheld it
across the centuries; Diogenes was its most characteristic embodi-
ment. Cynicism had a chequered history. Ascetic discipline might
flounder in mere squalor. Poverty could degenerate into mendicancy, and fraudulent mendicancy at that. The deliberate flouting of convention, *anaideia* and *anaischuntia*, seems at times even
in Diogenes to savour of self-advertisement.[3] The general ideal
remained, most potently perhaps in its influence upon the other
schools of thought. Autarcy was cultivated in the most anti-
Cynical places. To some extent, as we have indicated, this was a
natural response to the temper of the times. It is to Diogenes'
credit that he was the first to formulate it into a *Weltanschauung*.

Among the hedonists for example, we find Theodorus of
Cyrene standing between Aristippus and Diogenes. Aristippus
himself, a pupil of Socrates, had presented a philosophy of independence in his celebrated description of his relations with the
courtesan Lais, ἔχω ἀλλ' οὐκ ἔχομαι. 'I possess without being
possessed'[4] a statement on the face of it of appalling selfishness,
since its converse is that Lais is possessed without possessing. But
the radical hedonism of Aristippus had claimed pleasure for
the *summum bonum* and had opposed to it *ponos*, toil. Theodorus
significantly rejected this antithesis and substituted one between

---

[1] A. E. Housman, *A Shropshire Lad*, LXII. [2] D.L. VI 38.
[3] For an attack on Cynic excesses see Lucian, *Fugitivi*.
[4] D.L. II 74; cf. Ath. VIII 350 f; XII 544 d; XIII 588 e.

joy and grief. Like Diogenes he claimed the universe for his country, and rejected conventionalism. He carried the search for independence in some ways even further than Diogenes, rejecting even friendship as incompatible with the ideal of self-sufficiency, and disavowing belief in gods whose intervention it was outside the power of the wise man to control.[1] Epicurus, a greater man altogether, followed Theodorus in disbelieving in gods with power to intervene in human affairs, motivated no doubt by similar reasons. The Epicureans are classed as hedonists, but the centre of Epicurus' thought was not pleasure but tranquillity (*ataraxia*). Tranquillity is impossible as long as men are held down by fear and desire. The principal fears which haunt men are fear of death and fear of the gods. To this we may perhaps add fear of the unknown and fear of pain. The greatest means to eliminating these is scientific knowledge, which explains the unknown, and demonstrates that death is extinction and the gods remote and disinterested. When pain remains the sufferer can be comforted with the reflection that if it is long-lasting it will not be intense, and if it is intense it will not be long-lasting. Hence the *tetrapharmakon*, or fourfold cure—twelve words in Greek:

ἄφοβον ὁ θεός
ἀναίσθητον ὁ θάνατος
τὸ ἀγαθὸν εὔκτητον
τὸ δεινὸν εὐεκκαρτέρητον

'There is nothing to fear in God: there is nothing to feel in death: Good can be procured; Evil can be endured.' Desires can be analysed into those which are natural and necessary, those which are natural but unnecessary, and those which are unnatural and unnecessary. The disciplined life will lead to the elimination of all but the first and the compassing of desire into the narrowest possible circle. Epicurus disliked Cynic extravagances and called the Cynics 'the enemies of Greece',[2] but he cultivated autarcy as assiduously as they.

'We regard autarcy as a great good, not with a view to always making do with a little, but to finding a little sufficient if

[1] D.L. II 97–103; D. R. Dudley, *A History of Cynicism*, 104–6.   [2] D.L. X 8.

we have not got a lot, frankly realizing that it is the people who least need luxury who enjoy it most, and that only bagatelles are hard to come by whereas that which is natural is easy to procure. Plain fare gives as much pleasure as an expensive menu, when once the pain of want has been removed. Bread and water offer the keenest pleasure when a hungry man tackles them. So to accustom oneself to a simple, inexpensive régime provides all that is needful for health, and enables a man to face more readily the inescapable demands of life. It places us in a better position when we do occasionally come upon luxuries. It enables us to face fortune fearlessly.'[1]

The ultimate aim of tranquillity is the more generalized expression of this. The end of life with Epicurus, as with Diogenes, is to enable a man to face with tranquillity whatever may befall. Diogenes rejected political ties and lived in the open, Epicurus rejected political ties and retired to the cloister. And it was Epicurus who provided the great catch-phrase of autarcy when he said that the wise man would be happy even upon the rack.[2]

But it is among the Stoics that the influence of Cynicism is most clearly to be seen, and the Cynics often appear as the left wing of the Stoics; indeed in philosophers like Musonius and Epictetus the influences are hard to disentangle. The Stoics also in their own way cultivated autarcy, but they were free from the squalor to which the Cynics succumbed. Antisthenes had declared that virtue was sufficient in itself to ensure happiness.[3] Zeno, Chrysippus and Hecato echoed the sentiment, in almost identical words, though the later Stoics who were concerned to mellow and mediate Stoicism to Rome demurred, and added health, strength, and a means of livelihood.[4] We have Hecato's words:

'If greatness of soul (*megalopsuchia*) is sufficient in itself (*autarkes*) to raise us far above everything, and is a part of

---

[1] Epicurus, *Ep.* 3 *apud* D.L. X 130–1. Note however Sen. *Ep.* 9, where Epicurus criticizes Stilpo for saying that the wise man, being *autarkes*, needs no friends.
[2] D.L. X 118; cf. Cic. *T.D.* II 7, 17. [3] D.L. VI 11. [4] ib. VI 127–8.

virtue, then virtue also will be sufficient in itself (*autarkes*) to procure happiness and can despise all that seems troublesome.'

The Stoics were determinists, as we have seen. 'Ducunt volentem fata, nolentem trahunt' ('Fate leads the willing and drags the unwilling').[1] The external circumstances of our life, our wealth or poverty, our success or failure, are fixed by the deliberate foreknowledge of God. They are 'things indifferent', though, said the later Stoics, other things being equal, some might be 'preferred'. What God cannot and will not determine is the free response of our will to the circumstances in which we are placed. We are swept down willy-nilly by the irresistible flood of events—but it still matters whether we swim with the current or against it, and matters supremely to our happiness. The Stoic sought spiritual autarcy in the attitude of acceptance. To this end Zeno used similar practices of self-discipline to those of the Cynics, frugal diet, and exposure to the weather, so that an anonymous poet wrote of him:

> The cold of winter and the ceaseless rain
> Come powerless against him: weak the dart
> Of the fierce summer sun or racking pain
> To bend that iron frame. He stands apart
> Unspoiled by public feast and jollity:
> Patient, unwearied night and day doth he
> Cling to his studies of philosophy.[2]

One of the comic poets, Philemon or Posidippus, commented on Zeno's new philosophy. 'He teaches men to go hungry, and yet gets disciples.'[3] Discipline and toil were the motto of Stoic as well as Cynic. ἔκτισας αὐτάρκειαν, says a later Stoic, bursting into poetry about the founder of the school. 'You laid the foundation-stone of self-sufficiency.'[4] That this approach endured throughout the history of the school we can see by looking at Zeno's successor Cleanthes, who was renowned for his 'love of labour' to such an extent that he was nicknamed 'a second Heracles'.[5] Or we can skip four hundred years to the days of

---

[1] Cleanthes *apud* Sen. *Ep.* 107, 11. [2] D.L. VII 27, tr. R. D. Hicks.
[3] ib. [4] ib. 30. [5] ib. 168, 170.

the lovable moralist Epictetus, who is deeply imbued with Cynic doctrine, and praises their spirit of patient endurance,[1] and preaches the gospel of non-attachment. 'Stop admiring your clothes, and you are not angry with the man who steals them; stop admiring your wife's beauty and you are not angry at her adulterer. Realise that a thief or an adulterer has no place among the things that are your own, but only among the things that are another's and not under your control.'[2] He tells how a thief stole his iron lamp; so he replaced it with an earthenware one.

'Remember that you ought to behave in life as you would at a banquet. As something is being passed around it comes to you; stretch out your hand and take a portion of it politely. It passes on: do not detain it. Or it has not come to you yet; do not anticipate it in desire, but wait until it is opposite you. Do this with children, a wife, political office, wealth, and you will some day be worthy to share in the banquets of the gods.'[3]

He goes on to say that it is better still not even to take the dish when it is offered. In this he is unlike the other great Stoic of first-century Rome, Seneca. Seneca also preached non-attachment.

'All these fortuitous things, Marcia, that glitter about us,— children, position, wealth, spacious halls and vestibules packed with a throng of unadmitted dependents, a high reputation, a well-born or beautiful wife, and all else that depends upon uncertain and fickle chance—these are not our own but borrowed trappings; not one of them is given to us outright. The properties that adorn life's stage have been lent, and must go back to their owners; some of them will be returned on the first day, others on the second, only a few will endure until the end.'[4]

But Seneca became a millionaire, and justified his wealth on the grounds that it happened to come his way, and that he, being a philosopher, could use it more wisely than another. Epictetus was

[1] Arr. *Epict.* III 22, 100.   [2] ib. I 18, 11–2.
[3] Epict. *Man.* 15.   [4] Sen. *Ad. Marc.* 10.

more thorough-going in his pursuit of *apatheia*. In either case it is a philosophy of individualism:

'Everything with the Stoic turns on the individual. τὰ ἐπί σοι (the things in your own power), is the refrain of Epictetus' teaching. All is thrown upon the individual will, upon "the universal" working in the individual, according to Stoic theory, "upon me" the plain man would say.'[1]

There are many interesting instances of the impact made by the philosophy of autarcy. Two merit special attention. The first is Philo, an Alexandrian Jew, whose writing owes a great deal to Greek philosophy. Philo is scornful of the Cynics of his day (as indeed is Epictetus two generations later), but his ethical thought has been moulded by the Cynic wing of Stoicism, and there are significant parallels between his language and that of Musonius Rufus.[2] For him, as for the Stoics, virtue is the *summum bonum*, and he follows Diogenes in seeing the two chief means to this end as *askesis* and *ponos*.[3] Only God can possess the good without them. It is more than a little strange to find the paraphernalia of the philosophy of self-sufficiency attached to Judaism. More telling is the influence of Cynicism on Dio Chrysostom. Born in Bithynia towards the middle of the first century, of honourable family, he began his career by delivering sophistic discourses. His attacks upon the Stoic Musonius seem to have had the intensity of uneasiness, and he finally became a convert. At Rome he had the *entrée* into high society, but his outspoken criticisms of the emperor Domitian and his intimate association with one of the latter's victims led to his exile. For nearly fifteen years he was forced by circumstances to live out his philosophy. He was able to preach the higher tenets of Cynicism with integrity, because he was so patently living out in homelessness and poverty the independence he advocated. It was during this period that he delivered four sermons upon ethical subjects with Diogenes as his central

---

[1] T. R. Glover, *The Conflict of Religions in the Early Roman Empire*, p. 65.
[2] See Wendland, *Philo und die Kynische-Stoische diatribe*: Bréhier, *Les idées philosophiques et réligieuses de Philon*. [3] Philo *De fug. et invid.* passim.

illustration.[1] They are, as von Arnim said, marked by a 'radical Cynicism'. Recurrent is the comparison of life with an athletic contest,[2] a comparison St. Paul was also fond of making;[3] the implication that far more intensively disciplined training is needed for life than for athletics is obvious. The theme of the labours of life is also recurrent and explicit, as is the exaltation of Heracles. On the death of Domitian Dio's exile was rescinded and he returned to a position of wealth and influence. But he did not forget the religion of his days of hardship. He devoted himself to the service of his native town of Prusa, and in four sermons delivered before Trajan,[4] Diogenes is contrasted with Alexander, Heracles is exalted, the pursuit of possessions or security or power is attacked, and the life of unremitting labour is over and over again laid before the emperor.

The pursuit of autarcy is the general philosophy of the Greek world, and such of the Roman world as was under Greek influence, from the end of the fifth century onwards. But as a philosophy of life it laboured (the word is apt) under two main handicaps. In the first place it was essentially a response to a particular set of historical circumstances, long-lasting it is true, but ultimately temporary. It was a philosophy of a decadent age, using the word strictly and not as a term of loose vituperation. In so far as we can compare civilizations with individuals, we may say that Greek civilization passed through its period of greatest vitality and maturity in the fifth century. In the early fourth century the vitality remains but there are signs that it is cracking. Thereafter there is much that is thoughtful and much that is lovely but they are the products of a civilization that is ageing. Autarcy meets this condition if not with despair, at least with defiance. But it could never be the philosophy of a civilization in adolescence or an age of optimism.

But there is one more cogent reason why autarcy could not satisfy man's moral aspirations. It is a selfish philosophy by its very nature. It seeks to make the individual independent of cir-

---

[1] D. Chr. 6; 8; 9; 10. [2] D. Chr. 8, 13; 9, 11; cf. 3, 126.
[3] 1 Cor. IX 24–9; Gal. II 2; V 7; Phil. I 30; II 16; 2 Tim. II 5; IV 7; cf. Hebrews XII 1; Rev. VII 9. [4] D. Chr. 1–4.

cumstances, and in so doing must seek to make him independent of other people, for they are included in the circumstances. This is impossible. Man is not independent and can never be, and we have seen the confusion which the qualifications introduced by those who acknowledged this occasioned. But even if it were possible it would be undesirable. For morality subsists in relationship with others. Aristotle was right when he asserted as an ethical principle that man is a social creature, and wrong in his attempts to evade his own assertions. Of course to say this is not to deny the missionary sense shown by many who should by their own philosophy have been saving their own souls. We have seen the Cynics as preachers. The Stoics had an advanced sense of duty, originating in the thought that God has set a man in a particular place with a particular job to do, and we find, for example, Musonius Rufus risking his life by intervening in a Roman civil war somewhat as Mary Slessor stood between two armies of African warriors in Calabar. Even the Epicureans, who should have been pursuing tranquillity in retirement, possessed in lively measure what the Quakers call a concern. This is nowhere seen more powerfully than in the great inscription which was placed around the market-town of Oenoanda in Asia Minor by an Epicurean of the name of Diogenes (not to be confused with the Cynic). He is a loyal follower of Epicurus, whose doctrines were cherished by the school for centuries with little or no change. The inscription is fragmentary, but enough remains for us to see that it was a characteristic exposition of Epicurean philosophy. What is especially interesting is his reason for going to the expense, which must have been enormous, of this tremendous inscription. All mankind is sick, haunted by desire and fear. If there were only a finite number of individuals involved he would visit them personally. But all mankind is sick, and he is singularly moved by the spectacle, and out of his concern has recourse to the inscribed word in order to proclaim the prescription of salvation. Such actions are noble indeed, but they really run counter to the professed ethical basis of those who perform them.

If we would see what this philosophy of autarcy involved, we have to look at its treatment of the virtue of pity. It is not suggested that the Hellenistic world did not know compassion. That would be a folly of overstatement. At Athens there stood an altar dedicated to Pity. Dedications only begin in the fourth century, and it looks as if it may in that era have replaced an altar to the Twelve Gods. Statius has a sympathetic description of it; he calls Pity, significantly by the canons of his time, *Clementia*.[1] This altar was, however, certainly exceptional, and, Pausanias tells us, unique.[2] Demonax, himself a Cynic, when they proposed to celebrate the gladiatorial shows at Athens, told them that they would first have to remove the Altar of Pity.[3] The Epicureans did not disown compassion, and even advocated it,[4] which is one reason why Epicureanism is so much more attractive than Stoicism. Cicero, whose professed philosophy was a blend of Academic metaphysics and Stoic ethics, when it suited his brief declared that there was no more admirable virtue than pity.[5] Vergil, tenderest of poets, as his outlook moved from Epicureanism to Stoicism, decided to cast Aeneas into a Stoic mould. But the harshness of Stoicism was too rigid for him, and he permitted Aeneas to show pity, pity for the unburied dead which actually allowed him to criticize the government of the universe, and pity for Lausus in the act of killing him.[6] Bowra pointed out rightly that this is not utilitarian pity. It has no real fruits in action. Aeneas can neither help the ghosts nor spare Lausus.[7] The most he can do is to give up the body. This pity springs from the hidden wells of personality. The unknown artists of the Trajanic column showed Trajan receiving the Dacian surrender with courtesy and mercy—was not the Roman destiny 'parcere subiectis' as well as 'debellare superbos'?—and turning aside from the severed heads brought as spoil, and there is even a most tender portrayal of a Dacian chieftain turning away and hiding his tears as he receives the body of his son.

These things are true. But they do not spring from the philosophy of autarcy. They are in defiance of it. Aristotle, who took

---

[1] Stat. *Theb.* XII 481–505; see below, pp. 184 ff.
[2] Paus. I 17, 1; cf. D.S. XIII 22; Schol. Aesch. *Parapresb.* 2 § 15. Sextus Empiricus *Contr. Phys.* A 187 speaks of 'altars'. [3] Luc. *Dem.* 57.
[4] e.g. D.L. X 118. [5] Cic. *Pro Ligar.* 12, 37; but cf. *T.D.* III 9, 20; IV 26, 56.
[6] Verg. *Aen.* VI 332; X 821–4. [7] C. M. Bowra, *From Virgil to Milton*, 65–7.

too commonsensical a view of life not to accept the fact that
people do show pity and there must therefore be a place for it,[1]
showed his true philosophy when he said that the function of
tragic drama was to purge out of the system pity and fear.[2]
Tragic drama provides a harmless inoculation which will prevent
pity and fear assailing us in real life. Pity is classed with fear as an
undesirable emotion. Some psychologists have indeed suggested
that pity is a projection of fear. Thomas Hobbes, for example,
declared that 'Pity ariseth from the imagination that the like
calamity may befall himself'. We may recall Cyrus and Croesus.[3]
Aristotle, curiously, defined fear in terms of pity.[4] Zeno declared
that pity was a sickness of the soul, which no one would display
except a frivolous fool.[5] The reason is obvious. The man who
pities places his inner peace of mind at the mercy of things outside
his control. He is not *autarkes*. So with the later Stoics. Seneca tells
us to act helpfully, but says that to show pity is the mark of a
weak character, and one which the good man will avoid.[6] 'It is
only weak eyes which weep in sympathy.' Epictetus reinforces
this. 'If a man is unhappy, remember that his unhappiness is his
own fault, for God has made all men to be happy and free from
perturbations.' 'You must feel no anger, no rage, no envy, no
pity.' He suggests that the cause of pity lies in too rapid an assent
to the situation which confronts us; we see a poor man and feel
immediately 'he is wretched', but it is a vicious judgement. 'Say
to yourself, "It is the opinion about this thing that afflicts the
man". So far as words go, do not hesitate to show sympathy, and
even, if it so happen to lament with him. Take care, though, that
you do not lament internally also.'[7] Even the Neo-Platonists, who
enjoyed the noblest vision of the self-sufficiency of God ever
vouchsafed to the ancient world,[8] declared that 'it is weakness to
be touched with any feeling of pity for misery'.[9] If this be true of
the philosophers, it is scarcely to be wondered at that the politi-

[1] Arist. *N.E.* II 1106 b 19 and elsewhere. [2] id. *Poet.* 1449 b 27. [3] Hdt. 1, 86.
[4] Arist. *Rhet.* II 1382 b 26.
[5] Cic. *Pro Mur.* 29, 61; cf. *T.D.* III 9, 20–10, 21. [6] Sen. *De Clem.* II 5, 1.
[7] Arr. *Epict.* III 3, 17; III 24, 2; IV 4, 33; Epict. *Man.* 16.
[8] Plot. *Enn.* V 3, 13; 17; Iambl. *De Myst. Aeg.* VIII 2 αὐτοπάτωρ καὶ αὐτάρκης.
[9] Plot. *Enn.* I 4, 8.

cians used the brutal spectacles of triumphal procession and gladiatorial display as instruments of their popularity, nor that the common people rejoiced therein. Not till the heroic monk Telemachus flung himself to his death in the arena amid the vituperations of the crowd whose pleasures he had dared to interrupt, were the 'games' abolished. A Demonax might protest, a Seneca might write nobly without it affecting his actions. By and large, the ancient world in general and the Roman world in particular grew inured and indifferent to brutality. This is the outcome of autarcy, and, confronted with it, are we not bound to say with the Christian Ignatius that absence of compassion can only arise from falsity of belief?[1]

In fine, the choice is that which Ibsen declared in *Peer Gynt*. There the motto of the trolls was 'To thyself be enough'. But the motto of the humans was 'To thyself be true', and, however flounderingly the humans might behave, we cannot but see it as the nobler and higher aim.

[1] Ign. *Ad Smyrn.* 6, 2.

IX

ROMANA VIRTUS

'Moribus antiquis res stat Romana virisque.'

S O SAID ENNIUS in words which bit deep into the imagination of Rome, though whether 'moribus' meant customs
or character, or whether indeed language had learned the
sophistication which distinguishes what a man does from what he
is, remains not wholly clear. What is clear is that the classical
Romans, looking back on their history, saw in the traditional
qualities of their menfolk the element which had made Rome
great. Hence they exalted the memory of a Brutus or a Cincinnatus. The familiar *more maiorum* appears as early as Plautus.[1] By
the time of Cicero it has become a commonplace.[2] This traditionalism runs deep in the bed of the Roman story, deeper perhaps than the most all-embracing philosophy, as we can see if we
look at the upsurge of Stoicism in the first century A.D. This is
the period of the so-called 'philosophic opposition to the principate', the period of Thrasea Paetus and Helvidius Priscus. But
how far they were motivated by traditional republicanism, the
exaltation of the past, and the sense that particular emperors
lacked the ancient Roman virtues, and how far by Stoic political
doctrine, is a matter of academic dispute. It gives a false estimate
to emphasize one to the exclusion of the other. This is the age
when Cato appears as the characteristic Stoic saint, Cato who
combined the professions of Stoicism with the sturdy republicanism and pugnacious obstinacy of the ancient Romans.

Virtus is derived from *vir*, a male, and means 'manliness' in the
full sense of the word. Ancient Roman society had for its unit the
familia or household, a term much wider than our 'family' for it
included all those relatives, dependants and slaves who were

---

[1] Plaut. *Trin.* 1031.　　　　　　　　　　[2] Cic. *Ad Att.* I, I, I.

associated with the homestead; even the animals had their place in the *familia*. At the head of the *familia* stood the *paterfamilias*, and his authority was absolute, even to death, though it was kept by custom from being arbitrarily exercised, as all serious decisions would be taken through a council of relations. The *familia* was also a religious unit, observing particularly the worship of Vesta, the goddess of the hearth, the Penates or powers of the pantry, the Lares, who were originally spirits of the land round about but later were admitted into the house itself, and the Genius, the life-spirit of the family embodied in the father. Women at first had no legal position and no authority; they were absolutely under the thumb ('in manu', said the Romans) of the head of the house. But frequent absences of their master on military campaigns gave them considerable power, which led naturally to their acquiring legal rights. We have seen a similar process in our day and generation, when one world war won for women the vote, and two won them full status within the University of Cambridge. Cornelia, mother of the Gracchi, may be taken as representative of the best type of Roman matron.

The early Romans were citizen-farmers, and this affected their destiny. Rome itself as a site has certain obvious advantages. It combines the natural position of a hill-fortress with a command of the north–south traffic of the plain, which crossed the Tiber where the Isola Tiberina now stands, and an old salt-route from the Apennines down to the sea. Later the centrality of Rome in Italy and of Italy in the Mediterranean were to be major factors in the emergence of Rome to world dominion. That lay far in the future. In early days Rome was not obviously stronger than the Etruscan fortress of Veii, and certainly lacked many of the natural advantages of Campania in the south. She was involved in war after war, upon which her very survival depended, and Larth Porsinna and the Etruscans, and the Gauls in 390, came near to ending her history before it had well begun.

Virtus covers all that is meant by 'being a man' in this environment.

> *If you can fill the unforgiving minute*
> *With sixty seconds' worth of distance run,*

Yours is the earth and everything that's in it,
And—which is more—you'll be a Man, my son.[1]

Kipling's poem seems a little tawdry to us today, but a Roman would have understood it. An epitaph on the Appian Way for a cousin of Scipio Africanus who was praetor in 139 B.C. shows the Roman concept well, and its intimate connection with the *mos maiorum*:

> *virtutes generis mieis moribus accumulari,*
> *progeniem* [mi] *genui, facta patris petiei.*
> *maiorum optenui laudem ut sibei me esse creatum*
> *laetentur, stirpem nobilitavit honos.*[2]

The soldier, the farmer, the citizen, the father, had demands upon him which he had to fulfil. This was his *virtus*, and it may be approximately analysed into three separate qualities.

The first of these qualities is courage, *virtus* in the narrower sense, and here we are not wrong in saying 'the quality of a soldier'. We have already followed out the story of this in Greek thought. It is a just representation of the difference between the Greek and Roman approaches to remark that the Greek word for courage, though also deriving from the Greek word for man, never became extended to mean virtue in general. It is indeed more than a little ironic that a word of such cogency in moral philosophy and religious thought should in its early history reflect the military expediency of a small Italian city-state. The absence of primitive literary sources does not permit us to trace the literary development of the word against the background of social and political history. By the time Latin literature becomes articulate the word is already richly confused in meaning. Already Plautus can speak of the virtue (which ought to mean 'manliness') of some goods,[3] Cato of the virtue of an estate,[4] Cicero of a tree or house (though he is sensitive enough to notice the sole-

---

[1] R. Kipling, *If.*
[2] *C.I.L.* I 15. I owe the reference to my colleague Mr. H. F. Guite.
[3] Plaut. *Mil. Gl.* III 1, 131.
[4] Cato, *R.R.* I 2.

cism),[1] Livy of a ship,[2] Ovid of plants,[3] and Quintilian of oratory in all its forms.[4] We may speculate upon the process of development by which this took place, and though language does not always develop as logically as we theorists would like, we shall probably not be far out. *Virtus* means 'manliness'. For the early farmers this meant a capacity for hard work, an ability to endure the weather, and courage in facing robbers and wild animals. As the state grew in power and significance the need for these qualities remained, but they became overshadowed by the exigent demands of war. The man who showed his *virtus* was the military hero. Indeed in Plautus *vir* may simply mean 'soldier'.[5] The meaning 'courage' persists into classical Latin. Caesar, at the beginning of his commentaries, remarks that the Helvetii surpass the rest of the Gauls in courage, because they have to fight with the Germans almost every day.[6] From here the word branched out into three directions. The courage of a soldier is a narrow and limited thing. There is a more extensive and representative courage, and Cicero has an interesting discussion of the use of the word in which he points out that though all right ethical dispositions were in his days called 'virtues', the name, being derived from *vir*, man, whose peculiar virtue is courage, should be properly confined to a capacity to scorn death and bear pain.[7] This capacity is not merely to be shown on the battlefield. *Vir*, which may mean male as opposed to female, or adult as opposed to boy, can also mean man as opposed to mouse—human mouse that is. Secondly the thought of virility, literal and metaphorical, blends into the thought of power, and by the time of Plautus a colossal oxymoron produced the popular phrase 'virtute deum' ('by the power of the gods').[8] Finally as the citizen-soldier died away, and the military defence of Rome no longer became part of the normal obligation of citizenship, and, similarly, as Greek philosophy, from the end of the third century, began to make its im-

[1] Cic. *Leg.* I 16, 45.   [2] Liv. 37, 24, 1.   [3] Ov. *Met.* 14, 357.
[4] e.g. Quint. *Inst. Or.* 1, 5, 1.   [5] e.g. Plaut. *Am.* I 1, 65.
[6] Caes. *De B.G.* I 1.   [7] Cic. *T.D.* II 18, 43.
[8] Plaut. *Trin.* II 2, 65; cf. III 2, 17; *Aul.* II 1, 44; *Capt.* II 2, 71; *Mil. Gl.* III 1, 85; 90.

pact, thoughts turned to the wider destinies of man. *Virtus* began to represent *arete* as well as *andreia*. Manliness could be displayed in rebuffing moral temptation as well as facing physical foes. But *virtus* to the Roman was never merely a Greek concept, and Cicero contrasts it, as a peculiarly Roman quality, with Greek scholarship.[1] There is a 'virtue' of the mind and a 'virtue' of the body, Cicero says elsewhere, more under Greek influence, and the former is more important than the latter.[2] It was in fact the authority of Cicero which handed the word down to posterity in its wider ethical sense. Virtue is, philosophically speaking, 'a state of mind in conformity with reason along the lines of nature'.[3]

This was a philosopher's definition. Popularly speaking *virtus* still meant broadly 'courage', and as such it was personified and worshipped. Shrines were dedicated by victorious generals in time of war or immediately afterwards. In them *virtus* is found associated with *honos*, and indeed our English word 'honour' gives a fair idea of the overtones of the word in its normal usage. We have but to think of the familiar seventeenth-century words with which Lovelace justified his abandoning Althea to go to the wars:

> *I could not love thee, dear, so much,*
> *Loved I not honour more.*

or the twentieth-century description of the aviators who

> *Left the vivid air signed with their honour.*

There were at least two such temples in Rome. One, by the Porta Capena had been dedicated to Honos in 234 by Q. Fabius Maximus Verrucosus, and enlarged into a double shrine to both by M. Marcellus.[4] Another was somewhere near the Capitol and dedicated by C. Marius after his victory over the Cimbri and Teutones. 'Virtus colenda est, non imago Virtutis' is Lactantius' scornful comment[5]—'Revere virtue' (for so Lactantius understood the word) 'not her statue'. His criticism is unsympathetic and unjust. It is hard to take seriously these personifications, but

---

[1] Cic. *De Or.* III 34, 137. [2] Cic. *De Fin.* V 13, 38. [3] id. *De Inv.* II 53, 159.
[4] Liv. 25, 40, 2–3; 27, 25, 7–9; 29, 11, 13. [5] Lact. *Inst. Div.* I 20.

they show the sort of qualities which the political leaders desired
to propagate, and on the whole to which the people responded.
What is here significant is that the generic word *virtus* never shook
off its narrower associations, and one cannot help feeling that
there remained a certain narrowness in the character which the
Republican Roman honoured.

The second of these qualities is *pietas*. *Pietas* is not 'piety'; indeed Cicero at one point insists that proper behaviour in relation
to the gods is not *pietas* but *religio* (which is not what the manuals
of Latin Prose Composition say about the latter word); *pietas* is
proper behaviour towards parents.[1] Typical of this is Coriolanus'
acceptance of his mother's plea when all else had failed. So in
Seneca's play, when Theseus believes his son has dishonoured
him, he invokes Pietas before calling on Jupiter and Neptune.[2]
It is of course wider, even within the family, though Lewis and
Short, with a rare flash of humour, note 'Towards a husband
(rare)'.[3] In fact *pietas* is a sense of duty. If Kipling's verse represents *virtus*, Nelson's signal 'England expects that every man this
day will do his duty' is an expression of *pietas*. It is exercised within
what a Biblical scholar might almost call a covenant relationship.
It is as if when one entered into a certain relationship one covenanted to behave in a certain way within that relationship, whatever might happen outside. The three main fields within which
pietas might be exercised were the family, the state, and the divine
purposes. Ultimately the three were the same. The loyalty owed
to the state was only an extended form of the loyalty owed
within the family. The loyalty to the gods was only an extended
form of the loyalty to the state. Much ancient religion was political. This was markedly true at Rome, where as early as 496 we
find the government meeting a famine crisis by religious measures
in consultation with the Sibylline Books. In the fourth century
the pace was intensified, and new rites are introduced from
Greece to keep the people quiet—the *lectisternium* and *supplicatio*,
which involved procession, pageantry, and banqueting, and were
likely to be popular. The disasters of the Second Punic War fur-

---

[1] Cic. *Part. Or.* 22, 78.   [2] Sen. *Hipp.* 945.
[3] Lewis and Short, *Latin Dictionary*, s.v. *pietas*.

ther intensified proceedings. Omens and prodigies were widely recorded, ceremonial purifications, banquets, processions, sacrifices, dedications, vows, and games galore were put up to quieten the people, and in the darkest moment when self-control slipped Rome succumbed to the desire to try the Carthaginian way of human sacrifice. Roman religion more than any other exemplifies the dictum which Karl Marx borrowed from Canon Charles Kingsley about how readily religion becomes the opiate of the people. Polybius pointed out at some length how the ruling-classes used religion to avert revolution.

'I will venture the assertion that what the rest of mankind deride is the foundation of Roman greatness, namely superstition. This element has been introduced into every aspect of their private and public life, with every artifice to awe the imagination, in a degree which could not be improved upon. Many possibly will be at a loss to understand this: but my view is that it has been done to impress the masses. If it were possible to have a state in which all citizens were philosophers, perhaps we might dispense with this sort of thing. But the masses in every state are unstable, full of lawless desires, of irrational anger, and violent passion. All that can be done, then, is to hold them in check by fears of the unseen and other shams of the same sort. It was not for nothing but by deliberate design that the men of old introduced to the masses notions about the gods and the after-life; the folly and heedlessness are ours who seek to dispel such illusions.'[1]

So too Varro and Cicero.[2] Augustine attacks the pagan religion on the same grounds, that it is delusion imposed by the governing classes for their own ends.[3] He little thought that the same charge would be brought against his own religion. We cannot help, with Warde Fowler, regretting that the clean and healthy religion of farm and home, in which every aspect of life had its spiritual power, became overlaid by alien superstition fostered for political purposes. Which is not to deny that, let us say, Vergil sincerely

[1] Polyb. VI 56. [2] Aug. *C.D.* IV 31; Cic. *De Leg.* II 8, 19 ff.
[3] Aug. *C.D.* IV 32.

came to believe that Rome's destiny was decreed by heaven, and that therefore religion genuinely mattered. For the unscrupulous but superstitious Augustus, for the free-thinking Polybius, for the now devout Vergil, for the detached philosopher and fervent patriot Cicero, and for the unthinking masses, *pietas* towards the gods was a necessary part of patriotic *pietas*.

Two striking examples will serve to show the scope and limitation of *pietas*. The first comes from Catullus. Catullus' story is familiar and can be briefly told. He was a native of Verona, and came to Rome at the age of twenty-two, probably to complete his education. As a gauche young provincial he was received by Metellus Celer and his wife Clodia, fell helplessly in love with the latter, and prides himself on deceiving the husband behind his back. Meantime Catullus' brother had gone to Asia on the staff of Cicero's brother Quintus. There, near Troy, he died. Catullus' grief was real and bitter. It appears in a letter to his friend Manlius, and in the epitaph of singular beauty which he wrote later when visiting his brother's tomb. His parents needed him, and he them, and he returned to Verona. While he was there Clodia tired of him and started a new affair with Caelius Rufus. When Catullus returned to Rome Clodia denied him her presence. For a while he was torn between hate and love, but eventually, in one of the most tremendous poems ever written, cast her off.[1] This poignant outburst begins:

> *Siqua recordanti benefacta priora voluptas*
> *est homini, cum se cogitat esse pium . . .*

> *If it can please a man to recollect*
> *His deeds of kindness done, and to reflect*
> *That he has shown true loyalty in act*
> *And word unto his friends, nor in a pact*
> *Misused the gods to cheat his fellow-men,*
> *Your unrequited love should earn you then,*
> *Catullus, life-long joys in overflow.*

[1] This account is admittedly speculative, but it is soundly based, and there is no justification for the scepticism of R. G. C. Levens in M. Platnauer, *Fifty Years of Classical Scholarship*, pp. 284 ff.

It ends:

> *non iam illud quaero, contra ut me diligat illa,*
> *aut, quod non potis est, esse pudica velit:*
> *ipse valere opto et taetrum hunc deponere morbum,*
> *o di reddite mi hoc pro pietate mea.*

> *I ask no more that she be kind to me—*
> *Nor become chaste, for that could never be:*
> *Gods, from this festering wound give me release,*
> *If I have ever served you, grant me peace.*[1]

Catullus, a self-confessed adulterer, is claiming a release from the entanglement in which he has got himself, because of his *pietas*. It is plain that *pietas* is not a moral conception as we understand morals, and Baring's version is careful to bring this out. On the other hand it is equally clear that it is a moral conception as he understands morals. He claims to have lived his life 'puriter', that is 'without blemish'. In other words moral values have validity only within the natural covenant relationships as I have outlined them above. Between Catullus and Metellus Celer there was no binding relationship at all. If the dictionary says of *pietas* 'Towards a husband (rare)', it might well say 'Towards a mistress's husband (non-existent)'. Just where Catullus is claiming *pietas* is less clear, and Baring's version is here tendentious. We may, however, safely single out three aspects of his *pietas*. The first is what we would call his 'artistic' integrity. Some poets follow a divine inspiration, as we say, religiously. This is their divine mission. Others profane the gift they have been granted.[2] Some of the Augustan poets even speak of the poet as a priest.[3] Catullus claims to have followed his inspiration wherever it led. He has known no other calling from the gods. This he has known and accepted, and he has been loyal to it. Further this was a patriotic duty. For, though Catullus does not make the claim specifically, it is the implicit or explicit boast of almost every Roman poet from Ennius to Claudian that they write to the glory of Rome, either

---

[1] Cat. 76, tr. M. Baring.   [2] id. 14, 7.   [3] Hor. *Od.* III 1, 3; Prop. III 1, 3.

in their subject-matter, or in adapting the modes of Greek literature to the Latin language.[1] It is the overt pride of Catullus' contemporary Lucretius. 'I am among the first of all to be able to
turn philosophy into *my country's* language.'[2] Catullus was deliberately glorifying Latin literature by showing that it could accom-
modate itself to Alexandrianism. Secondly within the family he
has certainly shown *pietas*, and his affectionate 'desiderium' for
his brother is deeply moving.

> *Through many seas, my brother, and many a nation*
> *To this thy bitter burial I come,*
> *Bringing thy death its debt of lamentation,*
> *My last vain call to thee whose dust is dumb.*
> *Now, since a callous fortune has bereft us*
> *Each of the other, dear unhappy head,*
> *By that old custom that our fathers left us*
> *For the last mournful duties to the dead,*
> *Wet with my weeping take these gifts of me:*
> *Hail, brother, and Farewell—eternally!*[3]

Within the covenant-relationships of the family and of his divine
calling Catullus has done his duty. But there is a third aspect of
this *pietas* of Catullus. Between Clodia and himself there was a
covenant ('foedus')[4] and this is what he has immediately in mind
in his claim to have never misused the authority of heaven to
deceive a fellow-human in any covenant.[5] Furthermore, there is a
significant poem in which—poor self-deluded fool—he claims
that his love for Clodia was not the love of the man in the street
for a mistress, but that of a father for his sons and sons-in-law.[6]
This seems strangely frigid to the modern mind. The point is that
the son-in-law entered into the orbit of *pietas*. Catullus is suggesting that by a similar 'legal fiction' Clodia has entered into the
pietas-relationship with him. He claims that he has fulfilled the
obligations; she has not. The point remains the same. If there is a

---

[1] e.g. Verg. *Georg.* II 175–6; III 10–1; Hor. *Od.* I 26, 11–2; III 30, 10 ff; *Ep.*
I 19, 21 ff; 32–3. [2] Lucr. V 336–7. [3] Cat. 101, tr. F. L. Lucas.
[4] id. 109, 6. [5] id. 76, 3–4. [6] id. 72, 3–4; cf. 68, 142.

particular covenant-relationship there is an obligation of *pietas*. Outside that relationship there is no such obligation.

The second example is similar. In Vergil's epic it is Aeneas' destiny to found Rome. He is given the apparently stock epithet 'pius' and numerous generations of schoolboys have followed Charles James Fox in wearying of hearing him called 'pius Aeneas'; they have responded as the anonymous Athenian voter did towards Aristides. In the second book he makes good his claim to the title by the fervour of his patriotic defence, by his obedience to the call of heaven and his care for the gods of his home, and by his sense of responsibility towards his father and his son.[1] The fact that he loses Creusa, distraught though he is about it, shows the limitations of *pietas*. His return to look for her endangers his mission, and, though his attitude may partly spring from Vergil's sense of compassion, it also reveals an apparent weakness in Aeneas whereby he is distracted from his destiny through love of a woman, and thus anticipates the conflict of book four. In this, in many ways the greatest book of the poem, we see Aeneas dallying in Dido's court, making love to her, and actually building the walls of her Carthage when he ought to be founding Rome. Throughout this first part of the book he is never called 'pius', which shows that the epithet is not quite as conventional as some critics suggest. Indeed Addison had discerned this and remarked on it to Steele, who used the observation in the sixth number of the anonymous *Tatler*, thus betraying the authorship— a curious little byway of literary history. James Smith, of *Rejected Addresses* fame, also saw it, as an occasion for a witticism:

> *Virgil, whose epic song enthrals*
> (*And who in song is greater?*)
> *Throughout, his Trojan hero calls*
> *Now 'Pius' and now 'Pater'.*

> *But when, the worst intent to brave,*
> *With sentiments that pain us,*
> *Queen Dido meets him in the cave,*
> *He dubs him 'Dux Trojanus'.*

[1] For his filial devotion v. Sen. *De Ben.* 3, 37, 1.

And well he alters there the word:
For in this station sure,
'Pius' Aeneas were absurd
And 'Pater' premature.

The wit has seen half the point, but he has moralized 'pius' in a
direction the word will not permit. The point is that Aeneas is
neglecting his destiny. Jupiter sends Mercury to spur Aeneas back
to his true course, which, with the scornful word 'uxorius',
'woman's man', he does. Aeneas, horror-struck, vacillates, then
tells his men to prepare for departure and himself goes to essay
Dido. The queen has already realized what is afoot ('quis fallere
possit amantem?'), and in the scene which follows remonstrates
with him. At first she is gentle; it is pity, not anger, that is her cry,
and she pleads with him, partly for her own sake, but also, as
Landor saw, for 'hazarding his life by encountering the tempests
of a wintry sea'. Aeneas' words in reply are, in Landor's phrase,
'stiff, frigid, and artificial'. When a man says to his lover 'I shall
not regret the memory of you', or 'If I had my choice I should
be neither here nor where I am going, but in my old home', he is
not even tactful, let alone loving; when he lies three times about
the source of his divine call, he cannot expect to be convincing
when he comes to the truth. Dido very properly tells him what
she thinks of him, and Gilbert Wakefield refused to lecture on the
fourth book because this passage 'would lead to a discomposure of
decorum in a mixed assembly'. She flings herself out half-fainting
with a cry that he will pay the penalty: 'siquid pia numina pos-
sunt'.[1] The phrase deserves more attention than it has received,
since it plainly anticipates the apparent paradox that follows. The
covenant-relationship is two-way, but Dido has not discerned it
aright. Aeneas, despicable, says Page, odious, says Fox, is left alone.
And the next paragraph begins 'At pius Aeneas'.[2] One thing is
certain. This is not a stock epithet appearing in an unsuitable
context. It is placed purposively. Aeneas is not in the covenant-
relationship of *pietas* with Dido. His behaviour to her is irrelevant. His patriotic and divine duty, yes, and his duty to his family

[1] Verg. *Aen.* IV 382.   [2] ib. 393.

(for the thought of Iulus as founder of the Julian house is never far away) is to found Rome. He is back on the path of duty, and to *pietas* what happens to Dido does not matter. Of course it would destroy the power and pathos of this greatly human book to suggest that that was all. Vergil's intellectual assent is given to Aeneas' departure in fulfilment of his destiny, but his emotions are with Dido. It is from that conflict, from that 'odi et amo', from 'l'anti-Virgile chez Virgile' that the greatness of the poetry springs. Vergil has the gift of human sympathy which is the true secret of morals. But so far as the scope of *pietas* is concerned it is coldly true to say that Aeneas is bound by no ties to Dido, and his behaviour towards her should be governed by the *pietas* he owes elsewhere. If she stands in the way of those purposes, she must go, remorselessly.

There is thus a curious contradiction in the conception of *pietas*. It does genuinely represent an inward disposition and not merely an outward observance, and the heir who raised a monument EX PIETATE instead of EX TESTAMENTO indicated that he was acting out of real affection and not by reason of formal obligation. Further *pietas* is not an abstract virtue; it is realized in personal relationships, and is applicable to the confrontation alike of man and god and of man and man. In all this it seems to get down to the roots of morality. An interesting literary example of its exaltation is to be found in the *Aetna*, a poem written by an unknown author probably in the middle of the first century A.D.[1] The poem shows Epicurean influence, and contains a remarkable defence of scientific studies. It is for the most part a cold examination of the scientific explanation of volcano eruptions. But the culmination of the poem, and the note on which it closes, is the *pietas* of two lads who rescue their parents from the perils of an eruption. The human quality of *pietas* has more kindling power than the volcano. Again Statius has a fine picture of Pietas personified and mourning over the Theban civil war.[2] But the fact that it takes in some relationships only and leaves out others limits it hopelessly, for

[1] There is quite a lot to be said for the attribution to Lucilius; cf. Sen. *Ep.* 79, 5 ff. It cannot be by Vergil. Seneca refers to the incident, *De Ben.* 6, 36, 1.
[2] Stat. *Theb.* XI 457 ff. Cf. also X 780 ff.

over considerable areas of human behaviour it is either irrelevant or, worse still, treats people outside the covenant-relationship as instruments of an alien and narrow purpose.

One further stage in the history of *pietas* calls for comment. It became, as we shall see,[1] one of the four imperial virtues of Augustus. From this it came to be a natural term of adulation or of imperial propaganda with no necessary precision of meaning. Nerva appears as *piissimus*; his devoutness overcomes the normal limitations of grammar. Trajan succeeds him in imperial destiny and in the *pietas* which his coins proclaim. Antoninus bore the title Pius proudly and peculiarly. His full name IMPERATOR TITVS AELIVS CAESAR HADRIANVS ANTONINVS AVGVSTVS PIVS PATER PATRIAE is shortened on coins to ANTONINVS AVGVSTVS PIVS. He showed his loyalty in word and act alike to the memory of Hadrian which the Senate was prepared to objurgate, within his own family (he came to Hadrian's sick-bed supporting the steps of his father-in-law), in relation to his subjects—'the loyal master of his servants, in honour exigent to fulfil his devoir', said Weber,[2] —and towards the gods. But the title was given him especially in the light of his consecration of Hadrian, and the word has not yet lost its meaning. When Commodus becomes L. AELIVS AVRELIVS COMMODVS AVGVSTVS PIVS FELIX we begin to wonder; still more when he is described as the source or author of *pietas*. In the third century it is little more than a vague description of one aspect of imperial power. It becomes assimilated to *clementia*, and on the coinage of Caracalla, Gallienus or Claudius II represents little more than the indulgence of a conqueror towards those whom he holds in the palm of his hand. By the fourth century *Tua Pietas* is a vaguely honourable address for the emperor. Its noble and distinctive quality has fallen away.

The third quality is *gravitas*,[3] and if we seek once more for the English parallel we shall see it in the words

> *He nothing common did or mean*
> *Upon that memorable scene.*

---

[1] infr. p. 179.   [2] *C.A.H.* XI p. 327.
[3] See W. Kroll, *Kultur d. Ciceron. Zeit*, pp. 27 ff; M. Hadas, 'Gravitas Cousque' *C.J.*, 31 (1935), pp. 17 ff; H. Wagenvoort, *Roman Dynamism*, pp. 104 ff.

The closest English equivalent is 'dignity'. It has in it something of Aristotle's *megalopsuchia*, but it is more practically and actively conceived. It is a quality of demeanour, of presence. A Victorian Speaker of the House of Commons, summoned to the House because a free fight had broken out and the Deputy Speaker was helpless, had only to stand at the Bar of the House for the members to crawl back to their seats like whipped schoolboys. He had *gravitas*. In this sort of context it is almost what we mean by 'authority', and in Roman history is exemplified by the action of C. Popillius Laenas. A story of which the Romans never tired told how after Pydna the senate sent him with a dispatch to Antiochus of Syria, who himself had the title of God Incarnate (Epiphanes), commanding him to withdraw from hostilities against Egypt. As the god-king read the dispatch Popillius drew a circle in the sand around the spot where he stood and forbade him to break that circle until he had given a decisive answer. Such was the Roman's *gravitas* that Antiochus did not dare to refuse.[1] The Quakers sometimes speak about a 'weighty Friend'. That is literally and precisely *gravitas*.

There is an element of pomposity about *gravitas*; it is represented in Greek by *semnotes*, and contrasted with *philanthropia* or *humanitas*. Occasionally the two qualities are allowed to co-exist in a single individual, but this is generally either an expression of flattery, such as Cicero uses as counsel for the defence towards the president of the court,[2] or it is implied that one quality modifies the other,[3] or it is a matter for surprise and admiration—Cicero so characterizes Atticus's personality and Catullus's oratory.[4] This contrast seems almost to be associated with the battle between Roman traditionalism and Greek culture. At any rate *gravitas* is peculiarly linked with the traditions of Rome, and steps are taken to safeguard it against outside influences. Thus Livy records the action of the censor in 204 B.C. in depriving the majority of Roman citizens of their civic privileges, as in accord with the

[1] Liv. 45, 12; Polyb. 29, 27; Val. Max. 6, 4; Vell. Pat. 1, 10; App. *Syr.* 131. It should be added that Polybius attributes Antiochus' acceptance to the military situation rather than the Roman's demeanour.   [2] Cic. *Pro. Mil.* 8, 22.
[3] Vell. Pat. II 116, 3; Plin. *Paneg.* 4, 6.   [4] Cic. *De Lèg.* 3, 1; *De Or.* 3, 29.

gravitas of that age.[1] Valerius Maximus tells how the magistrates protected *gravitas* by refusing to use languages other than Latin even in addressing Greeks.[2] *Gravitas* is in fact peculiarly associated with the ancient offices of state, with judges,[3] with the censor,[4] and above all with the senate.[5] In this way it is frequently linked with *auctoritas*,[6] and *maiestas*.[7] Wagenvoort reasonably associates its development with the primitive concept of mana attaching to a person or institution.

Among our literary sources we have in Horace an indication of what *gravitas* means. Horace is usually associated with *levitas* rather than *gravitas*. One thinks of Sydney Smith's characterization of himself: 'My brother and I are a living contradiction of Newtonian law. He rises by reason of his gravity; I fail to rise by reason of my levity.' Horace was under the patronage of Maecenas, and therefore might be expected to support the reassertion of ancient Roman virtue by the imperial régime. But though he never went to the extent of Ovid who, when Augustus demanded didactic poems, wrote one on the science of winning and keeping a mistress, and though he was prepared to write in honour of the victory at Actium,[8] he also asserted his liberty,[9] and was not prepared to lay aside his lightness of touch and become a mere moralist of someone else's philosophy. Horace's levity can be seen in one of his most familiar poems 'Integer vitae'.[10] It is difficult to see how anyone has ever taken this seriously, but the opening lines have often been divorced from their context, and even taken as a philosophy of life, as by Clare in Hardy's *Tess of the D'Urbervilles*. Horace would have smiled to see his mock-heroic beginning treated so literally. The poem was in fact written, not as is often said, about a *demi-mondaine*, but about a little girl, Lalage (Chatterbox), perhaps the daughter of Horace's estate manager.

[1] Liv. 29, 37, 16.   [2] Val. Max. 2, 2, 2.
[3] Quint. *Decl.* 4, 13; 14, 1.   [4] Plin. *Ep.* 3, 20, 6; Flor. 1, 18, 22.
[5] e.g. Cic. *Ad Att.* 1, 14, 4; 1, 16, 5; 4, 2, 4; *Cat.* 1, 9; *Phil.* VII 27; *De Or.* 1, 31; cf. Ov. *Fast.* 4, 293; *Met.* 15, 590.
[6] e.g. Cic. *Ad Att.* 1, 14, 5; *Verr.* 2, 5, 54; *De Orat.* 2, 230; *De Inv.* 1, 109; cf. Plin. *Ep.* 2, 7, 4; 9, 23, 1.
[7] e.g. Cic. *De Am.* 96; *Div. in Caec.* 69; cf. Val. Max. 2, 2, 2.
[8] Hor. *Epod.* 9. *Od.* I 37.   [9] id. *Ep.* I 7.   [10] id. *Od.* 1, 22.

'The upright man need never fear, wherever he goes'—and here we have a parade of geographical learning borrowed from Catullus. This beginning ought indeed to lead to a poem of *gravitas*. We have had 'Who would true valour see?' followed by 'From Greenland's icy mountains'. What do we get? 'The upright man need never fear. *I* was going along, singing of Lalage, and met a wolf—and the wolf ran away.' The dog it was that died! Then another parade of learning about what a monstrous great beast it was. How will this end? With some whimsical speculations on the part of Providence in looking after the just? Not a bit of it; 'So put me at the North Pole or the Equator, and I'll go on singing of Lalage, bless her!' This is typical of Horace at his best. He starts with a theme that ought to be a theme of *gravitas* and gently, goodhumouredly deflates it.

In the six great 'Roman' odes which begin Book III, however, he changes his tune. Here he has decided, sincerely as we need not doubt, to play his part in the new propaganda. Here we have a sequence of six poems in the same metre on the same general subject, reviewing the ends, social, moral, religious, and political, which a good government will encompass, and offering the promise that Augustus will do so. Here we can see *gravitas* unalloyed. The poetry itself seems heavier, though this may be a subjective judgement.[1] In the third ode we have a characterization of *gravitas* itself.

> *Iustum et tenacem propositi virum*
> *non civium ardor prava iubentium,*
> *non voltus instantis tyranni*
> *mente quatit solida neque Auster,*

> *dux inquieti turbidus Hadriae,*
> *nec fulminantis magna manus Iovis:*
> *si fractus illabatur orbis,*
> *impavidum ferient ruinae.*

---

[1] But not purely. Cf. the line Hor. *Od*. III 14 dissentientis condicionibus; cp. also 47–8.

The man of firm and noble soul
No factious clamours can control;
No threat'ning tyrant's darkling brow
　Can swerve him from his just intent:
Gales the warring waves which plough,
　By Auster on his billows spent,
To curb the Adriatic main,
Would awe his fix'd determin'd mind in vain.

Ay, and the red right arm of Jove,
Hurtling his lightnings from above,
With all his terrors there unfurl'd
　He would, unmoved, unawed behold.
The flames of an expiring world,
　Again in crashing chaos roll'd,
In vast promiscuous ruin hurl'd,
Might light his glorious funeral pile:
Still dauntless, 'midst the wreck of earth he'd smile.[1]

The English loses effect by being verbose. The very concision of Latin makes for weightiness—the Spartans had a similar *gravitas*—and it was with Horace's words that Cornelius de Witte upon the rack defied his tormentors.

What emphasis the Romans put on *gravitas* we may glimpse in the subsequent history of the imperial régime. The grotesque, shambling, slobbering figure of Claudius lacked the *gravitas* expected of an emperor. So *gravitas* had to be induced by artificial means, by statues which idealized him, by the military glory of adding Britain to the empire, by titles—he was *imperator* no less than twenty-seven times. Nero's fall is significant. 'But in any event', writes Momigliano of his triumphal tour of Greece, 'the journey, though it may have excited Greece and made a deep impression on the East, had been most damaging for the prestige of Nero in the West.'[2] The Romans could forgive Nero his cruelties, but not his stage-appearances. They could forgive him for being a tyrant, but not for being a mountebank. They could forgive his offences against *humanitas*, but not his offences against

[1] Hor. *Od.* III 3, 1–8, tr. Byron.　　　　[2] *C.A.H.* X p. 737.

gravitas. Again, Juvenal is a satirist, and we must not be so heavy-handed as to ignore his use of the unexpected—*paraprosdokian*. Still, he himself claims that indignation is the mainspring of his writing ('Facit indignatio versum'),[1] and it is difficult not to feel that triviality arouses his indignation as much as cruelty. The woman who goes hunting, and the young aristocrat who drives himself instead of employing a chauffeur are set alongside the poisoner and the oppressor of the provinces.[2] A whole satire deals with a Privy Council summoned by Domitian to discuss the cooking of an unusually large fish.[3] Later again, Commodus displayed *virtus*, the *virtus Augusti*, by killing lions in the arena. But the emperor's desire to display his prowess *publicly* was contempt of *gravitas*,[4] and whomever else he offended, it was the old Roman traditionalists whose hostility killed Commodus, and after his death he was reviled as 'murderer and—gladiator'.[5]

This general treatment of *Romana virtus* can be summed up in the figure of M. Atilius Regulus. Regulus commanded the Roman troops in Africa during the first Punic War. Despite his victories at Ecnomus and Uthina he cannot be regarded as a fit commander of troops, and showed little or no comprehension of the situation in Africa. His desire to finish the war himself shows him a man of intense personal ambition. Instead he was involved in calamitous defeat, and taken prisoner. In short we have a man who was in moral behaviour, general competence, and imaginative sympathy not above average, and in some ways well below. Yet he recurs again and again in the pages of Cicero as the exemplar of *virtus*,[6] and Horace borrows him from Cicero as the type of patriotism.[7] Why? Because history, or legend, or a mixture of both,[8] told how Regulus, sent as envoy to Rome upon parole to return if the Carthaginian prisoners in Roman hands were not released, advised the senate not to release the prisoners, who were of more value to Carthage than he to Rome, and, being

---

[1] Juv. 1, 79.   [2] ib. 22–78.   [3] id. 4.
[4] S.H.A. *Comm.* 12, 12.   [5] ib. 18–19.
[6] Cic. *De Off.* III 26, 99 ff; cf. *Ad Att.* XVI 11, 4; *De Sen.* 20, 75; *De Fin.* V 27, 82; *Pro Sest.* 59, 127; *In Pis.* 19, 43; *Par. Stoic.* II 16.
[7] Hor. *Od.* III 5; cf. also Sen. *De Provid.* 9; *De Tranq.* 16, 4.
[8] cf. T. Frank in *C. Ph.* (1926), p. 311; E. Klebs in *P.W.* s.v. Atilius (51).

under oath, with unimpassioned countenance, returned to his own torture and death. Here we have *Romana virtus*—the courage which faced death unflinchingly, the loyalty to his country's interests and to his oath, the dignity of his demeanour. The appeal of Stoicism to Rome is easy to comprehend.

There is much to admire in the traditional Roman character, but it is admirable within narrow limits. Its virtues are sectarian rather than universal, within that public rather than personal, and within that again the virtues of a soldier rather than those of an administrator. They were not incompatible with the most flagrant immorality in other directions; they were not easily compatible with the gentler virtues of humility and compassion. Cicero comments on the difficulty of combining in one person the qualities of *humanitas* and *gravitas*.[1] As the empire prospered and was peaceful, we shall see other qualities thrusting themselves to the fore, generosity, and forethought, and clemency. In time of war and crisis the ancient character reasserted itself, if not in actuality, then in yearnings of memory. Sometimes in the complexities of empire it was sighingly idealized; later writers admired its *simplicitas* or single-mindedness. Sometimes a prophet of perspicacity might see the need to humanize it, as Vergil attempted to do when he endowed Aeneas with compassionate feeling and declared the Roman destiny:

> *But Romans, never forget that government is your medium!*
> *Be this your art: to practise men in the habit of peace,*
> *Generosity to the conquered, and firmness against aggressors.*[2]

Here are *virtus*, *gravitas*, and *pietas*—courage, authority, and the acceptance of destiny. But *parcere subiectis* is something new, and the whole is tinged with a love of peace which derives partly from Epicurean philosophy and partly from Vergil's own hatred of war. In itself the ideal was inadequate, but it was not ignoble, and the relationship implied in *pietas* was capable of an extension which it never received.

[1] Cic. *De Leg*. III 1. See above p. 173.   [2] Virg. *Aen*. VI 851–3, tr. C. Day Lewis.

X

THE VIRTUES
OF A ROMAN EMPEROR[1]

I
N THE YEAR 27 B.C., as he proudly records in the Res Gestae,[2]
the senate and people of Rome presented Augustus with a
shield formally testifying to his high qualities, 'virtutis clemen-
tiaeque et iustitiae et pietatis caussa'. It was of course a put-up job.
He had just proclaimed the formal restoration of the Republic.
The restoration was no doubt a sham, and the whole operation
must have been meticulously arranged beforehand. Augustus kept
the power, but he held it behind a façade of freedom, and he held
it as a commission from the senate and people. 'I transferred the
government from my own authority to the free disposal of the
senate and people of Rome' are his own words,[3] and the catch-
word of the restitution of constitutional government appears alike
in official and unofficial documents.[4] The shield was the public
recognition of his qualities; with the presentation was associated
a wreath of oak-leaves, given originally to one who had saved the
life of a fellow-citizen in war, as ten years later he was recalling on
his coinage;[5] the whole show was certainly stage-managed,
probably by Maecenas. It is important to recognize that the events
of 27 B.C. are transitional, and the clupeus virtutis is not to be taken
as a broadsheet of policy for the principate; it looks back as well

[1] The title and background of this chapter are taken unashamedly from M. P.
Charlesworth's brilliant Raleigh lecture on the subject, P.B.A. XXIII (1937),
pp. 105-33. See also his 'Providentia et Aeternitas', Harv. Theol. Rev. XXIX
(1936), 107 ff, and R. S. Rogers, Studies in the Reign of Tiberius. Charlesworth
was concerned with the method of imperial propaganda as well as its substance.
The emphasis here is different. A. D. Nock, 'A Diis Electa' H.T.R. XXIII (1930),
266 ff is useful on the later period.   [2] Aug. R.G. 34.   [3] ib.
[4] Vell. Pat. II 89, 4; Fasti Praenestini; Laudatio Turii.
[5] See C.A.H. Plates IV 198 o.

as forward.[1] It may be approximately said that of the virtues here enumerated two predominantly refer to past events, two prognosticate the future. We have already seen *virtus* and *pietas* as part of the traditional Roman character. It was Augustus' aim to seem to restore this, as part of the seeming restoration of the Republic. But valour and patriotism were desirable qualities to foster for the future as well. Further, in his public policy Augustus was a genuine traditionalist. On the whole he was a conservative by temperament; he was seeking stability; and he was seeking to rehabilitate those qualities which had made Rome mistress of the world. We find, says Adcock,

> 'in the first years of the Augustan age a consciousness of the greatness of the Republic. In the early books of Livy, in the *Odes* of Horace, and in the *Georgics* and *Aeneid* there is heard again and again the note of pride in the past, of belief in the people of Italy and in the sound old qualities of the Republican worthies.'[2]

Hence his similar care to restore religious forms and observances. Finally *virtus* and *pietas* spoke directly of Augustus' own past. He was not a soldier; he owed his victories to Agrippa. But he had to appear himself as conqueror. It must be he who had won his victories by courageous generalship, when Antony, the leading commander of the day, had fled ignominiously from Actium. In the wider sphere of *virtus* he had astonishingly shown manly qualities while still a lad; we are liable to forget that he was only eighteen at the time of Caesar's murder. In the years that followed only once, under defeat from Sextus Pompeius, did he flinch from that inexorable purpose and indomitable ambition which were to make him ruler of the world. *Pietas* too looked to the past. How far love or honour of the dead Julius truly spurred him on we cannot now tell. It should have done. He took the name of Caesar, and Antony remarked bitterly that the young man owed everything to his name; there was enough truth in the remark to make it barbed. Certain it is that it was in the name of duty and of

---

[1] The best treatments are those of E. Kornemann, *P.W.*, XVI, cols. 223–9; H. Markowski, *Eos*, XXXVII (1936), p. 109. But I cannot wholly agree with either. [2] *C.A.H.* X p. 586.

vengeance that he went to Philippi, and it mattered enough to him for the temple he vowed to Mars the Avenger to be dedicated forty years later; the long delay suggests that his *pietas* was worn on the sleeve rather than in the heart. Bullets at Perusia have been found inscribed MARS VLTOR and DIVOM IVLIOM, though the connection between the Perusine war and the duty to avenge Caesar is hard to discern. This loyalty to Julius was useful to him in other ways. He liked to style himself 'son of the divine Julius'; analogies with Heracles or Asclepius suggest that this may have presaged his future apotheosis. The *pietas* towards his adoptive father became subsumed in a wider *pietas* exercised towards Rome, and towards the gods who were lords of its destiny. It was his pose to have saved Rome, and whatever his methods and whatever his motives it was also his accomplishment. Hence his title of 'pater patriae'.[1] He was not a religious man. Suetonius tells a story of how he aped Apollo at a mock banquet of the Olympic gods.[2] The story is suspect, for whom would he permit to play Jupiter? —but to pass muster at all it must be *ben trovato*. Superstitious he was, and still more he knew with Polybius before him and Napoleon after him the political value of religion for the powers that be in the state.[3] He took the office of pontifex maximus, augur, quindecimvir, pontifex and fetialis, and held various other priesthoods.[4] He restored eighty-two temples, and was himself responsible for many new foundations, of which the most important were the temples to Mars Ultor, the great temple to Apollo, and new places of worship for Jupiter.[5] Still more, he was concerned to foster the sense that the destiny of Rome was a religious destiny. This is to be seen clearly in the pages of Vergil, where the prophecies of Rome's high calling are uttered in the spiritual environment of the sixth book, and the founding of Rome is declared to be the will of heaven. It is to be seen in Horace, the whilom Epicurean and sceptic, who cries that Rome will never be great again as long as the ancient temples remain unrestored. It is to be seen in the *Ludi Saeculares* of 17 B.C., the birthday of a new age, such as Vergil had conceived in the Mes-

[1] Aug. *R.G.* 35. [2] Suet. *Aug.* 70. [3] Polyb. VI 56.
[4] Aug. *R.G.* 7. [5] ib. 20, 21, 35.

sianic Eclogue, and Cleopatra had hopefully heralded in her
Sibylline prophecies. There were offerings to the powers of destiny and the goddess of childbirth, prayer for prosperity, cathar-
tic ritual, nightly offerings symbolizing the death of the old order,
and a new emphasis upon Apollo, the radiant god of light, culture and the peaceful arts, and peculiar patron to Augustus. All
this is woven with great skill into Horace's carefully scripted ode,
and in it the ancient traditions of Capitoline religion are linked
with a new moralism—Honour, Peace, Valour, Glory, and Chastity are exalted. Or we may see what Augustus was fostering in
the Altar of Peace, where the Emperor appears at worship as
primus inter pares, attended by the religious orders, the imperial
family, and the commonalty of Rome. The four great panels
represent Mother Earth, attended by the spirits of Air and Water,
in a peaceful pastoral scene; the arrival of Aeneas in Latium and
his sacrifice to the Penates (a cult which Augustus had restored);
the nurture of Romulus and Remus within the Lupercal (a shrine
which Augustus had restored); and Rome herself seated on a pile
of armour. The combination of patriotism and religion and the
emphasis upon the emperor's own initiative which others are
expected to follow is patent and pointed. Later, *pietas* stands
clearly for this combination of patriotism and religion, and
becomes linked with emperor-worship. As a coin-type it is often
found associated with priestly emblems.

Iustitia with *virtus* Augustus inherited from the Greek scheme
of the cardinal virtues; his selectivity is interesting. Here we are
dealing much more with a manifesto of future policy. As Charlesworth remarks, it is perhaps the most obvious virtue desiderated
in a ruler. 'Set justice aside', said St Augustine, 'and what are
kingdoms but great robberies?' Justice does not require lengthy
treatment here; it is important to observe that though philosophically *iustitia* represents the Greek *dikaiosune* the word itself has
a very different flavour.[1] The Latin word is connected with law,
and means conformity with law. Of course, in the hands of
philosophers and theologians the laws of God dominate the laws
of man, and it may even be said, as it was said by Heraclitus of old,

[1] See above, p. 42.

that human laws derive from divine law. This was not the intent
of Augustus' propaganda. A monarch might be arbitrary, despotic and tyrannical or he might submit himself to the rule of
law. Augustus was claiming to be a monarch of the latter sort,
and he did in fact on occasion appear in the courts as a private
individual in the course of judicial business. But if a monarch is
praised for his *iustitia*, it means that he is not constitutionally
bound to rule by law or there would be no need to praise him for
it. This was historically true, as Rome found to her cost when
faced with a Caligula. Further, *iustitia* in a monarch is not quite
the same as *iustitia* in a subject, for it is ultimately the monarch
who makes the laws. We need not be afraid of a certain cynicism
about imperial professions. Our motives are generally mixed and
an ordered society under the rule of justice was in the interests of
the Roman people as well as a security for Augustus' own power.
It is curious that Justice has little place upon the coins which were
such a potent instrument of imperial propaganda. Elsewhere it is
prominent. In A.D. 13 a statue was put up celebrating and per-
sonifying the Justice of Augustus; it was part of the policy of
getting as near as possible to deifying the emperor without actually
doing so in his lifetime. Tiberius celebrated the tenth anniversary
of the Ara Iustitiae Augustae with a coin showing the bust of
Justice and so inscribed.[1] Vespasian also celebrated the centenary
of the 'clupeus virtutis' with an unusual coin showing Justice
with corn-ears and a sceptre. It is interesting that Augustus is
never called 'iustus' in inscriptions. Tiberius receives the appella-
tions 'iustus' and 'iustissimus princeps'.[2] Later 'most just' is one
of the stock imperial designations. In the golden years at the
turn of the century it is especially to be seen. In between, Seneca
makes a point in praising—and preaching to—Nero, that there
is *law* to meet wrong.[3] One of the rare coin-types of IVSTITIA
is Nerva's; it proclaims a new beginning after the absolute
and irresponsible autocracy of Domitian. Nerva's successor
Trajan follows a similar vein of thought and speaks proudly
of 'the justice of our times'; that he meant it is seen in his de-

---

[1] C. H. V. Sutherland, *Coinage in Roman Imperial Policy*, pp. 97–8.
[2] *I.L.S.* 159; 3783. [3] Sen. *De Clem.* I 1, 8.

precation of 'witch-hunts' and anonymous accusations. 'They are the worse kind of precedent and alien to the spirit of our age.'[1]

It should be added that the descent of justice—'Astraea virgo' —from heaven symbolizes the return of the Golden Age—'Saturnia regna'. So in 40 B.C. Vergil, composing in the expectation of a son for Antony and Octavia, wrote 'iam redit et virgo, redeunt Saturnia regna'.[2] 'Virgo' is Justice. This return of Justice is associated, as Tarn has shown, with the ideal of sovereignty. These ideas were again prominent at the beginning of Nero's reign. The author of the second Einseideln eclogue takes up Vergil's words and applies them to his own day, 'Saturni rediere dies Astraeaque virgo'.[3] The author of the *Octavia* was similarly right in letting Seneca soliloquize about this vision, though there it is contrasted with Nero's reign of death and doom.[4] What is important for our purpose is that during the period of the early empire Justice is seen as a gift of heaven, associated with monarchical rule, and so maintained and even imposed.

Of Augustus' four virtues *clementia* is in many ways the most significant. We have seen how the Greek tradition tended to minimize the virtue of pity, because it made the inner well-being of the individual dependent upon factors outside his control. Clemency, though it is sometimes linked with pity, is quite a different concept. In clemency the motive of action is the inner disposition of the actor, not the condition of the object of his clemency. The concept came into political prominence with Julius Caesar. Caesar's policy of conciliation has been admirably studied by Ethelbert Stauffer,[5] and little is needed save to summarize his conclusions. It should be said at once that the phrase 'policy of conciliation' is just. Caesar, a strange enigmatic genius, knew when it was politic to be mild, but he could be ruthless if his interests seemed so to dictate. His most gallant opponent, Vercingetorix, was kept for years in chains to be borne in the triumphal procession of the most merciful Caesar, and then killed

[1] Plin. *Ep.* X 55; X 97.
[2] Virg. *Ecl.* 4, 6. For the occasion see W. W. Tarn, 'Alexander Helios and the Golden Age', *J.R.S.*, XXII (1932), pp. 135 ff.   [3] Anon. *Eins. Ecl.* 2, 23.
[4] [Sen.] *Oct.* 391–435.   [5] E. Stauffer, *Christ and the Caesars*, c. IV.

without scruple. He would massacre a tribe cheerfully, *pour encourager les autres*; his initial campaign against the Helvetii showed that; he treated the survivors with leniency, but they were only a third of the whole. Three years later when the Usipetes and Tencteri, in numbers he himself estimated at 430,000, crossed the Rhine, he seized their leaders by treachery, and ruthlessly wiped out the remainder, sparing not even women and children.[1] But his own account of his campaigns in Gaul while it reveals clearly and deliberately the power of the mailed fist ready to be clenched under the outstretched velvet, stresses with equal deliberation this policy of clemency. Time and again the tribes he conquers come to him with the words 'Deal with us in accordance with the mildness and generosity which are all your own', and he replies 'I will spare the town, not so much for its merits as for my customary policy'. When the civil war came Caesar repudiated the practice of the earlier dictator Sulla, who had engaged in an orgy of proscription and bloodshed. Instead he asserted in noble words, 'Haec nova sit ratio vincendi, ut misericordia et liberalitate nos muniamus' ('Let us show a new pattern of victory, with mercy and generosity for our defence'). In general in his behaviour towards Romans he practised what he preached. After Pharsalus he pardoned the surrendered with a speech about his leniency. When he burnt the Pompeian papers without examining them for the names of potential enemies, Pliny saw his action as the supreme example of his royal clemency. On his return to Rome he proclaimed an amnesty. 'Such', says Velleius Paterculus, 'was the clemency exercised by the great man in all his victories', and Dio Cassius adds, 'In these ways he showed up the infamous practices of Sulla, and earned the greatest praise not only for courage but also for mildness, difficult though it generally is for a man to behave the same in peace as in war.' Even Cicero, who had earlier referred to Caesar's 'insidiosa clementia' ('treacherous display of clemency'), and who was later to revile the great dictator after his death, is now found speaking publicly of his 'unique and unheard-of', 'wonderful and laud-

[1] Caesar may exaggerate his numbers: they show the impression of himself he was prepared to leave.

able' clemency, and describing Caesar as 'clementissimus dux' ('most merciful of leaders'). The senate decreed a temple to Caesar's divine clemency, on whose pediment was to be set a globe proclaiming that his clemency stretched from one end of the earth to the other, and this temple appears on coins with the inscription CLEMENTIA CAESARIS and, on the reverse, a scene from the October festival. But Caesar was murdered by a conspiracy led by Marcus Brutus, who had defied him in 59 by a display of militant republicanism and again in 45 by his eulogies of the dead Cato. On each occasion Caesar had spared him and honoured him. Caesar refused armed protection. 'I will rather be slain than feared, and build upon the clemency which I practise,' he said. So Cicero was right in his words: 'Clemency became the dictator's fate, his generosity became his destruction.' Even the Christian Orosius praised his spirit. 'He was destroyed in the effort to build the political world anew, contrary to the example of his predecessors, in the spirit of clemency.'

Octavian, the future Augustus, was heir to Caesar's name and fortune, but not to his greatness of character. Caesar had been ruthless to Gauls and Germans, but not to Romans. Young Octavian joined with Antony and Lepidus in the proscription and slaughter of thousands of Roman citizens, who by reason of wealth or policy stood in their way. No achievement of the emperor Augustus could eradicate this crime of the young Octavian. There is strong evidence of an attempt on his part to assassinate Antony.[1] At Perusia the loss of life was grievous, and Augustus was in a mood of merciless vengeance. He certainly executed some of the local magistrates and others. The story that he sacrificed them at the altar of the divine Julius is more controversial. It is fashionable to reject it, but the comparable act of Aeneas in Vergil's poem supports its historicity.[2] Whatever the truth there was not much evidence of *clementia* at Perusia. Of course when unscrupulous ruthlessness had won him the throne of the world he could afford to lay it aside, and use the propaganda of clem-

[1] Suet. *Aug.* 10; Cic. *Ad Fam.* XII 28, 2; *Phil.* III 19; Plut. *Ant.* 16; Appian *B.C.* III 39. Velleius II 63 denies the story.
[2] Suet. *Aug.* 15; Sen. *De Clem.* I 11; Appian *B.C.* V 48; Verg. *Aen.* X 517; XI 81.

ency, though conspirators against the régime, a Gallus or a
Murena, found little mercy at his hands. Suetonius declares that
there are many notable demonstrations of his clemency; the
examples which he gives are not particularly notable, and his
general policy is seen in his well-known rejoinder to Tiberius:

'My dear Tiberius, don't give way to your youth and get
overheated that there should be anyone who attacks me verb-
ally. I'm satisfied if we have a situation in which no one can
attack me physically.'[1]

Seneca was cynical about the whole affair. He divided Augustus'
life into a period of brutality in his youth and clemency in his old
age. But Augustus' clemency was not genuine, he suggests; it
was 'cruelty in weariness'.[2]

Whatever Augustus might say about his successor, clemency
was in fact a conspicuous virtue of Tiberius, as Rogers has well
argued.[3] It is a commonplace of modern historical studies that
Tacitus' portrait of Tiberius is conditioned by his own experiences under Domitian, that his interest in psychology which is
one of his high qualities as a writer and historian, sometimes mis-
leads him, and that his interpretation can be corrected from the
evidence he himself presents. The major count in the indictment
is the trials for treason which took place during the reign, and it is
true that an absolute monarch must bear ultimate responsibility
for these. But Tiberius' personal attitude to these trials, when it
can be traced, is almost always on the side of clemency. Drusus
Libo committed suicide; Tiberius swore that he would have inter-
ceded for the man's life.[4] Clutorius Priscus was summarily executed by the senate for writing a premature obituary of Drusus
Caesar; Tiberius ordered that henceforth there should always be
a stay of execution for ten days.[5] Vibius Serenus was convicted of
treason; Tiberius intervened for clemency.[6] Cominius Macer was
convicted of a libellious attack on Tiberius; Tiberius had learnt
Augustus' lesson to the point of conservatism, and pardoned him.
Tacitus comments, perversely, as Rogers says:

[1] Suet. *Aug.* 51. [2] Sen. *De Clem.* I, 9–11.
[3] R. S. Rogers, *Studies in the Reign of Tiberius*, pp. 35–59.
[4] Tac. *Ann.* 2, 31, 4. [5] ib. 3, 51, 2 f. [6] ib. 4, 30, 1 f.

'This action made it the more surprising that, cognizant as he was of better things and what good reputation attended clemency, he yet preferred the darker course.'[1]

It would be possible to quote other instances. Similarly in A.D. 26 Dinis, one of the ringleaders of revolt in Thrace, chose surrender, through long experience, says Tacitus, of Roman power and Roman clemency;[2] the collocation of power and clemency is significant.

Public recognition of Tiberius' clemency took place to our knowledge twice in his reign. A coin series, datable to 22/23, depicts busts of Tiberius full face on ornamented shields or medallions accompanied by the words CLEMENTIAE—S.C. and MODERATIONI—S.C. Sutherland, following Mowat, has reasonably suggested that the Senate, in A.D. 22, presented Tiberius with shields of Clemency and Moderation—an act of which an echo is preserved in the pages of Tacitus—and that the formal but well-earned honour once conferred, the Senate proceeded by means of their coinage to call wide public attention to the imperial virtues which their ceremonial action had just recognized.[3] This act is thus parallel with the presentation of the fourfold shield to Augustus. The qualities which Tiberius stresses are significant. *Moderatio*, which in Tiberius represents the strict limitation of honours accepted for himself or his family, is our old friend *sophrosune*, and it is conspicuous by its absence from the propaganda of Augustus. Velleius also speaks of his hero's *singularis moderatio*.[4] *Clementia*, however, is the more important, and six years later, when Tiberius spared the lives of Agrippina and Nero, despite their conviction for treason, the senate greeted this notable display of magnanimity by voting the erection of an altar to *Clementia*.[5]

The emphasis on *clementia* at the beginning of Nero's reign is

[1] ib. 4, 31, 1 f.   [2] ib. 4, 50, 2.
[3] C. H. V. Sutherland, 'Two "Virtues" of Tiberius: a Numismatic Contribution to the History of his Reign', *J.R.S.*, XXVIII (1938), 129–40. I accept his view of the date of these, as against M. Grant, *From Imperium to Auctoritas*, pp. 447 ff.
[4] Vell. II, 122, 1.
[5] Tacitus appears to be wrong in the date he gives for their trial. He is contradicted by Suet. *Cal.* 10, 1, and cf. his own words about *pavor internus* in 28. *Ann.* 4, 74, 1–3. See Rogers, op. cit., pp. 55–9.

well documented and important to understand. Tiberius was succeeded by the crazed Caligula, who called his senators traitors:
they humbly responded by praising his clemency. Much has been
done in recent scholarship to rehabilitate the memory of his successor Claudius. Claudius did not make a virtue of *clementia*; he
tried to treat the senate as equals not as subjects.

> 'It is extremely unfitting, Conscript Fathers, to the high
> dignity of this order that at this meeting one man only, the
> consul designate, should make a speech (and that copied exactly
> from the proposal of the consuls) while the rest utter one word
> only, "Agreed", and then after leaving the House remark.
> "There, we've given our opinion".'[1]

But however beneficial the reign of Claudius in many ways,
notably in the provinces and in legal development, he offended
the aristocracy. His physique and behaviour offended against
gravitas. He used *equites* for his advisers and freedmen for his
executive. And his freedmen—and wives—used murder and proscription behind his back to feather their own nests. The attitude
of Roman Society to Claudius can be seen in the *Apocolocyntosis*,
formerly attributed to Seneca, but probably by Petronius. In this
Claudius reaches heaven with a Homeric quotation. The next line
is, as the author points out, 'There I sacked a city and killed the
people'. The charge finally preferred against him is: ' Senators killed
35; *equites* 221; others as the sand in number.'[2] It was the sense
that they had been subjected to arbitrary authority which led
for the plea for *clementia* at the beginning of the new reign. We
may perhaps wonder whether there was not a note of fear for the
future as well as relief from the past. They cannot well have
known what to expect from Nero, who was scarcely more than a
boy, but Agrippina had just murdered Claudius, and it was
dangerous to cross her. So it is that Calpurnius Siculus combines
some charming pastoral writing with the most nauseating flattery
of the new régime, and writes:

> omne procul vitium simulatae cedere pacis
> iussit et insanos Clementia contudit enses.

[1] M. P. Charlesworth, *Documents illustrating the reign of Claudius and Nero*, no. 2.
[2] [Sen.] *Apocol.* 5; 11; 13–14.

('Clemency has commanded every vice which disguises itself as peace to remove to a distance, and has blunted swords drawn in madness').[1] Calpurnius had no originality as a thinker; he is merely parroting the catchwords of the day. It was Seneca who laid down the manifesto of the régime in the words which he addressed to Nero *On Clemency*. The author of the *Octavia* was right in putting into Seneca's mouth the words 'Clemency is a sovereign remedy for fearfulness'.[2] Our manuscripts of the treatise are incomplete, but the general drift is clear. The beginning is ominous. Nero is to look from his superior eminence at the masses, quarrelsome, rebellious and uncontrollable, bound for disaster if once they snap the yoke of authority. He is to say to himself:

'I have been selected to perform on earth the office of the gods, I am lord of life, death, and destiny. But I bear the sword of severity sheathed, and wear instead the breastplate of Clemency.'[3]

This is all right so far as it goes, but it is little more than a flourish of trumpets to open the royal address. We are soon on prudential and expediential grounds. The tyrant's 'oderint dum metuant' ('let them hate, provided that they fear') is morally abominable, but, more serious, it is injudicious. Cruelty raises hatred and breeds insecurity. Clemency creates security for the subject and so for the ruler. But what is clemency? Seneca proffers several definitions. It is '*sophrosune* in a situation where you could use revenge', or it is 'leniency shown by a superior to an inferior in determining punishment', or it is 'a tendency towards lenience in exacting punishment', or it is 'the sort of moderation which remits a portion of a well-deserved punishment'. It differs from pity, which Seneca as a Stoic writes off as mere sentimentality. It differs also from pardon; pardon releases a person from merited punishment, but clemency treats as he deserves a man who could but should not be dealt with severely. Its opposite is cruelty. Seneca is here tendentious and rhetorical. If he had been wanting to argue a different case he could have opposed to clemency not

[1] Calp. Sic. 1, 58–9.   [2] [Sen.] *Oct.* 442.   [3] Sen. *De Clem.* I 1, 1–4.

cruelty but justice, and made out an equally strong case against clemency along these lines. The principal point to notice in this treatise is that Seneca claims clemency as a fitting virtue for all men but especially commendable in a monarch.[1] When, however, he comes to concrete examples they are those of parent and child, or master and slave. Just as, in the familiar picture of English business life, the wife snaps at the husband, who takes it out of his secretary, who boxes the ears of the office-boy, who kicks the cat, so in a hierarchical society clemency can permeate down from the top. Historically, Seneca's words bore some fruit. It is impossible to whitewash Nero, though attempts have been made, but our sources are hostile and overstate the case against him, and there is no doubt that he was remarkably patient under lampoons and personal attacks.

Coins with the legend return under Vitellius, but then not again, I think, till the time of Hadrian. Hadrian, interestingly, pairs *Clementia* and *Indulgentia*. As Charlesworth remarks:

'Tiberius, Caligula, Nero, and Vitellius—the list has an ominous ring, and Tacitus uses the word *Clementia* to achieve some of his most ironical effects. In fact, *Clementia* had become too much a despotic quality; the mercy of a conqueror towards those whose life he holds in his hands, the gracious act of an absolute monarch towards his subjects. Possessing that significance it was wisely laid aside for a time until its unhappy memories, its ring of civil war and despotism, could be forgotten, and it could return again under Hadrian or under later emperors in an altered form as *Clementia Temporum*, "the mildness of the times".'

We may instance as typical a coin of Probus showing a divinity handing to the emperor the globe of the world. The inscription is CLEMENTIA TEMPORVM. 'But it is significant', Charlesworth proceeds, 'that it is one of the titles by which Diocletian or Constantine were [*sic!*] addressed, *Tua Clementia*—significant when we remember how absolute their power was.'[2]

That is well said. *Clementia* can only be exercised by a superior

[1] ib. I 3; 5.   [2] M. P. Charlesworth, *P.B.A.*, XXIII (1937), pp. 112–13.

towards an inferior. It is significantly attributed, as early as Plautus, to Neptune by a trader who has made a voyage without being shipwrecked; he had been in the god's power and the god had spared him.[1] It is an attribute of autocracy. Where autocracy was a factual reality it was well that it should be challenged by a vision of condescension and gentleness. Furthermore, as with the other imperial virtues, it was the aim of the more thoughtful and responsible monarchs to set an example to their less powerful entourage in their relations with their inferiors. Imperial propaganda of this kind was not merely the hopeful suppliance of subjects nor was it merely the self-glorification of arrogant Moguls. It was a deliberate attempt to lay down the spirit which should stir through the whole of society. But the movement followed a kind of spiritual Newtonian law, and operated downward only. It could not be a basis for mutual relationship.

One of the most important qualities a ruler was expected to manifest was *providentia* or foresight.

'In the late Republic,' writes Charlesworth,[2] 'PROVIDENTIA was the foresight which, whether manifested by the gods, or by men working as the intermediaries of the gods, helped to secure the continued and peaceful existence of the state, preserving it against external or internal dangers.'

Far away in the second century Scipio Africanus had spoken of the disposition of the Romans to favour the Greeks, to take all possible care for them, continually seeking to benefit them.[3] Cicero was inclined to attribute the preservation of the state during the Catilinarian conspiracy, sometimes to his own foresight, sometimes to that of the gods.[4] We are beginning to see a contrast between the *videre* of the old formula, 'videant consules ne quid detrimenti res publica capiat', which signifies the taking of steps in an immediate situation, and the new *providere*, which avoids the situation of crisis by planning and forethought. This con-

---

[1] Plaut. *Trin.* 827.

[2] M. P. Charlesworth, 'Providentia and Aeternitas', in *H.T.R.*, XXIX (1936), p. 108, an article of which I have made extensive use.

[3] Dittenberger, *S.I.G.* 618; see G. de Sanctis, *Atti d. Accad. d. Torino*, LVII (1921–2), p. 242.   [4] Cic. *Cat.* III 14; Quint. *Inst. Or.* X 1, 25.

cept of providential government, alike by the gods and by the human ruler, persists throughout the empire, and the shading into one another of the two ideas is important. It becomes linked with Stoic theories of the providence which God exercises over the universe, but in its application to the ruler it appears to be Roman rather than Greek, and does not form a part of the Hellenistic conception of monarchy. So after the turmoil of the civil wars the cities of Asia, decreeing that their new year shall start on Augustus' birthday, proclaim that Divine Providence raised up Augustus for the benefit of man.[1] The idea of the monarchical benefactor is Greek, but the idea of the Divine Providence may be Roman. Augustus correspondingly shows 'continual care' to benefit the provinces,[2] and in the early part of Tiberius' reign Augustus' providence is stressed upon coins in the imperial propaganda; this no doubt refers to his foresight in adopting Tiberius, and is designed to obscure the fact that he was very reluctant to do so.

In Tiberius' reign indeed *providentia* comes into its own as an imperial virtue. There was the restoration of the cities of Asia, which Strabo calls *pronoia*,[3] and his practice of retaining successful provincial governors in their posts, to which Josephus applies the terms *prometheia*.[4] There was his repeatedly expressed conception of the emperor's responsibility for maintaining the material well-being of his people.

'Italy's dependence on external sources, Rome's subsistence continually at the mercy of sea and storm—these are the problems about which there are no speeches. Yet without provincial resources to support master and slave and supplement our agriculture, our woods and country-houses could not feed us. That, senators, is the emperor's anxiety. Its neglect would mean national ruin.'

'As for myself, senators, I emphasize to you that I am human, performing human tasks, and content to occupy the first place among men. That is what I want later generations to

---

[1] *O.G.I.S.* II 458; cf. *Suppl. Epig. Graec.* IV 490.   [2] Dessau, *I.L.S.* 103.
[3] Strab. 13, 4, 8.   [4] Jos. *Ant.* 18, 172.

remember. They will do more than justice to my memory if they judge me worthy of my ancestors, provident of your interests, steadfast in danger, and fearless of animosities incurred in the public service.'[1]

There was the detection of Sejanus' treachery. Tiberius was far from Rome, but his watchful eye unmasked the malefactor and saved the state. Valerius Maximus speaks of Tiberius' 'caelestis providentia'.

'The eyes of the gods did not sleep, the heavenly bodies kept their accustomed power, and above all the author and protector of our security by divine wisdom took foresight that his great merits should not vanish in the collapse of the whole world.'[2]

He calls Augustus and Tiberius the country's divine eyes.[3] So at Corinth an altar was erected and priesthood established to Providentia Augusta and Salus Publica; the people of Interamna celebrated the escape with a dedication to Tiberius' Providence; in Crete, a senatorial province, this is coupled with the name of the senate.[4] Italica issued a coin bearing on the reverse an altar inscribed PROVIDENTIA AVGVSTA. It is reasonable to suppose that the Ara Providentiae Augustae at Rome dates from this same period.[5]

Claudius was genuinely diligent for the good of the empire, and it was no mere flattery when a governor told the Ephesians that the emperor had taken the whole human race under his protection,[6] or when a senatorial decree began 'cum providentia optumi principis tectis quoque urbis nostrae et totius aeternitati Italiae prospexerit'.[7] ('Since the foresight of our noble sovereign has been exercised in behalf of the very houses of our capital and the permanence of Italy as a whole.') It is more curious to find it under Nero, who was not thus diligent. Perhaps it was mere optimism which led the Alexandrian mints to turn out coins inscribed with 'the foresight of the new Augustus'. It was in his reign that the insinuating Tertullus, accusing Paul, spoke flatter-

---

[1] Tac. Ann. 3, 54; 4, 38.   [2] Val. Max. *Pref.*; IX xi Ext. 4.   [3] id. IV 3, 3.
[4] Dessau, *I.L.S.* 157; 158; cf. 3793.   [5] *C.I.L.* VI 2028 d 15; 2033 5.
[6] *S.E.G.* IV 516.   [7] Dessau, *I.L.S.* 6043.

ingly of the foresight of the governor Felix;[1] like master, like man. Later in the reign dedications to Providentia represent the unmasking of conspiracies. But Tiberius Julius Alexander in his edict to the Egyptians spoke of the beneficence and foresight of the emperor in a wider sphere; this may be Nero or Galba.[2] With the uncertainties that followed Nero's death foresight was especially demanded in the stabilization of the succession. When Galba chose an heir sacrifices were offered to Securitas and Providentia, but after his death his scheme collapsed, and the Stoic Musonius was twitted with having claimed that the world was governed by Providence; he dissociated any such belief from the fortunes of the emperor. The collocation of Greek and Roman ideas is important and interesting.[3] Vespasian secured the throne and stabilized the succession, and a remarkable outburst of coins proclaims the emperor's foresight. An early issue of Titus with this inscription shows him receiving the power from his father. Nerva too praises the foresight of the senate, and Pliny's *Panegyric* is eloquent upon the Divine Providence which established him. But the wider aim is not lost, and Domitian, without using the word, ends an edict: 'ut . . . provinciales nostri per benevolentiam nostram consultum sibi esse laetentur'[4] ('so that . . . our subjects may rejoice that through our kindness care has been exercised on their behalf'). A noble passage depicts the care for his subjects expected of Trajan.

'These are cares worthy of a *princeps*, even of a god, to reconcile rival cities, and to restrain arrogant peoples by reason as much as by authority, to prevent unfairness on the part of magistrates, to reverse anything done amiss, and lastly like some swift star to visit all places, to hear all things, and wheresoever your aid is involved to appear and stand by like a god.'[5]

With Trajan the theme pulsates through the imperial propaganda. It occurs on coins. An altar at Tarracina was dedicated to the emperor's foresight,[6] an arch at Ancona (commemorating the new harbour) to the far-seeing emperor.[7] Pliny takes up the theme

---

[1] Acts XXIV 3. [2] Dittenberger, *O.G.I.S.* 669. [3] Arr. *Epict.* XV 14.
[4] *C.I.L.* 13569. [5] Plin. *Pan.* 80. [6] Dessau, *I.L.S.* 282. [7] ib. 298.

in his letters,[1] and Dio Chrysostom's third speech on Kingship stresses the duty of the ruler to care for the weaker with the foresight nature herself shows.[2]

The paternalism of the second century was the great age of *providentia*, and Hadrianic issues attest both the providence of the gods and the foresight of the emperor; the two are scarcely to be separated. If Pliny encouraged Trajan to travel with the swiftness of a star, Hadrian fulfilled the promise. Three great journeys showed him exercising his *providentia*. The first, from 120 to 125, covered Gaul, Germany, Britain, Spain, Morocco, Africa, Asia Minor, the Euphrates, the Balkans, and Greece. The second, from 128 to 133, took in Greece, Asia Minor, and Egypt, and the third, from 134 to 135, was occasioned by the emergency in Palestine.

'A great series of coins,' says Charlesworth, 'the ADVENTUS series, shows us different provinces and peoples welcoming the advent of their emperor, kneeling as a suppliant figure before him and Hadrian is here dressed not as a general, but wears the toga—a peaceful citizen come on works of peace.'[3]

He himself declared that he had won more by peaceful means than the others by war. His administration was humane. Equity and intention became cardinal principles of law. 'Voluntas spectatur non exitus.' The famous story of the woman who told him that if he had not time for her complaints he had no right to be emperor indicates his conception of imperial responsibility—the *providentia* which cares for all his subjects. It is small wonder that Pausanias called him the ruler 'who gave the utmost to all for the happiness of his subjects'.[4] It could not so last; the journeys would have worn out a lesser man, and Antoninus preferred to stay at Rome, like a benevolent spider in the middle of his web, receiving and acting upon messages from all over the empire. But this concept of government is ultimately the same. Fronto, Marcus Aurelius and Aristides all praise the foresight of Antoninus.[5] Almost any action of the emperor is henceforth a manifestation of foresight.

---

[1] Plin. *Ep.* VIII 17, 2; X 54; 61; 77; 108.　　　　[2] D. Chr. III 43; 62.
[3] M. P. Charlesworth, *P.B.A.*, XXIII (1937), p. 118.　　　　[4] Paus. I 5, 5.
[5] Fronto 224 (Naber); M. Aur. *Med.* I 16, 2; Aristid. *Ad Rom.* 36.

'When Marcus and Commodus propose to cut down the expense of gladiatorial games their *providentia* is praised; it is to the divine *providentia* of Commodus that the oppressed coloni of the Saltus Burunitanus appeal; in the reign of Alexander Severus a coin depicts *Providentia Augusta* with the attributes of Annona; the *providentia* of Gordian is praised because he restored a road "diutina incuria prorsus corruptam" and it is to that same *pronoia* that the men of Scaptopara, distressed and ill-treated, apply for pity and protection.'[1]

Providentia deorum is almost a catchphrase of Aurelian's propaganda.[2] At the end of the century Diocletian puts PROVID DEORVM QVIES AVGG on his coins and shows Tranquillitas and Providentia facing one another, and dedications once again celebrate his foresight in bringing peace.[3] An orator addresses Philip the Arabian (as we may reasonably assume) in terms which compare the *providentia* of the monarch with the Divine Providence; the sovereign he says must resemble the Ruler of the Universe 'alike in his clemency towards and his care for all those whom he rules'. Panegyrists invoke Maximian as 'divinae providentiae Imperator', and speak of the way that neither the beauty of natural scenery nor famous cities nor victorious celebrations distract him from the never-ending tasks of government. His *providentia* and *auctoritas* are linked together, and he is invoked as 'Imperator Aeterne'.[4] Eumenius, in reopening the school at Autun, speaks of the four rulers in similar language.[5] Constantine and Licinius are welcomed as rulers whose *virtus* and *providentia* are steadily improving the lot of their subjects. The panegyrics of Constantine show the typical pattern of imperial virtues. *Clementia* (or *misericordia*, which, despite Seneca, comes to much the same thing, as an imperial attribute), *iustitia* and *providentia* rub shoulders together; in one passage of particular interest the emperor's forethought springs from his *philanthropia* and leads to the security of his people.[6] In the fourth century *Tua*

[1] M. P. Charlesworth, *H.T.R.*, XXIX (1936), pp. 119–20.
[2] A. D. Nock, *H.T.R.*, XXII (1930), pp. 266–8.
[3] Dessau, *I.L.S.* 618, 637; *C.I.L.* VI 1144. [4] Pan. Vet. VII 7, 12; X 5; XI 4.
[5] ib. IX 4; 8; 10. [6] ib. V 2; VI 3; 6; VIII 6.

Providentia is a normal mode of addressing the emperor, alongside *Tua Clementia* and *Tua Pietas*. With Julian we expect the maintenance of traditional Roman language with a sprinkling of Greek philosophy, and Mamertinus speaks of his 'ingenti divinaque providentia' ('foresight, great and godlike'). Elsewhere he attributes to him the four cardinal virtues, *providentia* appearing in the place of wisdom.[1] The concept remains even with the Christianization of the empire. Theodosius is protected by the forethought of the powers behind the universe.[2] In 450 Marcian made a pronouncement upon his imperial obligation: 'It is our care', he said, 'to provide for the benefit of the human race'—'utilitati humani generis providere'—'for this is what we aim at night and day, that all who live under our rule may both be defended by the protection of our army from the assaults of our enemies and may also enjoy peace, free leisure, and security.' Similarly Leo the Wise, in propounding a measure of reform, takes as his justification that 'all things have been made dependent solely on the providence and government of the sovereign'. As late as the eleventh century we find the Byzantine mystic Symeon evaluating the function of kingship as being 'to exercise providence over the subjects of his kingdom'. Charlesworth sums up this evidence with the pertinent comment: 'Monarchy, in fact, is providence.'[3]

Like *clementia*, *providentia* can be exercised only by a superior towards inferiors. It is an imperial attribute; indeed even more than *clementia* it is shown first by god to man, and so by the ruler who stands in the same relation to his subjects as god to man. From the ruler it passes down through the hierarchical structure of society, to the baron or patron, who again stands in the same relation to his dependants as the emperor holds towards the empire as a whole. It was one of the watchwords of paternalism. As an imperial ideal it was not ignoble. As an expression of God's relationship to man it retains some cogency. But it cannot express man's response to God. It does not cover the attitude of a dependant to a benefactor. It has no place in the normal interchange of a community of equals.

[1] ib. III 5; 21.
[2] ib. II 6.
[3] M. P. Charlesworth, *P.B.A.*, XXIII (1937), p. 126.

The Virtues of a Roman Emperor

Clementia and *providentia* then were two of the virtues which came to be newly stressed in imperial Rome. We may couple with them *liberalitas* or munificence. Augustus' lavishness in serving the multitude was a byword; he knew which side his political bread was buttered. He 'liked this sort of entertainment', says Tacitus, 'and thought it looked democratic to join in the people's amusements'.[1] He himself boasts of the numerous shows for which he was responsible, in the course of which some 10,000 gladiators fought and 3,500 wild animals were slaughtered. He also staged a naval battle as a spectacle, digging a lake for the purpose; thirty warships were involved, as well as smaller craft.[2] Spectacle is the opiate of the people. Suetonius says that he surpassed everyone in the frequency and variety of the performances he offered.[3] Eighty days a year were occupied in this way, apart from special celebrations. Recipients of the corn-dole were raised from 150,000 to 320,000 and though the figure was later stabilized at 200,000 it was a marked increase. The emperor gives a long list of his benefactions. Actual cash distributions between 29 and 2 B.C. seem to have amounted to something like 50 million sesterces; in all he claims to have given to the Treasury, the commons, and to discharged soldiers the remarkable sum of 600 million sesterces,[4] and this does not take account of the immense expenditure on restoring old buildings and erecting new, on constructing roads, aqueducts, and other public works. Augustus in short set the standards of a paternalistic empire. By contrast Tiberius had a reputation for parsimony.[5] None the less, *liberalitas* and *munificentia* are found not infrequently in our records of the reign even when these are hostile to Tiberius, and it is probable that he intended it to be one of the ideals of his rule. The reputation for miserliness came partly from that careful husbanding of imperial resources which left the state at his death in a healthy position financially, partly because he was, as a great soldier, temperamentally uninterested in the spectacles and perhaps also aware of their

---

[1] Tac. *Ann.* I 54. This and some of the other Tacitus translations in this chapter are taken from Michael Grant's excellent version.

[2] Aug. *R.G.* 22–3.   [3] Suet. *Aug.* 43–5.   [4] Aug. *R.G.* 15–18.

[5] Suet. *Tib.* 34; 46; Tac. *Ann.* I 54.

corrupting influence, partly because he was careful not to encourage extravagance and wastefulness among Roman society. Seneca tells an instructive story of him. Marius Nepos asked him to save him from his creditors. Tiberius requested a list of their names; this was apparently regarded as an unwarrantable inquisition. However, the list was supplied. Tiberius paid the debts and wrote to Nepos saying that he had done so and adding some insulting advice. Tiberius had in this way rescued Nepos from debt without putting him under any obligation to himself. One might think that this was commendable, but Seneca describes Tiberius' policy as censorship not generosity.[1] Velleius, who is biased in Tiberius' favour, speaks of his readiness to help needy senators, provided that it could be done without encouraging them to extravagant living,[2] and we need not doubt the truth of this. We know of his benefactions from his initial fulfilment of Augustus' legacies to the troops, doubled from his own resources, to his final legacies which included men whom Augustus had omitted.[3] When Claudius' house was destroyed by fire, Tiberius restored it out of his own *liberalitas*.[4] When Marcus Piso came from Syria as his father's forerunner, Tiberius rewarded him with *liberalitas* such as it was customary to show to young noblemen.[5] Even Tacitus speaks of his 'grata liberalitas' towards M. Aemilius Lepidus.[6] In A.D. 17 a disastrous earthquake occurred in Asia Minor. Tiberius remitted the taxes for twelve of the cities for a period of five years, and actually gave 10,000,000 sesterces for the relief of Sardes which had suffered most. The unsympathetic Tacitus calls this a 'magnifica largitio',[7] and it was typical of his dealings with such disasters in the provinces. 'The emperor's munificence claims for its sphere of action the losses inflicted by fortune, not merely on private citizens but on whole cities.'[8] So Velleius, admiringly. In A.D. 27 there was a serious fire on the Mons Caelius at Rome; Tiberius compensated the sufferers in proportion to their losses, and 'by his liberality even encouraged unknown victims to apply for help'. Suetonius in this context speaks of his *munificentia*;

---

[1] Sen. *De Ben.* 2, 7–8.   [2] Vell. II 129, 3.
[3] Suet. *Tib.* 48; 76; D.C. 59, 2, 1–3.   [4] Suet. *Claud.* 6, 2.   [5] Tac. *Ann.* III 8.
[6] ib. II 48.   [7] ib.   [8] Vell, II 126, 4.

Tacitus uses the same word and couples it with *largitio*; Velleius uses the central word *liberalitas*.[1] In short, says Tacitus, 'the emperor was prepared to spend in a good cause, and kept this good quality long after his others were gone'.[2] Tiberius was self-effacing, and this is one reason why *liberalitas* does not appear in inscriptions or coin-types during the reign, but his practice and example is clear.

The next landmark is Seneca's treatise *De Beneficiis*. This long and frankly tedious[3] document is of importance, because it is directed, not to the emperor, but to an unknown noble named Aebutius Liberalis; we may hope that he lived up to his name; Seneca describes him as naturally inclined to generosity.[4] We happily do not need to delay over the details of this treatise, over the analysis of gratitude and ingratitude, and such questions as whether a slave can be his master's benefactor, or whether a man can be his own benefactor. A benefaction is defined as an action of goodwill, which brings joy to the recipient and to the giver because of his act; it must be an act of a man's inmost nature, and not done contrary to his inclinations.[5] Its test is that a man forgets his own interests in order to be of use to someone else.[6] The benefactor should have an eye to the necessities of life, then to those things which are useful without being strictly necessary, then to those things which bring pleasure or happiness. In any event he should ensure that his gifts are durable—a test which leads Seneca into the fatuous doctrine that it is preferable to give statues to clothes, for the latter will soon wear out.[7] It is not easy to discern in the arid philosophy of this work anything of the noble paternalism prevalent fifty years later, or any real sense of human need or human solidarity. There is however one passage which merits attention. It comes in the course of a polemic against Epicurean views. According to Seneca the Epicurean view is that virtue is the slave of the pleasures, and when we give, we give only in the hope that our gifts will be requited. Seneca's answer is that God gives without the hope or expectation of any return.[8] The

[1] Suet. *Tib.* 48; Tac. *Ann.* IV 64; Vell. II 130, 2.   [2] Tac. *Ann.* I 75.
[3] As he almost implies himself: Sen. *De Ben.* 5, 1, 1.   [4] Sen. *De Ben.* 5, 1, 2.
[5] ib. 1, 6, 1.   [6] ib. 5, 11, 4.   [7] ib. 1, 11–12.   [8] ib. 4, 2–7.

passage is important for two reasons. In the first place, it shows clearly the hierarchical structure which infests this framework of thought which we are at present examining. The emperor stands to his subjects, the patron to his dependants, as God to mankind. Secondly, and more constructively, it introduces the religious dimension into ethics.

But the great age of the benefactions was the second century;[1] it is then, in Hadrian's reign, that *liberalitas* appears in the coin-legends. The picture we draw from Pliny's letters is confirmed by innumerable inscriptions. The emperors set the example. All, from Vespasian to Marcus Aurelius, gave liberal endowments for higher education.[2] Nerva initiated benefactions for the children of needy parents. We may discount much that Pliny says in his panegyric of Trajan, except in so far as it represents the frame-work of mind which it was imperial policy to foster. But in-scriptional evidence gives us factual detail.[3] Here we read of a large loan to landed proprietors, intended no doubt to stimulate local agriculture, the interest being five per cent instead of the usual twelve per cent. The income from the interest was then to be devoted to looking after three hundred poor children till the boys were eighteen and the girls fourteen. Hadrian extended Trajan's work in this field, and Antoninus and Marcus Aurelius established fresh foundations for girls.[4]

When we turn to buildings, the story is the same. Trajan, for example, built the great forum and column which bear his name, in the centre of Rome; he constructed aqueducts and baths, docks, warehouses, roads.[5] A list of Hadrian's works would be inter-minable. At Rome alone we may think of the Pantheon, and the Castel S. Angelo, the bridging of the Tiber, temples of Venus, Rome and Neptune, the restoration of Augustus' forum and Agrippa's baths. Outside Rome his biographer makes the per-tinent comment, 'He gave a public show and erected a public building in almost every city'.[6] This list of imperial benefactions

---

[1] Excellently treated in S. Dill, *Roman Society from Nero to Marcus Aurelius*.
[2] Suet. *Vesp.* 18; S.H.A. *Hadr.* 16, 8; *Ant. P.* 11, 3.   [3] *Or. Henz.* 6664.
[4] S.H.A. *Hadr.* 7; *Ant. P.* 8; *M. Aur.* 26.
[5] D.C. 48, 7, 15; Plin. *Paneg.* 29; 51.   [6] S.H.A. *Hadr.* 19, 2.

could, of course, be much extended. The most important fact about it was that it provided an effective example for others. They were men of wealth, and some not even unduly wealthy, and they showed a sense of the responsibilities attaching to wealth which is rare in any age. Of Pliny we know most: he tells us himself, and may be forgiven a certain pride; was he not anxious to emulate Cicero in all things? What is so impressive about Pliny's benefactions, which were mainly directed towards his home town of Como is, first, that they were sacrificial, for he was not so inordinately wealthy that he would not feel the money going, and, secondly, that they were so eminently sensible. Not for him the mimes and gladiatorial displays which perished as soon as they were presented; his gifts were indeed *mansura*—a library, the partial endowment of a school, a foundation to care for the children of the poor, a temple of Ceres with broad colonnades to shelter the traders at the great fair.[1] How many men of wealth can boast that they have used their money so wisely? Privately, he showed the same discerning benevolence, making up a dowry, helping a friend in imminent danger, relieving a young lady of inherited debts, offering to make the estate of Romatius Firmus up to equestrian dimensions, looking after his old nurse in her retirement.[2] It is a sustained record of thoughtful liberality.

Equally outstanding are the benefactions of Herodes Atticus later in the century. His munificence, writes Dill, 'was extended to cities in Italy, as well as to Corinth, Thessaly, Euboea, Boeotia, Elis, and pre-eminently to Athens. He gave an aqueduct to Canusium and Olympia, a racecourse to Delphi, a roofed theatre to Corinth. He provided sulphur baths at Thermopylae for the visitors from Thessaly and the shores of the Maliac gulf. He aided in the restoration of Oricum in Epirus, and liberally recruited the resources of many another decaying town in Greece. He was certainly benevolent, but he had also a passion for splendid fame, and cherished an ambition to realize the dream of Nero, by cutting a canal across the Corinthian Isthmus. But Attica, where he was born, and where he had a princely house on the Ilissus, was

---

[1] Plin. *Ep.* 1, 8; 1, 19; 4, 1; 4, 13; 5, 7; 7, 18; 9, 12, etc.
[2] ib. 1, 19; 2, 4; 3, 11; 6, 3; 6, 32, etc.

the supreme object of his bounty. In his will he left each Athenian citizen an annual gift of a mina. He would offer to the Virgin Goddess a sacrifice of a hundred oxen on a single day; and, when the great festivals came round, he used to feast the people by their tribes, as well as the resident strangers, on couches in the Ceramicus. He restored the ancient shrines and stadia with costly marbles. And, in memory of Rhegilla, his wife, he built at the foot of the acropolis a theatre for 6,000 spectators, roofed in with cedar wood, which, to the eye of Pausanias, surpassed all similar structures in its splendour.'[1] This is more vainglorious and less discriminating than Pliny. It is more munificent only in so far as it springs from almost boundless resources. It is full of all the dangers of irresponsible patronage. But on the whole its results were beneficial and, though the scale is exceptional, it is not atypical of the age.

Already in the first century these benefactions were beginning. We are apt to forget, amid the welter of his extravagance, the real generosity of Nero to the citizens suffering from the Great Fire, and indeed many of his plans for reconstructing the city were to the undoubted benefit of its inhabitants.[2] In the civil wars which followed Nero's death Cremona suffered terribly; its temples and forums were restored by private generosity.[3] Dio Chrysostom's grandfather expended his entire patrimony on public benefactions.[4] The elder Pliny tells us of two doctors, whose whole earnings, which were not inconsiderable, went in gifts to the city of Naples.[5] Later we find Ummidia Quadratilla presenting Casinum with a temple and amphitheatre,[6] an old officer of the fourth legion providing free bathing at Suessa Senonum for everyone including slave girls,[7] a priestess providing a temple at Calama in Numidia and being honoured with five statues in gratitude.[8] The mood of the period is indeed expressed in an insignificant epitaph. 'Bene fac, hoc tecum feres' ('Be generous; you *can* take it with you').[9]

---

[1] S. Dill, *Roman Society from Nero to Marcus Aurelius*, pp. 225–6; cf. Philostrat. *Vit. Soph.* 2, 1–6.   [2] Tac. *Ann.* 15, 39; Suet. *Nero* 16.   [3] Tac. *Hist.* 3, 34.
[4] D. Chr. *Or.* 46.   [5] Plin. *N.H.* 29, 5.   [6] *Or.* 781.
[7] *Or. Henz.* 2287.   [8] *C.I.L.* VIII 5366.   [9] *Or. Henz.* 6042.

The Virtues of a Roman Emperor

The opening words of Gibbon's monumental study of the decline of the Roman Empire are these:

'In the second century of the Christian era, the empire of Rome comprehended the fairest part of the earth, and the most civilized portion of mankind. The frontiers of that extensive monarchy were guarded by ancient renown and disciplined valour. The gentle, but powerful, influence of laws and manners had gradually cemented the union of the provinces. Their peaceful inhabitants enjoyed and abused the advantages of wealth and luxury. The image of a free constitution was preserved with decent reverence; the Roman senate appeared to possess the sovereign authority, and devolved on the emperors all the executive powers of government. During a happy period of more than four score years the public administration was conducted by the virtue and abilities of Nerva, Trajan, Hadrian, and the two Antonines.'

In his third chapter he elaborates this.

'If a man were called to fix the period in the history of the world during which the condition of the human race was most happy and prosperous, he would without hesitation name that which elapsed from the death of Domitian to the accession of Commodus. The vast extent of the Roman empire was governed by absolute power, under the guidance of virtue and wisdom. The armies were restrained by the firm but gentle hand of four successive emperors, whose characters and authority commanded involuntary respect. The forms of the civil administration were carefully preserved by Nerva, Trajan, Hadrian, and the Antonines, who delighted in the image of liberty, and were pleased with considering themselves as the accountable ministers of the laws. Such princes deserved the honour of restoring the republic, had the Romans of their day been capable of enjoying a rational freedom.

'The labours of these monarchs were overpaid by the immense reward that inseparably waited on their success; by the honest pride of virtue, and by the exquisite delight of beholding

205

the general happiness of which they were the authors. A just, but melancholy, reflection embittered, however, the noblest of human enjoyments. They must often have recollected the instability of a happiness which depended on the character of a single man. The fatal moment was perhaps approaching, when some licentious youth, or some jealous tyrant, would abuse, to the destruction, that absolute power, which they had exerted for the benefit of their people. The ideal restraints of the senate and the laws might serve to display the virtues, but could never correct the vices, of the emperor. The military force was a blind and irresistible instrument of oppression, and the corruption of Roman manners would always supply flatterers eager to applaud, and ministers prepared to serve, the fear or the avarice, the lust or the cruelty, of their masters.'

It is doubtful whether anyone would write in those words today; the passage is redolent with Gibbon's century and his own personality. But, granted its premisses, it is a shrewd and cutting characterization of the age in which the imperial virtues which we are studying in this chapter were supreme. It will not do to underestimate them. Within its limitations the age was one of remarkably widespread prosperity and happiness. It shows paternalism at its highest. But it carried within itself the seeds of its own decay, and that plain historical fact shows why these imperial virtues could never become the basis of universal morality.

First there appears at times an intolerable self-contradiction in the paean of panegyric lavished upon these princes of paternalism; it lurks behind the conscious irony of Gibbon's judgement, though he did not see it. It can best be seen in Pliny's words to Trajan: 'Iubes esse liberos; erimus' ('You command us to be free; free we shall be').[1] Such freedom is illusory; it depends upon the continued goodwill of the emperor.

Secondly, there is the fact which modern moralists rightly deplore, even when their analysis is itself defective, that charity (in its crude sense) is no substitute for equity. There is something pathetic in the spectacle of men of vast riches in a world of mal-

[1] Plin. *Paneg.* 66, 4.

206

distribution throwing a sop to the Cerberus of their conscience by redistributing some part of their excess, or the men of power in a world where power is inequitably divided claiming it as a virtue that they have refrained from an arbitrary use of that power.

Thirdly, paternalism, however noble, can only go a limited distance in building up a sense of responsibility. In a world of 'haves' and 'have-nots' the example of a beneficent monarch can extend widely among the other privileged oligarchs. But it does not start at the grass-roots. This is the trouble with *providentia*. The emperor takes so much thought for his subjects that he deprives them of the faculty of taking thought for themselves and for one another. This is the meaning of Mill's epigrammatic saying that a good despotism is worse than a bad despotism; it is more enervating.

Fourthly, the imperial virtues are all, by their very nature, the virtues of one whose authority is absolute. Here Gibbon's analysis comes to the fore. The strength of the second century lay in the nature of the succession, each emperor adopting his best successor. As soon as the hereditary principle reasserts itself through the pathetic and over-praised person of Marcus Aurelius, the system is doomed. The exercise of the paternalistic virtues presupposes a situation in which the person who is not governed by those virtues can do untold damage.

Finally, all the imperial virtues look downwards. This gives them one solid strength. They can be seen as reflections of God's attitude to his world, and Stoic and Cynic moralists were not slow to draw the lesson. But they are subject to the same defect which we have seen infecting the Greek virtue of *philanthropia*, which also became a standard attribute of the better Hellenistic monarch. They are all condescending. They cannot be part of man's response to God, nor the cement which binds together a society of equals.

XI

THE CONTRIBUTION OF
JUDAISM[1]

ANY STUDY OF the way in which Christian values ousted
earlier value-schemes in the ancient world must take some
account of Judaism. It is true that Judaea lies geographically
aloof from the main centres of the Graeco-Roman world. It is true
that the Jewish intellectual and spiritual development presents us
with a similar sense of isolation, not least because of the exclusiveness of the Jewish tradition; it is only in the later period that Persian and Greek ideas modify the picture, and then peripherally
rather than centrally. But it is also true that Christianity emerged
in a Jewish environment and its characteristic emphasis cannot be
well understood except against that background. Hosea is not far
from the mind of Jesus. Furthermore in dispersion the Jews were
not a negligible element in the Roman dominion. At Alexandria
they formed a considerable section of the population. At Rome
they were expelled from time to time. Juvenal's famous complaint
that the Syrian Orontes has flooded into the Tiber no doubt
includes the Jews among other Eastern immigrants; he knows
something of them as does Horace before him.[2] Intrinsically, they
have an interesting and important contribution to make to this
pattern of ideas.

The ethical code of Judaism is laid down, often in minute detail,
in the Law. Such a scheme had manifest advantages. It ensured
that the content of Jewish ethics was concrete and not merely
abstract. After all, it is by their fruits that people are known. But
it had its disadvantages. The emphasis was on outward observance, and that was compatible with decidedly unethical inner

---

[1] I owe a major debt in this chapter to N. H. Snaith, *The Distinctive Ideas of the
Old Testament.*   [2] Juv. 3, 62; 3, 296; Hor. *Sat.* I 5, 100.

attitudes. Hence Jesus, in the Sermon on the Mount, restates the commandments with a deeper insight and an inward emphasis.

> 'Ye have heard that it was said by them of old time, Thou shalt not kill. . . . But I say unto you, That whosoever is angry with his brother without a cause shall be in danger of the judgement. . . . Ye have heard that it was said by them of old time, Thou shalt not commit adultery. But I say unto you, That whosoever looketh upon a woman to lust after her hath committed adultery with her already in his heart.'[1]

Of the decalogue, only the first and last commandments have any inward reference. Of course it may be said that the whole of the Law hangs upon the first commandment, and this is no doubt in theory true. But—as Clough was to see in his own professedly Christian generation—theory and practice did not always conform.

> *Thou shalt have one God only; who*
> *Would be at the expense of two?*
> *No graven images may be*
> *Worshipped, except the currency:*
> *Swear not at all; for, for thy curse*
> *Thine enemy is none the worse:*
> *At Church on Sunday to attend*
> *Will serve to keep the world thy friend:*
> *Honour thy parents; that is, all*
> *From whom advancement may befall:*
> *Thou shalt not kill; but need'st not strive*
> *Officiously to keep alive:*
> *Do not adultery commit;*
> *Advantage rarely comes of it:*
> *Thou shalt not steal; an empty feat,*
> *When it's so lucrative to cheat:*
> *Bear not false witness; let the lie*
> *Have time on its own wings to fly:*
> *Thou shalt not covet, but tradition*
> *Approves all forms of competition.*[2]

[1] Matt V 21–2, 27–8, etc.   [2] A. H. Clough, *The Latest Decalogue.*

Furthermore the legalistic approach to morality blunted the sense of proportion. 'Whosoever offendeth in one point is guilty of the whole Law'—and that point might be a profound issue of morality or a trivial ritual observance. Prophets and psalmists alike pointed out that the laws enjoining external purity were only important in so far as they led to a genuine purity of life and spirit, but their lesson seems to have struck home to comparatively few in practice. It is Jesus' repeated criticism of the religious leaders of his own day that they are so absorbed in external observances that they forget the things which really matter.[1]

To say this is in no sense to deny or to underrate the high morality of the Mosaic code. Jesus himself declared that he came not to destroy it but to fulfil it. To a young man who asked him the way to eternal life his first injunction was to observe the decalogue, and only when it was clear that the inquirer was basing his life on these principles did Jesus go further and lay upon him a deeper, and more sacrificial, demand.[2] The two great commandments of Christ are both to be found in the Pentateuch; what is significant is that he singles them out and exalts them above the others.[3] Perhaps the most notably distinctive injunction in the books of the Law is care for strangers and foreigners. This is seen as part of a general duty to help the needy, but it is specifically linked with the fact that the Israelites had themselves known what it was to be foreigners in a strange land. God, it is said,

'executes the judgement of the fatherless and widow, and loves the stranger, giving him food and clothing. So too you ought to show love towards the stranger, for you were strangers in the land of Egypt.'[4]

'You must not hate the Edomites, for they are your brothers; you must not hate the Egyptians, for you were strangers in their country.'[5]

'The stranger who lives with you shall be to you as one born

[1] e.g. Matt. XV 2; XXIII 25; Luke XI 38–9.   [2] Mark X 17–22.
[3] Mark XII 28–34; Deut. VI 4; Lev. XIX 18.
[4] Deut. X 18–19.   [5] ib. XXIII 7.

among you, and you shall love him as yourselves, for you were strangers in the land of Egypt. I am the Lord your God.'[1]

Here we have the two springs of moral action, the imaginative understanding of and self-identification with the other person. It makes the prudential morality of later Judaism seem shoddy and shabby.

'If your enemy be hungry, give him bread to eat, and if he be thirsty give him water to drink; for in this way you heap coals of fire upon his head, and the Lord shall reward you.'[2]

It is more than a little strange that a religion which so mightily exalted God—'My thoughts are not your thoughts, neither are my ways your ways,' saith the Lord—should take the Divine Being as the standard of human morality, but it was so, and not a few of the contradictions which have bedevilled Christian ethical thinking arise from the attempt to hold together that fact with belief in a God who is 'wholly other'. The result has generally been the rejection of a genuinely Christian ethic and the substitution of some form of worldly wisdom.[3] The conclusion is manifestly false. The legitimate analogy between divine and human action is drawn time and again in the Old Testament. A notable example is Hosea discerning in his relations with his wayward wife something of God's dealing with Israel, and then changing the image from marital to parental love. Another is in the book of Jonah where God uses the prophet's attitude to the gourd as a parallel to his own attitude to Babylon. Hence it is that Leviticus can declare, 'You are to be holy even as the Lord your God is holy.' Jesus, to whom God's Fatherhood of his earthly children was not analogical but direct and immediate, took up these words and extended them. 'You are to be perfect, even as your Father in Heaven is perfect.' It follows that in seeking to analyse and examine the moral values which appear in the religious ethic of Judaism we have to start from the nature of God, and see how the Jews applied their vision of God's nature to man's calling in this world. Three aspects of this especially demand our attention.

[1] Lev. XIX 34.   [2] Prov. XXV 21–2; cf. regrettably Rom. XII 20.
[3] See for example the ethical writings of Reinhold Niebuhr.

The first of these is righteousness (*tsedeq*). The root meaning of the word appears to be 'straightness', though this cannot be said to have been certainly established.[1] *Tsedeq* is the norm of conduct in this world. This norm depends upon God; Hebrew thought could not, like Greek thought, accept the idea of a power behind God to which even God must conform. The revolutionary transformation of religious thought by the great eighth-century prophets consists centrally in the fact that they moralized the idea of God's holiness by linking it with righteousness. Holiness (*qodesh*) has as its central note the idea of separation.[2] In the Old Testament it comes to denote the peculiar quality by which God is God. It has a general reference to what Rudolf Otto has taught us to call the 'numinous'; its particular application is to Yahweh alone. The fact however that God is separate does not mean that He is remote; it merely marks off God from man. 'I am God and not man, holy, in your midst.'[3] The God of the Old Testament is not the Creator conceived by the eighteenth-century Deists, who winds up Paley's watch and then abandons it upon the desert island of eternity to look after itself. He is not the Aristotelian pure Form engaged in unending self-contemplation so that his thinking is a thinking upon thinking. (It is a tribute to the ingenuity of the scholastics that they succeeded in identifying this abstract entity with the Biblical God.) He is not one of the indifferent deities of the Epicureans.

> *Who haunt*
> *The lucid interspace of world and world,*
> *Where never creeps a cloud, or moves a wind,*
> *Nor ever falls the least white star of snow,*
> *Nor ever lowest roll of thunder moans,*
> *Nor sound of human sorrow ever mounts to mar*
> *Their sacred everlasting calm.*[4]

[1] Delitzch, *Commentary on the Psalms* I 84 as against Skinner, 'Righteousness' in *H.D.B.* IV 274.

[2] Von Baudissim, 'Der Begriff der Heiligkeit in Alten Testament', *Studien zur semitischen Religionsgeschichte* (1878) II 20; as against the view which derives it from a root meaning 'bright'. [3] Hos. XI 9.

[4] Tennyson, *Lucretius*, quoted by H. W. Robinson, *The Christian Doctrine of the Holy Spirit*, p. 76.

He is the living God, active within His world. He has His will for this world; its standard is *tsedeq*. 'The holy God is sanctified in righteousness.'[1] Hence unrighteousness cannot abide His presence. The supreme account of the holiness of God comes in Isaiah's vision 'in the year that King Uzziah died'.[2] The whole passage is instinct with the sense of the numinous. But what is Isaiah's response to the vision?

> 'Woe is me! for I am undone; because I am a man of unclean lips and I dwell in the midst of a people of unclean lips; for mine eyes have seen the King, the Lord of hosts.'

There are three things of great importance about the Jewish conception of righteousness. In the first place it is directly dependent upon God. Snaith writes, with deep understanding, of the eighth-century prophets:

> 'Their whole attitude was dependent directly upon their new-found knowledge of God. This knowledge was religious rather than speculative. By this we mean that their knowledge was not based upon any notion of the best human conduct, nor upon theories of "the good for man". Their insistence upon the necessity of the humanitarian virtues did not rest upon any theory of the equality of man, nor upon any conviction as to the brotherhood or solidarity of mankind, even though that might include in practice, as often still it does, only men of their own race or colour or class. They made no idealization of human conduct. The idea of the Supreme God as the god of virtue, in whatever sense, may have arisen among other peoples as an idealization of human conduct on the part of the philosophers, but this was not the case in respect of these prophets. The standard by which they judged was not an ethical code. Their standard was what they themselves knew of the very Nature of God Himself. It was because they were so passionately religious that they were so insistently ethical. Knowledge of God came first, and the understanding of right action second.'[3]

[1] Isa. V 16.   [2] ib. VI 1-13.
[3] N. H. Snaith, *The Distinctive Ideas of the Old Testament*, p. 60.

It follows that sin is not primarily transgression but rebellion, a fact which is unfortunately obscured by those mistranslations of the Old Testament which are familiarly read in our churches.

'I have nourished and brought up children and they have rebelled against me.'[1]

'For the rebellion of Jacob is all this, and for the sins of the house of Israel.'[2]

'For I know how manifold are your rebellions and how mighty are your sins.'[3]

Isaiah's famous plea for true repentance shows his conception of the content of righteousness together with this equation of sin and rebellion.

'Wash you, make you clean; put away this evil of your doings from before mine eyes; cease to do evil; learn to do well; seek judgement, relieve the oppressed, judge the fatherless, plead for the widow. Come now, and let us reason together, saith the Lord: though your sins be as scarlet, they shall be as white as snow; though they be red like crimson, they shall be as wool. If ye be willing and obedient, ye shall eat the good of the land; but if ye *refuse and rebel*, ye shall be devoured with the sword: for the mouth of the Lord hath spoken it.'[4]

Secondly, the content of *tsedeq* is ethical—'justice, honesty, and fair dealing between man and man'.[5]

'Wherewith shall I come before the Lord, and bow myself before the high God? Shall I come before him with calves of a year old? Will the Lord be pleased with thousands of rams, or with ten thousands of rivers of oil? Shall I give my first-born for my rebellion, the fruit of my body for the sin of my soul? He hath shewed thee, O man, what is good; and what doth the Lord require of thee, but to do justly, and to love mercy, and to walk humbly with thy God.'[6]

[1] Isa. I 2.   [2] Mic. I 5; cf. III 8.   [3] Amos V 12.   [4] Isa. I 16–20.
[5] N. H. Snaith, *The Distinctive Ideas of the Old Testament*, p. 59.
[6] Mic. VI 6–8.

The prime usage of the word is perhaps closer to 'orderliness'; it would be legitimate in Hebrew to speak of the *tsedeq* of a mechanism which worked properly. But when the question is asked 'How will the world of human relations work properly?' the answer immediately acquires an ethical flavour. In Amos the ethical content is more than usually clear, for offence against righteousness is specifically and almost strangely said to be rejection of the law of God.

'Thus saith the Lord: For three rebellions of Judah and for four, I will not turn away the punishment thereof; because they have despised the law of the Lord and have not kept his commandments.'[1]

Hence his mighty cry, 'Let judgement run down as water, and righteousness as a mighty stream.'[2] A tremendous passage in Isaiah with its grim punning, carries the same lesson. 'He looked for judgement (*mishpat*) but behold oppression (*mispach*); for righteousness (*tsedaqah*) but behold a cry (*tse'aqah*).'[3]

Thirdly *tsedeq* is not legalistic. It is not coldly impersonal. It is linked with a burning compassion for the oppressed. This was realized even by the Greek translators of the Old Testament, who several times render *tsedeq* by *eleos* or *eleemosune*, 'pity'. It is interesting to observe that in Jesus' words, 'Take heed that you do not perform your righteousness before men',[4] a variant reading would replace 'righteousness' by *eleemosune*, 'charity'. When we examine the actual proclamation of the prophets this general tendency is clear. It is most explicit in Amos, who continually fulminates against the rich.

'Thus saith the Lord: for three rebellions of Israel and for four, I will not turn away the punishment thereof; because they sold the righteous for silver, and the poor for a pair of shoes; that pant after the dust of the earth on the head of the poor, and turn aside the way of the meek.'[5]

Of all the great prophets Amos is pre-eminently the prophet of *tsedeq*. But the story is there in them all.

[1] Amos II 4.   [2] ib. V 24.   [3] Isa. V 7.   [4] Matt. VI 1.
[5] Amos II 6–7; cf. V 11–12; VIII 4–6.

'Thy princes are rebellious, and companions of thieves: every one loveth gifts, and followeth after rewards: they judge not the fatherless, neither doth the cause of the widow come unto them. Therefore saith the Lord, the Lord of hosts, the mighty One of Israel, Ah, I will ease me of mine adversaries, and avenge me of mine enemies: and I will turn my hand upon thee, and purely purge away thy dross and take away all thy tin: and I will restore thy judges as at the first, and thy counsellors as at the beginning: afterward thou shalt be called The city of righteousness, the faithful city. Zion shall be redeemed with judgement and they that return of her with righteousness.'[1]

It remains to notice one strange but vital stage in the development of the word, which is associated with the unknown and unnamed prophet of the exile, who, because his writings were attributed to Isaiah, is sometimes called Deutero-Isaiah.[2] In this sublime genius Hebrew monotheism reached its most exalted point. He knew the grandeur of God transcendent; he knew the nearness of God immanent. He knew the redemptive value of suffering. With him the *tsedeq* root is used for 'victory' and even for 'salvation'. Even in the earlier prophets the word has tended to be associated with salvation. The line of thought seems to be that the establishment of *tsedeq* represents the *triumph* of God and the *salvation* of His people. But Deutero-Isaiah goes further.

'Assemble yourselves and come; draw near together, ye that are escaped of the nations; they have no knowledge that set up the wood of their graven image, and pray unto a god that cannot save. Tell ye, and bring them near; yea, let them take counsel together: who hath declared this from ancient time? who hath told it from that time? have not I the Lord? and there is no God else beside me; a *righteous* God and a Saviour; there is none beside me. Look unto me and be saved, all the ends of the earth: for I am God, and there is none else. I have sworn by myself,

[1] Isa. I 23–7.
[2] It is possible that the unknown prophet belongs to the period of the return from exile, not the exile itself. See C. C. Torrey, *The Second Isaiah*.

the word is gone out from myself in *salvation*, and shall not return, That unto me every knee shall bow, every tongue shall swear. Surely shall one say, in the Lord have I *victory* and strength; even to him shall men come and all that are incensed against him shall be ashamed. In the Lord shall all the seed of Israel be *victorious*, and shall glory.'[1]

In this key-passage the derivatives of *tsedeq* are rendered according to their probable meaning in the context, and italicized. The exciting feature of this passage is that the prophet does not say that the establishment of *tsedeq* in Israel shows the victory of God, but that the victory of Israel through God shows the *tsedeq* of God. It is a thought which had been anticipated by Jeremiah, who gives to God the new name of 'Jehovah our *tsedeq*', because of the salvation of Judah and preservation of Israel.[2] Deutero-Isaiah may well have this passage in mind. This association of *tsedeq* with victory and salvation is seen in another key-passage towards the end of the most famous of the Servant songs in Deutero-Isaiah. The passage is much disputed, and has been frequently emended, but it seems to mean 'The *righteous one*, my servant, will make many victorious.'[3] So time and again: 'My *tsedeq* is near; my salvation is gone forth.'[4] The result of this curious development was to deepen the religious meaning of *tsedeq*, but to weaken its moral power. A generation or two later Zechariah is writing in familiar and much mistranslated words, 'Behold thy king cometh unto thee, *tsaddiq* and saved.'[5] *Tsaddiq* here does not mean 'righteous' but 'victorious'. The insight of Amos has not been wholly abandoned but it has been radically changed, and *tsedeq* has lost its place in this particular investigation. None the less the influence of the Septuagint, which rendered *tsedeq* by *dikaiosune*, and thus produced a conflation of Greek ethical speculation with Hebrew religious insight, should not be forgotten, and this combination, with the all-important element of salvation, goes far to explain the difficulties in Paul's doctrine of *justification* by faith; if we look at the later meanings of *tsedeq* the difficulties fall away.

We turn now to *chesed*. In our familiar versions this is usually

---

[1] Isa. XLV 20–5. [2] Jer. XXIII 6. [3] Isa. LIII 11. [4] ib. LI 5. [5] Zech. IX 9.

represented by 'mercy' or 'loving-kindness'. The former of these is inadequate, the latter (Miles Coverdale's word) is much better. Luther daringly made *chesed* equivalent to the New Testament 'grace'. In this he was not wrong, in so far as the word is applied to God. Of man, as Snaith rightly saw, it is closely equivalent to the Latin *pietas*. *Tsedeq*, though a religious term, perhaps depicts God's will for man, rather than His own nature. *Chesed* denotes a quality of God's attitude to man, which must be reflected in man's attitude to God and to his fellows. The word appears to mean originally 'keenness' or 'eagerness'.[1] Its distinctive quality in Hebraic usage arises from the fact that like *pietas*, it is operative only within a particular covenant-relationship.[2] It is selective in the field of its activity and never indiscriminate. Sometimes it means loyalty to an agreement.[3] A particularly interesting example comes in a familiar passage in Deutero-Isaiah: 'All flesh is grass, and all its *chesed* is as the wild flower. The grass withers, the flower fades.'[4] Man has no reliability, no permanence, no steadfastness, no enduring loyalty; these are found only in God.

The peculiar quality of Jewish religion is due to the fact that the Jews stood in a covenant-relationship with their God. Chemosh was the god of Moab, and his destiny and theirs were inextricably intertwined. But Yahweh was not dependent on Israel in that way. He was perhaps originally a power of the mountain, and the god of the Kenites. But as the Israelites passed Mount Sinai He took with them a solemn covenant that they should be His people and He should be their God. The importance of this free relationship for the religious development of the Jews can hardly be overstated. For it meant that the relationship between God and man, being free and not constrained by the sort of inevitability which bound Chemosh to Moab, left room for ethical development. One could hardly describe the religion of the tribes round about Israel as ethical. Furthermore it meant that

[1] So Gesenius, *Thesaurus*, p. 502.
[2] W. F. Lofthouse, '*Chen* and *Chesed* in the Old Testament', *Zeitsch. f. d. altt. Wissenschaft*, vol. 20, pt. 1, pp. 29–35.
[3] 1 Sam. XX 14–16.   [4] Isa. XL 6–7.

the God of the Jews was not bounded by the Jews and this enabled the universalism and ethical monotheism towards which Amos took the next great step when in the name of Yahweh he condemned Moab for atrocities committed against Edom. Says Snaith:

'Out of these first distinctive ideas of the Covenant between Jehovah and Israel, four points of importance arise. Firstly, Jehovah existed before Israel. Secondly, if He once existed without them, He could do so again. Thirdly, if He chose them, He could also reject them. Fourthly, He was different from other gods in the demands He made upon His people as their part in the Covenant. These four points are of the utmost importance. Without them, Israel's religion could never have grown to what it actually did become. The development is wholly wrapped up with the special relations between God and His people. These relations were centred in, and summed up in the Covenant. The Covenant involved these four special and peculiar conditions.'[1]

The great prophet of the *chesed* of God is Hosea: He married a woman named Gomer. She bore him three children, but after six years deserted him for another man. But she fell out with this other man, and, abandoned and defenceless, became a slave. In this situation he found her. Hosea, hurt but all the while sensitive to God, came to discern through his own agony great spiritual truths. Gomer had abandoned him. Just so, only in a much greater way, Israel had abandoned Yahweh. And how greatly the patience of Yahweh exceeded his own. He had put up with Gomer and her infidelity for six years; Yahweh had put up with the infidelities of Israel for six hundred. What was the basis that held them together through this strained and strange relationship? It was *chesed*, the love of commitment, the commitment of the covenant, the commitment of marriage. That love is not broken when the one loved turns aside.

'Then said the Lord unto me, Continue to love Gomer despite all her adulteries, according to the love of the Lord

[1] N. H. Snaith, *The Distinctive Ideas of the Old Testament*, p. 108.

toward the children of Israel, who look to other gods and love flagons of wine. So I bought her to me for fifteen pieces of silver and for an homer and a half of barley; and I said unto her Thou shalt abide for me many days; thou shalt not play the harlot, and thou shalt not be for another man: so will I also be for thee. For the children of Israel shall abide many days without a king, and without a prince, and without a sacrifice and without an image, and without an ephod, and without teraphim. Afterward shall the children of Israel return, and seek the Lord their God, and David their king; and shall fear the Lord and his goodness in the latter days.'[1]

God does not throw over Israel. On the contrary, there is to be a new and deeper covenant.

'And in that day will I make a covenant for them with the beasts of the field and with the fowls of heaven, and with the creeping things of the ground: and I will break the bow and the sword and the battle out of the earth, and will make them to lie down safely, And I will betroth thee unto me for ever; yea, I will betroth thee unto me in *tsedeq*, and in judgement, and in *chesed*, and in mercies.'[2]

God's love is unswerving. Hosea's vision is caught by other writers. 'The Lord shows *tsedeq* in all His ways and *chesed* in all His works.'[3] That is one of the Psalmists. And here is Jeremiah:

'Go and proclaim these words toward the north, say, Return, thou backsliding Israel, saith the Lord; and I will not cause mine anger to fall upon you: for I show *chesed*, saith the Lord, and I will not keep anger for ever.'[4]

Was it not Jeremiah who supremely took up Hosea's vision of the new covenant?

What then is man's response? Hosea speaks of Israel's rebellion. 'There is no truth, no *chesed*, no knowledge of God in the land.'[5] The true *chesed* of man towards God is acknowledgement of Him and loyalty to the covenant-relationship. The *chasidim* were later

---

[1] Hos. III 1–5.   [2] ib. II 18–19.   [3] Ps. CXLV 17.   [4] Jer. III 12.   [5] Hos. II 1.

a separatist and puritanical party among the Jews. But apart from any specialized meaning the *chasid* is always the man who seeks to be faithful to the covenant, and to perform loyally, piously, his humble duty towards God. 'The Lord preserveth the *faithful*.'[1] 'The Lord loveth judgement and forsaketh not his *saints*.'[2] 'Gather my *saints* together unto me: those that have made a covenant with me by sacrifice.'[3] 'All thy works shall praise thee, O Lord; and thy *saints* shall bless thee.'[4] From different ages the cry is united. But for the prophets the covenant of sacrifice was not enough.

'Will the Lord be pleased with thousands of rams, or with ten thousands of rivers of oil? He hath shewed thee, o man, what is good; and what doth the Lord require of thee, but to do justly, and to love *chesed*, and to walk humbly with thy God.'[5]

So it shall be in the day of glad reunion, when God's *chesed* to His people is revealed through all their backsliding: '*Chesed* and truth are met together; *tsedeq* and peace have kissed each other.'[6] In practical terms the fruits of *chesed* shown by man to man are not different from those of *tsedeq*. The demands of covenant-love are righteousness, equity, compassion. Here through Jeremiah God proclaims what his people must do to receive the blessings of the covenant:

'Amend your ways and your doings, and I will cause you to dwell in this place. Trust ye not in lying words, saying The temple of the Lord, the temple of the Lord, the temple of the Lord, are these. For if ye thoroughly amend your ways and your doings, if ye thoroughly execute judgement between a man and his neighbour, if ye oppress not the stranger, the fatherless and the widow, and shed not innocent blood in this place, neither walk after other gods to your hurt, then will I cause you to dwell in this place, in the land that I gave to your fathers for ever and ever. Behold ye trust in lying words that

[1] Ps. XXXI 23. [2] ib. XXXVII 28. [3] ib. L 5.
[4] ib. CXLV 10. [5] Mic. VI 7–8. [6] Ps. LXXXV 10.

cannot profit. Will ye steal, murder, and commit adultery, and swear falsely and burn incense unto Baal, and walk after other gods whom ye know not, and come and stand before me in this house, which is called by my name, and say, We are delivered to do all these abominations? Is this house, which is called by my name, become a den of robbers in your eyes? Behold, even I have seen it, saith the Lord.'[1]

The passage might be paralleled from almost any of the great prophets. But *chesed* is not *tsedeq*. It is warmer altogether and more closely denotes an inward disposition which reveals itself in action and in life. It is in fact the nearest the Old Testament can approach to the Christian *agape*. It is not the least of these gropings towards it, and of all the great figures of the Old Testament Hosea seems closest to the mind of Jesus, and his words were not far from Jesus' memory at any time.

But the insight was for centuries lost, or at least obscured. *Chesed* depended upon the covenant, and it was inevitable that as the idea of the covenant changed the idea of *chesed* should be modified also. After the return from exile the Jews, having taken down their harps and struck up again the songs of the Lord, found that little but hardship awaited them. There were compromises, influences from outside, from Persia, from Greece. 'Under the rule of the nations, the Jews greatly modified the traditions of their forefathers.' Against these influences stood the Law, and the most fervent supporters of the Law stood for the segregation of the true Jews alike from the Gentiles and from the mixed population of Palestine. The Law was their distinctive mark. Only within rigid obedience to it could the Jews remain true to the original covenant, to their historical traditions, and to all that marked them off as a Chosen People. Hence the *chasidim* of later Jewish history are the party which stood for absolute loyalty to the covenant in narrow obedience to the Law. We cannot say that they lacked fervour; very much to the contrary. But they lost their sense of proportion, and the original insight from which their loyalty sprang had to be restated—and demonstrated—in other and deeper terms.

[1] Jer. VII 4–11.

There is a third concept of some importance upon which we must touch. This is the root '-h-b, giving the noun 'ahabah, and it is the most general word for 'love' in the Old Testament. Its normal usage is wide and free; it can be used of love of persons, and also of love of food or of sleep.[1] It is the central word in that greatest of love-poems, *The Song of Songs*. It stands in contrast to *chesed* in that it represents a love that is unconditioned. That is to say that it is prior to and deeper than *chesed*. God chose Israel before He entered into the covenant with her; the choice sprang from 'ahabah. It was not determined by anything Israel had done, nor by anything Israel was, nor by anything else. His love was undetermined, unfettered, inexplicable. It is among the Deuteronomic writers that this conception finds its most frequent and mighty exposition.

'Thou art a holy people unto the Lord thy God: the Lord thy God hath chosen thee to be a special people unto himself, above all people that are upon the face of the earth. The Lord did not set his love upon you nor choose you, because ye were more in number than any people; for ye were the fewest of all people; but because the Lord loved you, and because he would keep the oath which he had sworn unto your fathers, hath the Lord brought you out with a mighty hand, and redeemed you out of the house of bondmen, from the hands of Pharaoh king of Egypt.'[2]

'Speak not thou in thine heart, after that the Lord thy God hath cast them out from before thee, saying, For my righteousness the Lord hath brought me in to possess this land; but for the wickedness of these nations the Lord doth drive them out from before thee. Not for thy righteousness, or for the uprightness of thine heart, dost thou go to possess their land: but for the wickedness of these nations the Lord thy God doth drive them out from before thee, and that he may perform the word which the Lord sware unto thy fathers, Abraham, Isaac, and Jacob. Understand therefore, that the Lord thy God giveth

[1] e.g. Gen. XXVII 4; Hos. III 1; Prov. XX 13.
[2] Deut. VII 6-8.

thee not this good land to possess it for thy righteousness; for thou art a stiff-necked people.'[1]

'Behold, the heaven and the heaven of heavens is the Lord's thy God, the earth also with all that therein is. Only the Lord had a delight in thy fathers to love them, and he chose their seed after them, even you above all people, as it is this day.'[2]

'Nevertheless the Lord thy God would not hearken unto Balaam: but the Lord thy God turned the curse into a blessing unto thee, because the Lord thy God loved thee.'[3]

We are not so very far from

'God commendeth His love toward us in that, while we were yet sinners, Christ died for us.'[4]

This love is not conditioned by human merit. At most we can say that God looks not at achievement but at potentiality, and sees deeper than any what are the potentialities of a man or a nation. But it is rather true that this love springs from something deep in the nature of God. In this sense it is almost akin to *eros*. There is a yearning in God that needs satisfaction. It is a yearning of creativity; God is satisfied when He sees that it is good. So with His love of Israel. Time and again God is said to act 'for His own sake' or 'for His Name's sake'.[5] 'His nature and His Name is Love.' The type of His love is that of a parent for a child, but even that image is inadequate, for His love is more deep and lasting than a mother's.[6]

Israel's response is likewise that of love.

'Hear, O Israel: the Lord our God, the Lord is One: and thou shalt love the Lord thy God with all thine heart, and with all thy soul, and with all thy might. And these words, which I command thee this day, shall be in thine heart.'[7]

[1] ib. IX 4–6.   [2] ib. X 14–15.   [3] ib. XXIII 5.   [4] Rom. V 8.
[5] e.g. 2 Kings XIX 34; XX 6; XLIII 25; XLVIII 11; Ps. XXIII 3; XXV 11; XXXI 3; LXXIX 9; CVI 8; CIX 21; CXLIII 11; Isa. XLVIII 9; Jer. XIV 7; XIV 21; Ez. XX 9; XX 22; XX 44.
[6] cf. Isa. XLIX 15; Hos. XI 1–4; Jer. XXXI 9, etc.   [7] Deut. VI 4–6.

The last commandment makes it clear that whereas the love of God for Israel is paternal, unconditioned and free, the love of Israel for God is to be filial, responsive and obedient. So it is that in the longest and most Deuteronomic of the Psalms we read no less than eleven times of Israel loving the commandments of God.[1] This response to God's love is naturally seen within the covenant-relationship. 'O love the Lord, all ye his saints';[2] that is the *chasidim*, who are faithful to the covenant. This comes out with great clarity in Deuteronomy.

> 'Know therefore that the Lord thy God, He is God, the faithful God, which keepeth covenant and mercy with them that love Him and keep His commandments to a thousand generations.'[3]

The important thing to observe is that the normal secular use of *'ahabah* does not permit its application to the attitude of an inferior to a superior. It is never used of the love of a child for a parent, nor of the love of a wife for a husband (both in the Old Testament being relationships of dependence). It is once and once only used of the love of a slave for his master.[4] Its central usage is of the condescending love of a superior for an inferior. It is however freely used of love between equals, and is the word of the great commandment: 'Thou shalt love thy neighbour as thyself.'[5] In this element of condescension, *'ahabah* could seem to be like *philanthropia*. But it can, especially in a religious context, be used of the response to this condescending love; only the response is generically different from the love which called out the response. The Septuagint rendered *'ahabah* by *agape*, but in its Christian sense *agape* has much deeper implications.

The exclusiveness of the Jews prevented them from exercising a wide influence in the Graeco-Roman world, but even had they been less exclusive, it is doubtful whether they would have made much headway. They worked within a different framework of thought, and among the Greeks and Romans it is only occasionally, with a Pindar, say, or a Zeno, and then only with major

---

[1] Ps. CXIX, e.g. 127.   [2] Ps. XXXI 23.   [3] Deut. VII 9.
[4] Deut. XV 16.   [5] Lev. XIX 18; cf. XIX 34.

qualifications, that we feel ourselves in touch with the same thought-world. That which was good and true in Jewish thought needed mediating to the Mediterranean peoples, and Christianity proved the mediator. The exaltation of God in Jewish religion made it difficult for them to derive a basic moral attitude from their vision of God's attitude to man. Hence *'ahabah*, the election-love which represents the very nature of God, when applied to man, slides over into *chesed*, the loyal fulfilment of covenanted obligations, and *chesed*, when it requires definition, is seen in turn in terms of *tsedeq* which, while remaining theocentric, expresses, I think, at first at least, God's will rather than His nature. What is more, though all these words denote an attitude of mind which comes out in living actions, as the original inspiration dims and fades their fulfilment comes to be seen more and more in terms of legalistic obligation rather than the freedom of responsive love. 'Shall these bones live?' A new inspiration, a new vision, a new statement, a new demonstration were needed. This was to come in the context of Judaism through the person of Jesus of Nazareth, and to spread from there throughout the Mediterranean world.

XII

AGAPE[1]

A T THIS POINT we may take stock. We have examined in some detail the principal moral values of the ancient world, and found that they were all, through different defects, incapable of providing that basis for an universal morality for which people were seeking. Sometimes we have found them linked with a particular pattern of society, and inoperative once those conditions had disappeared. More often the failure of an apparently promising concept has shown, explicitly or implicitly, the nature of the object of our search, and we may usefully draw out some of these implications.

In the first place man, throughout ancient history, is conceived as belonging to a community of gods and men, or of God and men. Actual atheism is rare in the ancient world, and the word 'atheist' was freely applied to those who, like the Christians and Epicureans, attacked the religious beliefs of orthodox paganism, however fervently they might believe in their own gods. Once reflective philosophy examines this situation it is clear that morality cannot be divorced from religion. Hence Plato's criticisms of Homer, and the variously allegorical attempts to defend the poet. Even the Epicureans, who came closest to constructing a system of morality in purely human terms, spoke of 'effluxes' from the gods which might affect the righteous for good—

> 'for the gods, ever familiar with their own virtues, receive men like themselves, and reject as alien all that are not of this character.'[2]

---

[1] Innumerable writers have treated the subject of Christian love. The treatment here is my own analysis of the New Testament evidence, and does not profess to go beyond that. I have, however, drawn on what I have written in *Studies in Christian Social Commitment*, *The Enthronement of Love*, *Christian Faith for To-day*, and elsewhere. [2] D.L. X 124.

The basis of morality, according to this view, is to be sought in the nature of the divine being. But a difficulty at once emerges. The attitude of God to men is inevitably one of condescension. Is condescension really the basic social attitude? Possibly, said the ancients, and under the Roman Empire government was humanized because of such beliefs, though the social structure in which they took their place was unsound. The view could not be sustained: it was limited and oligarchic. And it could not apply to man's response to God. That seemed to be essentially one of aspiration, *eros*. But that in its turn was inapplicable to God, though Plotinus made an exalted effort so to apply it. The Jews came nearest to solving this dilemma; in the Graeco-Roman world the most fruitful concept was *philanthropia*. This failed at the last, partly because of its very nature it could not express man's response to God, partly because it never shook off the sense of superiority which accidentally adhered to it, partly because there was no precisely suitable Latin equivalent. On such small accidents of language does the development of our thinking depend.

Secondly, there is the fundamental paradox of morality. Man is man in society, as Plato and Aristotle knew, and morality is social morality. And yet our ethical categories have to make room for the individual who stands separate from his fellows, the Protestant, the Nonconformist, the martyr. The basic moral relationship must be potentially reciprocal. In this sense *philia* is by far the most important of the values which we have examined, and the Epicureans in their stress upon it deserve far more credit as moralists than is commonly accorded to them. Burnaby is undoubtedly right in suggesting that *philia* is a more fruitful concept for Christians than Christian teachers have yet realized. But a potency, as Aristotle puts it, is a potency both to be and not to be; it may not be actualized; the *dunamis* may never become *energeia*. *Philia* and *homonoia* are excellent descriptions of the proper social relationship when it is actualized. But they are by their nature reciprocal; it takes two to make a friendship just as it takes two to make a quarrel. The basic moral attitude is one which will create a friendship if it is reciprocated, but which will remain valid even if it is not reciprocated.

Thirdly, much of our desirable behaviour may be usefully expressed through particular moral principles. But our true norm runs deeper than this. Mere legalism is not enough, however high the standard of social behaviour which emerges from it; the Pharisees are here a warning. Further, a moral standard which demands introspection as its test is likely to lead to an immoral egocentricity. The essential moral situation, as Martin Büber has done most to remind us, is that of a Thou confronting an I, and it is in such personal encounters that morality has its roots, whether between God and man, man and God, or man and man, not in an abstract self-realization nor in the fulfilment of certain rules.

These conditions were met by the Christian *agape*. The verb from which it is derived is an old word with an interesting history. It occurs once only in the Homeric poems.[1] In classical Greek it is not uncommon. Sometimes it is used interchangeably with *philein*.[2] More often it seems to imply regard rather than affection, and, as Gildersleeve remarks, it is 'a colder word than φιλεῖν and less intimate'. He suggests that the Christian choice of it rather than *philein* was due to the fact that the latter had associations with kissing.[3] This may have been a factor, but it was not more than a small one, and we can see three others of greater significance. The first was the very fact that the word was colourless. It had few associations, and the fact that it had hitherto been cold enabled the Christians to endow it with their own warmth.[4] Secondly, such associations as it had acquired favoured the particular flavour and connotation of the Christian virtue, for it had come to mean not so much 'to be affectionately disposed towards' as 'to be patient with', 'to put up with'.[5] Thirdly, *philia*, as we have said, was essentially reciprocal, and *agape* was not.

The noun *agape* indeed scarcely existed; it was, it has been said, 'born within the bosom of revealed religion', though that is an

---

[1] Hom. *Od.* 23, 214.   [2] Xen. *Mem.* II 7, 9; 12.

[3] B. L. Gildersleeve, *Justin Martyr*, p. 135. 1 Peter V 14 actually has φίλημα ἀγάπης, as I am indebted to Mr. H. F. Guite for reminding me.

[4] cf. R. H. Strachan in *Expos.* VIII vii 263–7.

[5] e.g. Dem. I 14; VI 15 and elsewhere.

over-statement.[1] There are only three alleged examples of its use before the Christian era outside Judaic circles, and in all the reading is extremely doubtful.[2] It is for the Christian a back-formation from the verb, replacing the pagan *agapesis*.[3] It does occasionally—fourteen times to be precise—appear in the Septuagint meaning 'sexual love'. In Wisdom it appears as love towards God and love of Wisdom,[4] and Aristeas also uses it in the higher sense.[5] It was no doubt the Alexandrian Jews of the first century B.C. who laid the foundation for its later use. It is said in one reputable work of reference that it is not found in Philo or Josephus.[6] This is not so, for Philo links together the two attitudes of man towards God—love (*agape*) and fear.[7] This usage cannot be derived from the Septuagint, unless from the book of Wisdom, and we must presuppose some Jewish antecedents now lost to us. To all intents and purposes it is a Christian word, but it is not to be divorced from those ideas of love which we have been studying in the Judaic tradition.

The first fact about Christian love is that its standard, origin, and basis is found in the nature of God. 'God is Agape' is the great Christian affirmation.[8] He is 'the God of love and peace'.[9] From this basic fact follow certain corollaries. Love cannot be defined, for to define is to place limits upon and it is impossible to place limits upon God. It may be apprehended but not comprehended. It may be exemplified but not exhausted. Further, Love is to be seen in the nature of God primarily and only secondarily in His relations with men. It follows that in the ethic of Love there is no place for legalism—or rather the place of legalism is limited and not central. This may be seen alike in the gospels where Jesus replaces the old covenant of the Mosaic Law by the new covenant which Jeremiah had foreshadowed,[10] giving deeper and more searching commandments than the Law had known, and in the epistles, where in the response of Love to Love Paul finds a freedom he has never experienced under the Law. Again, because Love

---

[1] cf. Moulton and Milligan, *Vocabulary of the Greek Testament*, s.v.
[2] *P. Par.* 49³; *P. Berol.* 9859; Phild. *Lib.* p. 520.   [3] e.g. Arist. *Met.* I 980 a 22.
[4] Wisd. III 9; VI 18.   [5] 229.   [6] Hastings *D.C.G.* s.v. Love.
[7] Philo *Quod Deus immut.* xiv 69.   [8] 1 John IV 8.   [9] 2 Cor. XIII 11.
[10] Jer. XXXI 31-3; Matt. V passim; Barn. IV 8.

is rooted in God's nature, independently of the fact that there are such creatures as human beings, it escapes that element of condescension which frustrated the spread of other useful concepts. God can love man—yes, but man may also love God. What is more, because it is God's nature to love, Love is not determined by the character of its object. It may be called out by qualities in the recipient. 'The Father Himself loves you, *because* you have loved me and have believed that I come from the Father.'[1] But it may also be freely given. It is not for any merit in the Prodigal Son that the Father has been watching for him and runs to meet him.[2] 'God shows His love for us in that while we were yet sinners Christ died for us';[3] that is the great text which displays the free nature of the Love of God.

Love then is in its first sense a state, an attitude, a spirit, an alignment of the personality, what Aristotle would call an *hexis*. But as Aristotle sensibly remarked, virtue which is never practised is no virtue, and the second characteristic of Christian love is that it appears more often as a verb than a noun. It is an activity not an abstraction. When certain theologians try to oust Love from its position of ethical centrality and replace it by a 'justice' of which the New Testament never speaks, they commonly accuse their opponents of abstract theorizing and claim for themselves a concrete and particular commitment. In truth it is 'justice' which is the abstraction and 'love' which denotes an active personal commitment, for 'justice' is an abstract noun and 'love' an active verb. 'Have love in your hearts', said a great French preacher once from an English pulpit, and then corrected himself. 'No, I do not mean that. I do not know what the heart is except an organ for pumping blood round the body. Have love in your lives.' 'The first thing', said Ignatius Loyola, 'is that love ought to be placed in works rather than in words.' 'Love proves itself by deeds', said that most lovable of the saints, Thérèse of Lisieux. When the scribe asked Jesus to elaborate his Great Commandments, He told the story of the Good Samaritan. He ended his illustration, not with the words 'That is who your neighbour is', nor with the words 'That is what love means',

---

[1] John XVI 27.   [2] Luke XV 20.   [3] Rom. V 8.

but by the injunction 'Go and act'.[1] The most fearful words in the Gospel are these: 'Not everyone that says to me "Lord! Lord!" shall enter the Kingdom of Heaven, but he who does the will of my Father who is in heaven.'[2] In the Upper Room on the night of His betrayal Jesus spoke to his disciples of love, but He first demonstrated the activity of love by washing their feet. The words 'If I then, your Lord and Teacher, have washed your feet, you also ought to wash one another's feet', are not to be dissociated from the words 'This is my commandment, that you love one another as I have loved you'. He goes on to associate His teaching of love with the practical example of His laying down His life.[3] Love is dynamic; therein lies its power.

The third fact about Love is that it is an active verb requiring an object. Some theologians have seen in the need that the Love of God shall have an object the motive power behind the creation. Love is expressed through personal relationships. These relationships are many, and worth careful analysis. First Love is directed by God towards man.

'In this is love, not that we loved God but that He loved us and sent His son to be the expiation for our sins.'[4]

'As the Father has loved me, so have I loved you; abide in my love.'[5]

'But God shows His love for us in that while we were yet sinners Christ died for us.'[6]

'For I am sure that neither death nor life, nor angels, nor principalities, nor things present nor things to come, nor powers, nor height, nor depth, nor anything else in all creation, will be able to separate us from the love of God in Jesus Christ our Lord.'[7]

'God who loved us and gave us everlasting consolation and hope through grace.'[8]

[1] Luke X 37.   [2] Matt. VII 21.   [3] John XIII 14; XIV 15–24; XV 9–14.
[4] 1 John IV 10.   [5] John XV 9.   [6] Rom. V 8.
[7] Rom. VIII 39.   [8] 2 Thess. II 16.

It is a little curious that no such expression is attributed to Jesus in the synoptic gospels, but I do not think that its Christian authenticity can be seriously questioned. Secondly, men, kindled by God's love for them, direct their love towards Him.

> 'You shall love the Lord your God with all your heart, and with all your soul, and with all your mind. This is the great and first commandment.'[1]

James speaks naturally of loving God.[2] So does Paul himself.[3] So Jesus, when He has claimed that whoever has seen Him has seen the Father, goes on to tell the disciples that if they love Him, they will keep His commandments.[4] At the last He three times, asks Peter whether he loves Him (ἀγαπᾷς με).[5] On the whole the gospels do not dwell very much upon man's love for God, speaking rather of faith or trust. Ritschl writes:

> 'Love is reserved as the characteristic of God and God's son in the foundation and guidance of the congregation, while of its members faith or trust in God and His Son is demanded.'[6]

Others have put the view that love towards God must be called out spontaneously and naturally as the response to God's love for man, and if it does not so arise it is idle to seek to elicit it by exhortation.[7] The truth is surely that love towards God is the great commandment alike of Judaism and Christianity, and, once stated, it tended to be taken for granted. John in his first letter, that great paean of Christian love, speaks of that love towards God which is genuinely shown only when a man loves his brother also, and emphasizes that our love springs from God's; 'We love, because He first loved us.'[8]

When we turn to human relationships we are impressed by the comprehensive scope of love. It is to be directed first within the fellowship of the Church, as the binding force and characteristic of the new society.

---

[1] Matt. XXII 37; cf. Luke X 27.   [2] James II 5.
[3] Rom. VIII 28; 1 Cor. II 9; VIII 3.
[4] John XIV 8–15; cf. XIII 34.   [5] John XXI 15–17.
[6] Ritschl, *Rechtf. v. Vers.* II 100 f; cf. Wendt, *Lehre Jesu* II 227.
[7] e.g. B. Weiss, *Bib. Theol. of N.T.* § 25 b.   [8] 1 John IV 19–21; V 1–3.

'A new commandment I give to you, that you love one another; even as I have loved you, that you also love one another. By this all men will know that you are my disciples, if you have love for one another.'[1]

This was borne out in the history of the Church. The spread of Christianity can be attributed in no small measure to two factors, the bearing of the Christians in face of death (martyrs means witnesses), and the example which wrung from the pagans the reluctantly admiring confession, 'How these Christians love one another!' Here we have love reciprocated. But love is not always and inevitably so requited, and love is enjoined secondly towards our neighbour.

'If anyone says, "I love God", and hates his brother, he is a liar; for he who does not love his brother whom he has seen, cannot love God whom he has not seen. And this commandment we have from him, that he who loves God should love his brother also.'[2]

John in that passage may have had love within the Church in the forefront of his mind,[3] Jesus, however, gave His second commandment, 'You shall love your neighbour as yourself.'[4] Barnabas goes further: 'You shall love your neighbour more than your own life.'[5] The neighbour is shown in the parable of the Good Samaritan to be the man we happen to rub up against in life, who has no claims on us except those of need, who might himself despise and offend us ('Jews have no dealings with Samaritans'),[6] and who may or may not show gratitude.[7] This would seem to be comprehensive enough. But to emphasize still further that Love is unrestricted in its object, does not depend on merit in the recipient, and is not merely to be exercised when there is some hope of its being returned, we have the specific command 'Love your enemies'.[8] The point here is that Love is a redemptive power, even if it seems wasted in the immediate

---

[1] John XIII 34-5; cf. Rom. XII 10.   [2] 1 John IV 20-1.   [3] ib. V 1.
[4] Matt. XXII 39.   [5] Barn. XIX 5.   [6] John IV 9.
[7] Luke X 29-37.   [8] Matt. V 44.

context. 'If you love those who love you, what reward have you? Do not even the tax-collectors do the same?'[1] The word for enemies—*echthroi*—is a comprehensive word which includes personal and political enemies and the context with its reference to the juridical rights of the Roman soldiery points the same lesson. 'You are to be all-embracing, as your heavenly father is all-embracing'[2]—that does not exhaust the meaning of the word *teleios*, usually rendered 'perfect', but it is included within it. As God sends His sun and rain impartially upon the moral and the immoral, churchmen and criminals, saints and sinners, so is our love to be extended alike to the moral and the immoral, the deserving and the undeserving.

The fourth fact about Love is that it is laid upon the Christian believer as his ethical principle in the world as it is. It is needful to say this because of the misguided interpretations of some theologians who have tried to minimize the force of the commandment to love. On the one hand there are those who believe that Jesus expected the end of the world, the day of the Lord, and the Final Judgement to ensue shortly. They therefore suppose that he put forward an *Interimsethik*, valid only in those limited and peculiar circumstances. Others have brought Jesus' ethical teaching under the limitations of his humanity, and have supposed them to represent words of worldly wisdom applicable to an agricultural society in first-century Palestine, but by no means applicable to the complex industrial society of modern Europe or America. Both alike ignore the fact that the ethical teaching of Jesus is rooted and grounded not in the nature of the alleged 'interim' nor in the structure of society which he knew, but in his understanding of the nature of God.[3] Others (and it must be admitted that these include a high proportion of professing Christians) have supposed that Jesus was saying something like 'Wouldn't it be nice if we all loved one another!' They go on to add that as we live in a wicked world in which we do not all love one another, the command to love is irrelevant. Until all practise love, no one needs. Few non-Christians would suppose Jesus to be saying anything so fatuously bathetic. A very cursory glance at the fifth

[1] ib. V 46.　　　　　[2] ib. V 48.　　　　　[3] ib. V 44.

chapter of St Matthew's Gospel shows that the way of love is laid upon the Christian disciple, not in the land beyond the stars where everyone loves each other, but in this wicked world where toughs strike you in the face, and soldiers conscribe you to carry their packs.

Fifthly, then, what is the nature of this Love? I have said already that it cannot be defined, but something of its nature can be indicated. It starts in personal encounter, the outreaching of one personality to another. One of the most significant remarks in the early strands of Christian tradition is that of the evangelist on Jesus' reaction to the rich young ruler: 'And Jesus looking upon him, loved him.'[1] In this connection it is useful to recall a passage from Shelley's *Defence of Poetry*:

> 'The great secret of morals is love: or a going out of our nature and an identification of ourselves with the beautiful which exists in thought, action, or person not our own. A man to be greatly good must imagine intensely and comprehensively: he must put himself in the place of another and of many others; the pains and pleasures of his species must become his own. The great instrument of moral good is the imagination. and poetry administers to the effect by acting upon the cause. Poetry enlarges the circumference of the imagination by replenishing it with thoughts of ever-new delight, which have the power of attracting and assimilating to their nature all other thoughts. Poetry strengthens the faculty which is the organ of the moral nature of man in the same way as exercise strengthens a limb.'

We might quibble at the cult of beauty in that passage, but in his emphasis on imaginative out-reaching Shelley is wholly right. This aspect of Love is often called compassion or sympathy; both words mean literally the power of identifying oneself with the experiences of another, and may include the power to suffer with another person.

Some people have spoken of the Law of Love, but that is really a misnomer and indeed a contradiction in terms, though it has

[1] Mark X 21.

some scriptural precedent in James's description of the command to love our neighbour as 'the royal law'.[1] But the whole question of the relationship between the ethical principle of Love, and the familiar ethical precepts calls for further examination. We notice that Jesus claimed that he had not come to overthrow the Mosaic Law, but to fulfil it,[2] that when the rich young ruler, asked what he must do to inherit eternal life, Jesus' first answer was 'Obey the Ten Commandments',[3] and that Jesus' own characterization of the two Great Commandments singles out two passages from the Books of the Law.[4] When he criticizes the scribes and Pharisees, his words are significant.

> 'Woe to you, scribes and Pharisees, hypocrites! for you pay tithe of mint and dill and cummin and have neglected the weightier matters of the law, justice and mercy and faith; these you ought to have done without neglecting the others.'[5]

Thus Paul also says that the whole law is fulfilled in the commandment to love our neighbour,[6] and describes Love as the fulfilling of the law.[7] But we notice that there are occasions when Jesus breaks right through the normally accepted ethical precepts in the interest of a higher commitment. It was his indifference to the minutiae of the Law which went far to rouse the opposition of Pharisees and Sadducees. Here he might justly have claimed that the precepts he broke through were trivial and of no ethical significance. His challenge to the normal practice of Sabbath-keeping was in fact a challenge to re-examine the ethical basis of that practice.[8] Sometimes he went further. Whatever the precise purport of those very difficult words, 'If any one comes to me and does not hate his own father and mother and wife, and children, yes, and even his own life, he cannot be my disciple',[9] they certainly mean that there are occasions when one must break the salutary fifth commandment to honour one's father and mother. The contradiction is the more striking since this is the first com-

---

[1] James II 8.   [2] Matt. V 17.   [3] Mark X 19.
[4] Matt. XXII 37–40; Deut. VI 5; Lev. XIX 18.
[5] Matt. XXIII 23.   [6] Gal. V 14.   [7] Rom. XIII 10.
[8] e.g. Mark II 27–8; Luke VI 5; XIII 15; John V 18.   [9] Luke XIV 26.

mandment with promise, and the promise as well as the commandment is negated. The words are exaggerated; Jesus, like all
Jewish teachers, drove his points home with exaggerated emphasis. The point is that affection for some humans must not stand
in the path of *agape*, and it warns us not to identify Christian love
with such affection. Further, through much of the Sermon on the
Mount the refrain recurs, 'You have heard that it was said . . .
but I say to you, . . .'[1] Sometimes the words of Jesus give a new
and deeper meaning to the old commandment. It is not enough
to refrain from adultery: we must refrain from the thought of it.
It is not enough to refrain from murder; anger may be spiritually
tantamount to homicide. Sometimes the new way contradicts the
old. We are to love our enemies not hate them. Almost all the
new commands deal with an inner attitude which cannot be
legalistically tested. Hence St Augustine's famous paradox, 'Love
God, and do what you like', for if you truly love God the rest
follows. The general conclusion is clear. Ethical precepts—and we
may include such concepts as the cardinal virtues—are valuable as
guides, but they must not be taken as stringent rules, and may
have to give way to the claims of a higher principle. That principle is Love. It embraces the narrower precepts but transcends
them.

Can we then say more about the peculiar activity of Love? In
speaking of compassion we have begun to anticipate the answer.
Here is Paul's description of Love in his letter to the Church at
Corinth.

> 'Love is patient and kind; Love is not jealous or boastful; it
> is not arrogant or rude. Love does not insist on its own way,
> it is not irritable or resentful; it does not rejoice at wrong, but
> rejoices in the right. Love bears all things, believes all things,
> hopes all things, endures all things. Love never ends.'[2]

Elsewhere he says:

> 'Let love be genuine; hate what is evil, hold fast to what is
> good; love one another with brotherly affection; outdo one
> another in showing honour. Never flag in zeal, be aglow with

[1] Matt. V 21–2, 27–8, 31–2, 33–4, 38–9, 43–4.   [2] 1 Cor. XIII 4–8.

the Spirit, serve the Lord. Rejoice in your hope, be patient in tribulation, be constant in prayer. Contribute to the needs of the saints, practise hospitality. Bless those who persecute you; bless and do not curse them. Rejoice with those who rejoice, weep with those who weep. Live in harmony with one another; do not be haughty, but associate with the lowly; never be conceited. Repay no one evil for evil, but take thought for that which is noble in the sight of all. If possible, so far as it depends on you, live peaceably with all. Beloved, never avenge yourselves but leave it to the wrath of God; for it is written "Vengeance is mine, I will repay, says the Lord". No, if your enemy is hungry, feed him; if he is thirsty, give him drink; for by so doing you will heap burning coals upon his head! Do not be overcome by evil, but overcome evil with good.'[1]

The whole passage may properly be regarded as an expansion and analysis of what Paul understands by Christian love. The essential points we have noted are there—the mutual love in the Church, the unrequited love shown outside, the imaginative outreaching to those who joy or sorrow, the active nature of Love—together with some prudential morality which Paul has borrowed from Proverbs. But, this apart, the general tenour is reminiscent of the passage in the Sermon on the Mount which includes the injunction of love towards enemies. Paul's 'Do not be overcome by evil, but overcome evil with good', perhaps helps to explain Jesus' μὴ ἀντιστῆτε τῷ πονηρῷ,[2] commonly translated 'Resist not evil', sometimes (taking the dative as masculine) 'Resist not one who is evil' or even 'Resist not Satan', but perhaps meaning (in the light of this passage) 'Do not resist by evil means'.

Throughout all these passages we can discern a common theme. Love is concerned with means as well as ends. In the Christian conception the world, however fallen, remains God's. The lilies are His handiwork, and not a sparrow falls to the ground without Him caring.[3] Man is made in the image of God; he remains potentially the child of God; and, though he may have become evil, He still knows how to give good gifts to His children.[4] The

[1] Rom. XII 9–21.   [2] Matt. V 39.   [3] Matt. VI 30; X 29.
[4] Gen. I 27; John I 12; Matt. V 45; Luke XI 13.

world in short is God's, and will only work in God's way. Love, we have said, starts from personal encounter, and from the sense of identification with another or others. Arising from this understanding comes the desire for the highest well-being of the people involved in any situation. That result will not be achieved if the means used are wrong. In this context some of the phrases we have glanced at take on a new meaning. 'Love is patient. . . . Love bears all things.' 'Hate what is evil, hold fast to what is good. . . . Never avenge yourselves. . . . If your enemy is hungry, feed him. . . . Do not be overcome by evil, but overcome evil by good.' The peculiar quality of Christian love in action is its use of suffering as a means of redemption. Those who have dared to speak sentimentally of Christian love have been far from the truth. Dostoevsky in one of his novels speaks of the searing quality of love. William Temple, speaking at Jerusalem on the words 'God is Love', castigated those who

> 'tried to make the great truth comfortable for themselves. If they really believed it, it would frighten them out of their wits. All that was opposed to love was doomed to destruction. "Perfect love casteth out fear". But the imperfection of their love gave them every reason to regard this truth as very terrifying.'[1]

We can see this quality in the love of Jesus. He whips the Pharisees with his words as with a cat-of-nine-tails and cries out the woes to which the scribes had doomed themselves by their hardness. Even in its gentleness this love is fearful. The young man of great possessions came to Jesus and told of his acceptance and practice of the Law of Moses from his youth up. 'And Jesus, looking upon him, loved him, and said to him "One thing you lack".'[2] Love itself provides the trial which the young man fails. It was no maudlin sympathy from Jesus that made Mary of Magdala wash His feet with her tears and dry them with her lovely hair.[3]

In these passages we see that Love may sear its object. But it is with the deeper truth that we are concerned. Love may itself be

---

[1] *Report on Jerusalem Conference*, I, 379.
[2] Mark X 21.   [3] Luke VII 48; John XI 2; XII 3.

seared. Love will not use evil means to encompass a good end. 'The end justifies the means' is philosophical nonsense (for the means shape the end, and if the means are baneful, though the aim may be justified, the result will not be); in Christian theology it is blasphemy. 'For nothing in the world neither for love of any creature, is evil to be done', said Thomas à Kempis. The means which love uses is suffering. The Christian has always seen in the crucifixion of Jesus the supreme exemplar of that love which refuses to meet evil with evil, sin with sin, and the sword with the sword, and overcomes instead by redemptive suffering. 'Greater love has no man than this; that a man lay down his life for his friends.'[1] 'But God shows His love for us in that while we were yet sinners Christ died for us.'[2] 'It was fitting that He, for whom and by whom all things exist, in bringing many sons to glory, should make the pioneer of their salvation perfect', or complete, or all-embracing—'through suffering'.[3] 'I live by faith in the Son of God who loved me and gave himself for me.'[4] 'By this we know love, that he laid down his life for us; and we ought to lay down our lives for the brethren.'[5] That Love suffers is the universal witness of the New Testament. Such suffering is not undertaken in the calculation that it will move men's hearts. It may do, but to count on it is sentimentalism and a return to the idea of a love which is merely reciprocal. He who treads this path is not to expect quick or facile results. Indeed the immediate consequences may be disastrous. Good Friday seemed to be the end of Christianity, and even though Jesus may have peered through the veil of the future towards Easter, it does not seem that his disciples were able to follow his gaze. But trodden this path must be by the Christian believer. 'If any man would come after Me, let him deny himself and take up his cross and follow Me.'[6]

I do not propose to follow the theme of *agape* beyond the times of the New Testament. That has been done by scholars subtler, abler and more widely read than I.[7] Their story belongs more

[1] John XV 13.   [2] Rom. V 8.   [3] Hebr. II 10.
[4] Gal. II 30; cf. Eph. V 2; V 25.   [5] I John III 16.
[6] Mark VIII 34; Matt. XVI 24; Luke IX 23.
[7] e.g. A. Nygren, *Agape and Eros*; M. C. D'Arcy, *The Mind and Heart of Love*; J. Burnaby, *Amor Dei*; D. de Rougemont, *Passion and Society*.

properly to the Middle Ages than to the Ancient World. I have said enough to show that *agape* fulfilled all the conditions which were only partially realized by earlier gropings towards this central moral value. What is more in its doctrine of redemptive suffering it added a new factor of some weight in a world which was dominated by a suffering which it could only either grimly accept with the Stoics or hopelessly evade with the Epicureans. In cold historical fact this is one part of the reason why *agape* ousted those earlier values in the minds of thinking men, as the philosophical conversions of the second century may remind us, whereas to the poor and uneducated it had a thrilling relevance such as they had scarcely before experienced save perhaps in the friendship of the Epicureans' Garden. The other part of the reason is that the early Christians were prepared to live and die by their faith. The outreaching of their love in life, and the courage with which they faced death as a further extension of the way of love, won from the Roman world, as it had won from Saul of Tarsus, a reluctant admiration which soon became allegiance. T. R. Glover truly characterized the whole process when he said: 'The early Christians out-thought, out-lived, and out-died their pagan contemporaries.' It did not last. Before many centuries had passed philosophical confusion had syncretized *agape* with *eros, philia, philanthropia*, and even some of the narrower virtues. The imperious demands of military expediency, and the governmental traditions of a régime which was Christianized without becoming Christian, played down the election of suffering rather than violence, and the refusal of *agape* to use means less than the highest. It was not long before theologians were found to defend the new practice (in perfect sincerity), exalt justice above love in the ordering of society, and put forward a Ciceronian ethic in the name of Christ. What was worse, Christian became to Christian more hateful than a foe, and the words 'How these Christians love one another!' originally the product of reverent wonder, were repeated with bitter sarcasm. Such a story of decay belongs to the pathology of religious thought, and does not concern us here.

But this is not all there is to say. The study of the ancient world is justified only in so far as it is relevant to life in the modern world. This does not mean that we are to read back our own pre-occupations into the ancients without more ado. We have to study their preoccupations and the conditions which moulded their thought. We have to learn to ask their questions and not merely our own. But Thucydides, wisest of historians, claimed that his work was a permanent possession because, amid all the chance of human history, there was one constant factor, human nature. 'Mankind advances,' said Goethe, 'but man remains the same.' Our quest today is not alien from the quest we have here been studying. 'Who will show us the good?' Not the Homeric aristo-cracy, or the Age of Escapism, or the Imperial Hierarchy of Rome for they were too dominated by their own peculiar circumstances, though we can still learn from them. Throughout this study there is good sense and nobility, and truth to be glimpsed and accepted with gratitude from our forbears, and lessons to be learned from their limitations. The love which completed their quest fulfilled not merely the accidental associations of the ancient world, but the permanent conditions attaching to any such ethical search. If those who still profess the name of Christ could recapture it in thought and life they might bring hope and purpose to the modern world as their predecessors did nineteen centuries ago.

INDEX

Index

Benefaction, 201–4
Bernard, S., 48–9
Bias, 54
Bithynia, 153
Böckh, A., 24
Boeotia, 203
Boule, 16
Bowra, C. M., 156
Bruderhof, 72
Brutus, 159, 186
Büber, Martin, 229
Burnaby, J., 228
Burnet, J., 63
Bury, J. B., 25
Butler, Bishop, 31
Byzantine Empire, 113, 114
   Byzantium, 122

Caelius Rufus, 166
Caesar, Julius and Antony, 73; and Cicero, 131; and *virtus*, 162; and Augustus, 180–1; and *clementia*, 184–186
Calama, 204
Caligula, 183, 189
Callicles, 35
Callinus, 20
Calpurnius Siculus, 189–90
Camillus, M., Furius, 129
Campania, 160
Canusium, 203
Capitol, 163
Caracalla, 105, 131, 172
Cardinal virtues, ch. III passim.; and Julian, 198; as rules, 238
Carthage, 169
   Carthaginians, 165, 177
Cary, M., 133–4
Castel, S. Angelo, 202
Casinum, 204
Catiline, 66, 130–1, 192
Cato, the elder, 161
   the younger, 157, 186
Cattulus, 76, 166–9, 175
Catullus, 173
Celsus, 111
Cephalus, 43
Cephisodotus, 122
Cerberus, 207
Cercidas, 13
Ceres, 203
Cervantes, 89
Chachrylion vase, 76
Chaerephon, 139

Chemosh, 218
Chesed, and Jewish thought, 217–22; and *tsedeq*, 221–2; and *'ahabah*, 223
Chance, 135
Chaos, 81
Chariton, 127
Charlesworth, M. P., 182, 189, 191, 192, 196, 197
Charmides, 77
Chase, A. H., 74
Chastity, 182
Chilon, 54
Chinese philosophy, 39–40
Christian apologists, 131
Christianity predominance of, 9; and *philanthropia*, 111, 114; emergence of 208; mediator, 226; and adoption of *agape*, 229; and meaning of *agape*, 230–242; spread of, 234
Chrysippus on *arete*, 20; in Cicero, 65; and friendship, 68; and Eros, 96; and *homonoia*, 126; and autarcy, 150
Cicero, Marcus on mean in vice, 36; in Athens, 38; on Cephalus, 43; on cardinal virtues, 45–8; influence on Christianity, 48, 50; on Bias, 54; on friendship, 65–7, 70, 72, and Matius, 73–4, and *humanitas*, 116–7; and *concordia*, 130; on Socrates, 136; and pity, 156; and *more maiorum*, 159; and *virtus*, 161, 163; and *pietas*, 164, 166; and religion, 165; and *gravitas*, 173, 178; and Regulus, 177; on Caesar, 185–6; and *providentia*, 192; and Pliny, 203; and Christianity, 242
Cicero, Quintus, 166
Cimbri, 163
Cincinnatus, 159
Claudian, 167
Claudius, I, 176, 189, 194
Claudius II, 172
Cleanthes, 68, 126, 151
Clement of Alexandria, 83, 111
Clementia, and Augustus, 48; and *philanthropia*, 105, 115; in Statius, 156; and *pietas*, 172; and virtues of emperors, 184–92, 197; and *providentia*, 198–9
Cleobulus, 54
Cleomenes III, 105, 135
Cleopatra, 128–9, 182
Clodia, 166–8
Cloud-cuckoo-land, 94
Clough, A. H., 209

Index

Index

Index

Index

Index

Index

Date Due